DEVELOPING SPEED

SECOND EDITION

National Strength and Conditioning Association

Ian Jeffreys

EDITOR

HUMAN KINETICS

Library of Congress Cataloging-in-Publication Data

Names: Jeffreys, Ian, editor. | National Strength & Conditioning
  Association (U.S.)
Title: Developing speed / National Strength and Conditioning Association ;
  Ian Jeffreys, editor.
Description: Second edition. | Champaign, IL : Human Kinetics, [2025] |
  Series: Sport performance series | First edition published in 2013. |
  Includes bibliographical references and index.
Identifiers: LCCN 2023058561 (print) | LCCN 2023058562 (ebook) | ISBN
  9781718207059 (paperback) | ISBN 9781718207066 (epub) | ISBN
  9781718207073 (pdf)
Subjects: LCSH: Physical education and training. | Athletes--Training of. |
  Physical fitness--Physiological aspects. | Muscle strength. | Speed. |
  BISAC: SPORTS & RECREATION / Training | SPORTS & RECREATION /
  Bodybuilding & Weightlifting
Classification: LCC GV711.5 .D477 2024 (print) | LCC GV711.5 (ebook) |
  DDC 613.7/11--dc23/eng/20240212
LC record available at https://lccn.loc.gov/2023058561
LC ebook record available at https://lccn.loc.gov/2023058562

ISBN: 978-1-7182-0705-9 (print)

Senior Acquisitions Editor: Roger W. Earle; **Managing Editors:** Kevin Matz and Shawn Donnelly; **Copyeditor:** Marissa Wold Uhrina; **Indexer:** Dan Connolly; **Permissions Manager:** Laurel Mitchell; **Senior Graphic Designer:** Sean Roosevelt; **Cover Designer:** Keri Evans; **Cover Design Specialist:** Susan Rothermel Allen; **Photograph (cover):** © Human Kinetics; **Photograph (interior):** © Human Kinetics, unless otherwise noted; **Photo Asset Manager:** Laura Fitch; **Photo Production Specialist:** Amy M. Rose; **Photo Production Manager:** Jason Allen; **Senior Art Manager:** Kelly Hendren; **Illustrations:** © Human Kinetics unless otherwise noted; **Printer:** Versa Press

We thank Matthew Sandstead, NSCA-CPT,*D, Scott Caulfield, MA, CSCS,*D, TSAC-F,*D, RSCC*E, and the National Strength and Conditioning Association (NSCA) in Colorado Springs, Colorado, overseeing (Matthew and Scott) and hosting (NSCA) the photo shoot for this book.

Human Kinetics books are available at special discounts for bulk purchase. Special editions or book excerpts can also be created to specification. For details, contact the Special Sales Manager at Human Kinetics.

Printed in the United States of America   10 9 8 7 6 5 4 3 2 1

The paper in this book is certified under a sustainable forestry program.

Human Kinetics
1607 N. Market Street
Champaign, IL 61820
USA

United States and International
Website: **US.HumanKinetics.com**
Email: info@hkusa.com
Phone: 1-800-747-4457

Canada
Website: **Canada.HumanKinetics.com**
Email: info@hkcanada.com

DEVELOPING SPEED

SPEED

SECOND EDITION

Contents

Introduction

Ask athletes what aspect of performance they would like to improve the most and their answer normally is running speed as having greater speed affords them greater options, both offensively and defensively, to impact in a game. Indeed, the importance put on testing for speed in many sports further attests to the fact that speed is considered a major factor in differentiating between being a great athlete and being a good athlete. In practically every sport, we can see instances of where speed directly impacts a game: the striker in soccer beating the defender to the ball and scoring the winning goal, the tennis player running down a crosscourt shot before playing a winner down the line, or the wide receiver outrunning the defense for a game-winning touchdown. Thus, we are always looking for ways of getting faster.

So the critical question naturally becomes, can we get faster? For a long time, speed was viewed as a genetic trait that could not be improved. However, this belief has been found to be false, and although genetics play a role in determining the top speed an athlete can reach, speed is now considered a trainable component. The key is that we need to follow a well-designed and scientifically based training program. This is where this book comes in. In the following pages we will present the information a sport coach or strength and conditioning professional needs to be able to create such a program. However, simply getting faster in a speed test is only a part of a bigger picture. There is now a greater realization that the way in which speed has traditionally been viewed and measured presents a limited perspective and misses much of the nuance of sport-specific speed. With the traditional emphasis on linear speed, as measured by speed tests such as the 40-yard (37 m) dash, track and field models of speed have often guided speed training methodologies. Although these models still have many valuable applications to speed development, it is always important to keep in mind that a key qualifier is how well any improvement in speed transfers directly to sport performance. Here application is related to the achievement of a sport-specific task and is often specific to the context that speed is expressed or demonstrated. As a result, considerations of how speed is applied in specific sports should always be the priority, and interestingly this then adds further opportunities to enhance sport-specific speed.

This book is specifically designed to address the full gamut of speed training from a traditional linear speed approach through to how best to deliver sport-specific applications. Essentially, it is designed as a journey; initially looking at the determinants of linear speed and moving progressively through to their applications. As a result, that pathway provides coaches with the tools to improve speed—in any sport. Further, this book purposely blends science with practice, providing detailed background knowledge on the nature of speed mixed with advice and information of how to develop speed across a range of sports. To achieve this, the book gathers some of the world's leading authorities in speed development. These experts span the spectrum from top speed scientists through to highly skilled and experienced practitioners. The result is a book that provides information drawn from the latest research and scientific constructs underpinning speed training with the insights of accumulated decades of practical experience of how speed can be enhanced in a range of contexts. This dual yet sequential approach allows coaches to make informed decisions about training and to enable them to adapt programmatic models to directly address their specific needs that, in turn, develop faster athletes and directly enhance their performance.

Key to Diagrams

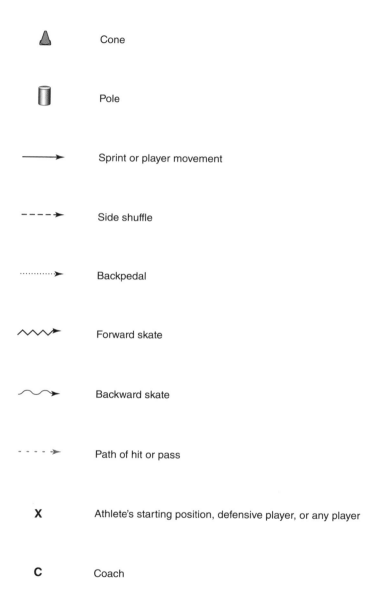

Cone

Pole

Sprint or player movement

Side shuffle

Backpedal

Forward skate

Backward skate

Path of hit or pass

X Athlete's starting position, defensive player, or any player

C Coach

CHAPTER 1

The Nature of Speed

Ian Jeffreys

It is often said in sporting circles that speed kills, and without doubt, the expression of speed is central to many key tasks in sport. Indeed, the high value placed on fast athletes and the extensive use of speed tests to identify talent and monitor performance in most sports further attests to the importance placed on speed in multiple sports. But what is meant by the expression "speed kills," and is it always true that the fastest athlete wins? This chapter will examine the nature of speed and its underpinning constraints and explores how sport-specific speed differs from what we traditionally regard as speed.

Taken to its extreme, if speed were the most critical component in sport, talent identification would be easy: A coach could go to the nearest track meet, select the fastest athletes, and convince them to play for his or her team. However, it is never that simple. Allied to speed must be the ability to deliver on the field, and this requires a multitude of skills and capacities, of which speed is one. There are numerous examples of athletes with exceptional speed scores on tests of linear speed being outperformed by an athlete whose underpinning speed capacities as measured by their 40-yard (37 m) dash are more limited but whose other capabilities can make up for this perceived lack of speed. Similarly, an athlete with exceptional underpinning speed may appear to be an exceptional performer one week but ordinary the next. Now, this does not mean that speed is unimportant; indeed, underpinning speed always will be an important tool in any athlete's armory. What it does indicate is that a sole focus on developing underpinning speed may be insufficient and that it is also important to ensure that this speed can be directly used in the attainment of the sport's key tasks. However, this requires that we take a different perspective on speed development, moving from a focus on speed as a universal capability, totally determined by a score on a linear test, to a capacity that is contextual and used to carry out key tasks within a specific sport.

Much remains to be understood about the precise application of speed in sports. Many of the concepts discussed later in this chapter under the banner of constraints, such as cognitive capacities, defy measurement, and as a result these constraints receive far less analysis of their impact and of how to develop them than the more traditional approach to speed. Given its greater body of evidence, track speed offers a logical place to commence a journey into speed development.

WHAT IS SPEED?

Any discussion on improving running speed must start with an examination of what linear speed is. In scientific terms, speed equals distance divided by time, and expresses how far an object can move in a given period of time, normally measured in meters per second. However, in performance terms, coaches seldom use a direct measure of speed but instead use a time taken to cover a given distance. Football athletes, for example, may not know the maximal speed they can run but can easily tell you their 40-yard time, while track athletes will tell you how fast they are over 100 meters.

CAN SPEED BE IMPROVED?

Whether we use actual running speeds or times for a given distance, what is critical from a training perspective is whether these can be improved and, if so, how. Whereas speed once was seen as largely a genetic trait limited by factors such as muscle fiber type and anthropometrical makeup, today we recognize that a well-structured and scientifically sound training program can improve

Usain Bolt's speed is a combination of genetic traits and speed training.

Ian Walton/Getty Images

speed—a program that this book will provide. However, although speed can be improved individually, it is inaccurate to suggest that everyone has the capacity to become a sprint champion. A genetic ceiling exists for the top speed an athlete can reach (similar to other characteristics such as strength), therefore limiting the ability of the vast majority of people to become an Olympic 100-meter champion. However, while this ceiling exists, it is likely that only a few people actually reach their ceiling. This is clearly demonstrated by the improvements that elite sprinters make throughout their careers. If top sprinters, with their training aimed specifically at speed development, take years of training and practice to reach full genetic potential, then clearly, the likelihood of athletes involved in other sports reaching their speed ceiling is much lower. As a result, the majority of athletes have a large potential to improve speed, and speed development programs are fundamental to any total performance enhancement program.

THE NATURE OF SPRINTING

Although genetic limits provide a theoretical ceiling for speed capacity, the focus of a speed development program is improvement of this capacity and especially how it relates to sport performance. This requires an examination of the nature of running speed and identifying the elements that can be enhanced through training. In this way, athletes and coaches can focus on the elements they can adapt, which then become the focus of a speed improvement program.

While the focus of this book is how to develop sport-specific speed, as mentioned earlier little research has been conducted into how speed is expressed directly in sport settings. However, a large body of work exists in track and field and in scientifically based measurements of linear speed. For this reason, we will examine sprinting, with the aim of developing generalizations that can apply to speed development in specific sports. The aim of sprinting is to move horizontally from one point to another as rapidly as possible, and generating horizontal velocity is vital. This requires generating an impulse (measured as the force applied multiplied by the duration of the force application into the training surface) to move the body horizontally and the ability to maximize the effectiveness of this movement.

Sprinting can be viewed in two ways. In one school of thought, sprinting is a finely coordinated motor skill, emphasizing finely tuned movements. In another view, sprinting is a ballistic activity, with the body driven forward as a projectile (with both feet leaving the ground at certain points) in a series of muscular efforts. While these views may appear diametrically opposed, they are both true. Sprinting depends on skilled movements, and it also depends on ballistic forces. Therefore, training for speed is multidimensional and must involve a range of activities that address all of the factors that contribute to speed. One of the greatest skills in developing speed is choosing the activities that best meet the needs of an athlete at a given time and to coordinate these into an effective training program. This requires an understanding of how motion is achieved.

BIOMECHANICS OF SPEED

Given that horizontal propulsion is generated during the stance phase and the result of the application of impulse, an important consideration is how force application directly affects speed expression. This requires a delve into the realm of biomechanics. Biomechanics is the study of forces and their effects on living systems (9), and because forces determine motion, a fundamental understanding of the biomechanical principles that affect speed can assist coaches and athletes in developing running speed.

In 1687 renowned British scientist Sir Isaac Newton published his famous book, commonly referred to as *Principia*. Published in Latin, the language of science at that time, the book contained his three laws of motion, the fundamentals of which still hold true today and contribute greatly to understanding the training concepts for speed development. Newton's three laws of motion—the law of inertia, the law of acceleration, and the law of action and reaction—translated into English read as follows:

▶ *Law 1—law of inertia.* A body continues in its state of rest or of uniform motion in a straight line unless it is compelled to change that state by forces impressed upon it.

▶ *Law 2—law of acceleration.* The change of motion of an object is proportional to the force impressed and is made in the direction of the straight line in which the force is impressed.

▶ *Law 3—law of action and reaction.* To every action there is always an opposite and equal reaction or the mutual actions of two bodies upon each other are always equal and directed to contrary parts.

At first, these may appear to be overly scientific and have little relevance to speed training. However, when examined more closely and worded more simply, they play a vital role in planning effective speed training. An understanding of these rules, together with the application of their impact, will help coaches and athletes make informed decisions in many elements of speed development.

The first law of motion states that when motion needs to be started or changed, a net force must be applied. In terms of running speed, this net force comes from within the body in the form of a muscular action, so every time an athlete wants to start moving or change the motion (e.g., increase speed, decrease speed, or change direction), the athlete needs to generate a net force. Without the application of a net force, motion cannot be initiated or changed. A change in the direction or quantity of motion is termed *acceleration*; any acceleration requires the application of a force.

This leads to the second law of motion, where the rate of change in motion (acceleration) is proportional to the amount of net force applied. This is a cause-and-effect relationship, where a net force directly causes acceleration. This is indeed one of the most important messages an athlete or coach needs to take onboard when designing a speed training program: The rate of acceleration depends on the magnitude of the net force applied. The second law of motion is summarized by the following equation:

$$\text{Net Force} = \text{Mass} \times \text{Acceleration}$$

In terms of running, body mass can be assumed to be constant; therefore, acceleration is directly dependent on, and proportional to, the magnitude of the net force applied. The ability to generate a net force effectively and rapidly is essential.

This also brings up another important element for long-term speed development: the role of mass, or the athlete's weight. Increased mass requires greater net force to achieve a given acceleration. Therefore, when athletes use resistance training, they must make sure an increase in body weight coincides with an increase in strength. Increasing muscle size without also increasing the ability to produce force does nothing to improve the ability to accelerate. Strength training for speed development should focus on increasing rapid force-producing capacity (i.e., rate of force development), not on increasing muscle size. However, the caveat to this is that in many collision sports such as football or rugby, mass can be beneficial. This is because the momentum the athlete can bring into the collision often determines the outcome of that collision. Given that momentum is the product of mass and velocity, there are probably optimal mass and speed combinations for athletes involved in these collision sports.

The key message of the third law of motion states that for every action there is an equal and opposite reaction; that is, force comes in mirrored pairs. This is illustrated when running forces from the feet are applied downward and backward into the ground, which then reactively pushes the athlete upward and forward with an equal and opposite force. This brings into focus the importance of the direction of the application of force as well as its quantity and where force needs to be applied in a direction opposite to the intended direction of motion. Speed, therefore, is maximized when both the quantity and direction of the force are optimal.

Taking all of these laws together, it can be seen that ground forces largely determine acceleration and running speed. Thus, improving the application forces into the ground needs to be a major focus of any speed training program. More detailed information on the impact of force on speed will be discussed in chapter 2.

MECHANICAL DETERMINANTS OF RUNNING SPEED

Movement is clearly driven by the application of forces, so how are these concepts applied in the generation of speed? Classically, running speed has been defined as the product of stride rate (also called *stride cadence* or *stride frequency*) and stride length (6). *Stride rate* refers to the number of strides taken per second, and *stride length* refers to the distance traveled by each stride in yards or meters. The product of these variables (i.e., stride rate × stride length) gives a mathematically accurate calculation of running speed. Therefore, the focus of speed training has been on improving stride rate, improving stride length, or improving both. However, recent research suggests that while improving these factors plays a role in determining running speed, they may provide misguided advice when developing speed training programs (6).

In particular, the concept of stride length, traditionally measured as the distance between each successive foot contact, can be problematic. Too much focus on artificially lengthening an athlete's stride can result in placing the foot ahead of the athlete's center of mass. This position compromises the athlete's ability to generate force and ultimately slows running speed. Instead, an effective stride length should be the focus. This is the distance traveled by the athlete's center of gravity per stride. An effective stride length is generated by applying a force into the ground (pushing off the ground) and propelling the athlete forward rather than reaching forward with the legs in an attempt to pull the athlete forward. The athlete's force-producing capacities are fundamental to achieving optimal stride and length and maximal speed.

Stride rate is a function of contact time (the time spent on the ground with each stride) and flight time (the time spent in the air on each stride). Research has shown little variation in flight time between runners of different speeds, and the greatest variations in stride rate are a result of differences in ground contact time (12). Therefore, efforts to improve stride rate should predominantly focus on shortening ground-contact times rather than focusing on cycling the legs faster, unless there is a clear issue that limits performance. However, here again a challenge may present itself where an overemphasis on producing a faster stride rate may result in reduced ground force application and thus a reduced stride length (5). Finding the optimal balance will always be important.

Stride length is largely a function of the impulse and velocity generated at toe-off. The velocity of the athlete's center of gravity, which is a key factor in dictating stride length, does not alter between successive steps. Instead, it is generated by the impulse applied during the time the athlete's foot is in contact with the ground (the stance phase). Therefore, efforts to enhance stride length by technical means during the flight phase, the time the body is not in contact with the ground, are limited and should instead focus on applying impulse and generating velocity during the time the athlete is in contact with the ground.

PHASES OF A RUNNING STRIDE

The discussion of stride length and stride rate requires an analysis of the phases of a running stride. Each running stride can be divided into two components: a stance phase and a flight phase. These phases are outlined in figure 1.1. The stance phase occurs when the athlete's foot is on the ground and consists of the time between the initial contact with the ground and the subsequent toe-off.

Figure 1.1   Running stride consists of a three-part stance phase: the *(a)* early stance, *(b)* midstance, and *(c)* late stance, followed by *(d)* the flight phase (of the next step).

The stance phase can be further divided into an early stance, a midstance, and a late stance. During the early stance, when the foot makes contact with the ground, the athlete's body absorbs the landing forces, which can vary from two and a half to five times the body weight, depending on the speed and distance of a sprint (6). The leg muscles absorb the landing forces through eccentric actions, which lengthen the muscles and result in the rapid generation of elastic energy. This landing force has the potential to cause significant braking forces unless the athlete has the strength capacities and the required muscle stiffness to effectively recoil like a spring (5). Importantly, athletes with these physical capacities are able to exploit this elastic energy when entering mid- and late stance. During the midstance the athlete switches from absorbing force to exerting a concentric force, which shortens the muscles and generates maximal vertical force. The elastic energy generated in the early stance can contribute to the force applied through the mid- and late stance. In late stance, the body accelerates forward as a result of the concentric forces generated.

The flight phase is the period between toe-off and the next foot contact (see figure 1.2). During this phase the athlete makes no contact with the ground so in essence is in flight. Velocity during the flight phase cannot be increased, and the athlete must reposition the leg in preparation for the next foot contact. An inability to reposition the leg effectively results in suboptimal ground contact in the next stance phase and therefore limits speed expression. Because athletes can propel themselves forward only when their foot is in contact with the ground, the stance phase is typically the main focus of speed enhancement programs.

Figure 1.2 Sprinting technique at maximum velocity. In this illustration, the left and right legs show the phases of the running stride: (i) early flight, (ii) midflight, (iii) late flight, (iv) early stance, and (v) late stance.

Adapted by permission from G. Schmolinsky, *Track and Field: The East German Textbook of Athletics* (Toronto: Sport Books, 2000), 122-123.

ACCELERATION VERSUS MAXIMUM SPEED

While *speed* is a relatively generic term and means many things to many people, when developing an effective development program, it is important to differentiate between the different components of running speed—acceleration and maximum speed. Although often used interchangeably by commentators, these are different capacities with different mechanical goals and thus differing mechanical constraints. Consequently, methods to develop acceleration and maximum speed differ in their construction, and the ability to differentiate between them allows coaches to target their training to the capacity most important for the athlete. In simple terms, acceleration is the rate of change of velocity, or how quickly an athlete can increase the velocity of the motion. Maximum speed is the highest instantaneous speed that an athlete can attain.

Because acceleration is a change in velocity, and because velocity has both a magnitude and direction associated with it, acceleration changes when an athlete changes the magnitude of the motion (how fast he or she is running), the direction of the motion, or both. In terms of running, anytime the body starts, speeds up, or changes direction, it is accelerating. Given the number of direction changes in most sports, together with the number of times the rate of velocity needs to change, acceleration plays a crucial role in speed performance in sport. This is further emphasized by the fact that elite sprinters have been shown to take up to 60 meters (66 yards) to reach top speed, and while this distance is normally shorter for field sport athletes, it still takes a considerable distance for most athletes to reach their maximum speed (11). Given the typical distances run in sport and the limits of court dimension in other sports, such as tennis and basketball, acceleration may play a more important role than maximum speed in these sports.

However, maximum speed can still play an important role in sport, even if the distances run are relatively short. This is because athletes can still reach a high

While attaining maximal speed is limited by the size of the court, Kevin Durant uses his acceleration speed to outmaneuver his opponent.

proportion of their maximal speed in a relatively short distance. Figures from the International Associations of Athletics Federations have shown that during his 100-meter final in the Beijing Olympics, Usain Bolt achieved 73% of his maximum velocity at 10 meters, 85% at 20 meters, 93% at 30 meters, and 96% at 40 meters. He attained maximum speed at 60 meters (1). Therefore, developing maximum speed should still be included in the training for most sports, but the relative importance of the two should dictate the time spent on each.

GRAVITY AND FORCE APPLICATION

In addition to the laws of motion, Newton's scientific legacy has had another important impact on speed development: the law of gravity. Whatever the sport, athletes are subject to a gravitational force that causes acceleration toward the earth at a rate of 9.8 meters (10.7 yards) per second per second. As we have discussed, sprinting is concerned with maximizing horizontal impulse. However, sprinters also need to ensure that they exert sufficient vertical force to overcome gravity and create sufficient time to reposition their legs effectively for the successive stride.

Therefore, the ideal force vector is one in which sufficient vertical force is applied to enable leg repositioning, with the remainder applied horizontally to provide propulsion. In reality, it is impossible to independently alter the horizontal and vertical aspect of the resultant force vector. The direction of the net force, therefore, depends on body position (which in turn affects the angle of force application into the ground), the overall force the athlete applies, and the muscles activated.

GROUND CONTACT TIME

Because the application of force is fundamental to running speed, and because force can only be applied when the foot is on the ground, we will examine the ground contact times during pure acceleration, transition acceleration, and maximum speed. Ground contact times are at their greatest during the initial part of a sprint (approximately 0.2 second) and decrease as a sprint continues, lasting approximately 0.12 second at the later parts of acceleration, then decreasing further to 0.09 to 0.10 at maximum speed (figure 1.3). This has important consequences for force-producing capacity. Because impulse is the force applied multiplied by the duration of force application, when ground contact time decreases, the net impulse also decreases. Therefore, during acceleration, greater ground contact times allow for greater impulse, so force can be directed both vertically and horizontally.

However, as speed increases and ground contact time decreases, more force is needed vertically to overcome the force of gravity, and less is available for horizontal propulsion. There comes a point at which ground contact time is so short that all of the force equals what is required to overcome gravity, and at that point, no additional force can be directed toward horizontal propulsion (2). At this point the athlete can no longer accelerate and has attained maximal speed (2).

As mentioned previously, stride length and stride rate are factors that affect running speed. Overall stride rate is related closely to ground contact times, and stride length is related to the impulse produced during ground contact. Thus, a key element of speed may be the ability to produce more force in a shorter time (i.e., rate of force development). Faster sprinters consistently demonstrate shorter ground contact times than slower sprinters, indicating their enhanced ability to exert force rapidly (13, 14). This requires the development of appropriate strength and power characteristics, including optimal stiffness and eccentric and concentric force capacity.

Figure 1.3   Ground contact time is greatest during acceleration.

Adapted by permission from G. Schmolinsky, *Track and Field: The East German Textbook of Athletics* (Toronto: Sport Books, 2000), 122-123.

Part of a sprinters' ability to shorten ground contact times may be caused by their ability to terminate the stance phase earlier, allowing them to cycle the leg through as efficiently as possible (6). This earlier termination of the stance phase has been shown in both acceleration and maximum-speed running. This appears to be achieved by the initiation of hip flexion before the completion of the stance. Additionally, it requires high levels of stiffness in the knee and ankle to allow for the rapid absorption of the eccentric landing forces, the activation of the stretch-shortening cycle (SSC), and subsequent concentric force production (6).

Although athletes apply an impulse to the ground during the stance phase, the flight phase also plays an important preparatory role for effective force production. At high velocities, athletes must reposition the swing leg rapidly in order to prepare for the next stance phase. This becomes increasingly important as ground contact times decrease and the athletes have to apply predominantly vertical forces to overcome gravity. This rapid cycling action requires a triple flexion of the hip, knee, and ankle, which results in shortening the lever (where the mass of the leg is placed closer to the glutes) and allowing a rapid recovery cycle (cycling the leg through to the next stance phase). This ability needs to be developed through appropriate technical development.

DIRECTIONAL FORCE APPLICATION

Because the horizontal and vertical aspects of force cannot be split, the athlete needs to generate forces that reflect the relative importance of each. One of the major ways to do this is through posture. The changes in posture during a sprint are dictated by the direction that the force needs to be applied. In the early phases of a sprint there is little momentum, so an athlete needs to generate forward momentum. This requires that force be applied horizontally and vertically to overcome the influence of gravity. In the initial acceleration phase, horizontal and vertical forces are equally distributed, resulting in a forward lean at a 45-degree angle (see figure 1.4). At this time, ideal running technique involves a piston-like action, enabling the generation of the forces needed to drive horizontally and vertically. The technical acceleration exercises in chapter 4 develop this piston-like action.

However, as athletes approach top speed, they have produced considerable horizontal momentum, and the major requirement is to overcome gravity in order to allow for an effective leg cycle. In this situation, the resultant forces are predominantly vertical (see figure 1.5). This line of force application and the application of optimal posture are explored further in chapters 2 and 3. Similarly, the technical exercises for maximum speed in chapter 4 are aimed at developing this vertical technique and rapid cycling action of the leg.

Figure 1.4 Initial acceleration posture.

Figure 1.5 Maximal speed posture.

WHAT IS GAMESPEED?

Gamespeed can be described as "a context-specific capacity, where an athlete uses movement of optimal velocity, precision, efficiency, and control to interact with the environment in order to maximize the performance of a sport-specific task" (7). A number of key aspects of this description guide us toward a more inclusive understanding of the application of speed and in turn help us understand some of the anomalies of the application of speed in sport.

First, gamespeed is context specific. In this way, the application of speed varies between and, importantly, within sports. Consequently, we can never presume that an athlete with excellent track speed will necessarily be able to apply that speed in the context of a sport. A running back, for instance, may be able to demonstrate a blazing top-end speed if he is able to get into the secondary, but unless he also possesses the skills to navigate the earlier parts of the play, where different movement capacities may be needed, he may never get the opportunity to apply his top speed.

Navigating these earlier parts of the play may require a different movement skill set, perhaps a more controlled run of optimal velocity where he has to interact with the environment, demonstrating control of his movements, reading the movements of his teammates and opponents, and adjusting the speed and direction of his movements accordingly. This may require combining his speed with shape shifts to wrongfoot the opposition in an attempt to create daylight, with the ultimate goal of picking up as many yards as possible. Clearly, having high end speed for this athlete can be transformative, but in and of itself it may be insufficient to be fully effective. Crucially, although speed and agility typically have been considered separate capacities—indeed this book focuses on speed as a separate entity—true gamespeed does not differentiate between the two. If we take the example of the running back's play, movement happens as an integrated whole, where speed is combined with aspects more associated with agility such as changing direction, adjusting body shape, and so on. To separate these out is to miss the crux of the movement itself. To evaluate speed in context, it is useful to look at the factors that potentially limit gamespeed.

THE CONSTRAINTS OF GAMESPEED

The constraints of gamespeed are thought to lie in three broad categories: environmental constraints, task constraints, and organismic constraints (figure 1.6) (7). This is important because the factors that explain the application of speed are not solely determined by an individual's capacity but also by the task he or she has to perform and the environment he or she faces.

Unlike linear speed, which is very much mechanically based, gamespeed is multidimensional with potential constraints lying in a range of areas, many

Figure 1.6   The constraints of gamespeed.

relating to context. As a result, and unlike in track with a sole focus on the individual, it is impossible to fully explain gamespeed performance from a purely individual perspective. Instead, to fully understand the application of gamespeed, it is critical to ascertain how the context in which the athlete is performing and the tasks the athlete is trying to carry out directly affect the application of speed. This is why an effective speed development program can never be separated from its underpinning purpose and why understanding context is crucial (8). Undoubtedly, arming an athlete with greater speed capacities is an important goal of training, but unless these can be applied in context, they will never be fully effective. In the running back example, simply giving greater and greater linear speed capacities may have limited impact unless the athlete also develops the skills required to navigate the early parts of the play and the ability to create the space into which to accelerate.

Understanding context requires us to consider the task and environmental constraints that are present at any given time. The task constraints refer to what needs to be achieved and factors such as the rules of the activity that govern how this can be achieved. Task constraints often interact with environmental constraints to dictate the external environment the athlete will have to navigate. Some environmental factors will be relatively stable throughout a contest, such as the playing surface, temperatures, weather conditions, and so on, while others will fluctuate to a far greater degree. The formation of the opposition, any play called, and the individual matchups all can affect speed application. Again, in the running back example, when the opposition uses blitz defenses, a screen pass may allow the running back to get into an open secondary more easily than when playing against a defense set up to defend the run. Similarly, he may perform better on a team with a pass-based offense than on one geared for a running game, because he would face different defensive setups often more conducive to getting into the secondary.

Once the context of the sport is considered it is possible to evaluate how the individual needs to interact with the context and how their individual capacities will affect this interaction. These individual limits to performance are termed *organismic constraints* and can be classified under four types: (6)

Clive Brunskill/
Getty Images

Coco Gauff has excellent gamespeed, running the width of the court in seconds to return a shot.

1. *Perceptual constraints.* The application of speed in many sport contexts involves manipulating and responding to the unfolding environment. This requires the ability to identify and focus on the key stimuli that inform decisions.

2. *Cognitive constraints.* Effective decision making not only involves the capacity to perceive crucial stimuli, but also relies on the ability to process the incoming information, differentiating and using this information to make effective decisions.

3. *Physical constraints.* The application of speed relies not only on effective decision making, but also on the capacity to execute movements. As will be highlighted later, movement ultimately relies on the application of force, and thus the ability to apply force of the optimal magnitude, in the optimal direction, and from effective starting positions is fundamental to effective speed application.

4. *Motor control constraints.* Applying force of the optimal magnitude, in the optimal direction, and from effective starting positions does not depend just on an athlete's physical constraints, it also requires optimal body alignment and the application of effective technique that facilitates speed. The ability to select and apply effective motor programs is also an important constraint to speed performance.

Now the relative importance of these constraints clearly will depend on context. In track and field, where a predetermined task is performed in response to a relatively fixed stimulus, physical and motor control constraints predominate. However, in team sports, the relative importance again is contextually specific, and athletes will be able to succeed at a task with a more individualized skill set. For example, in soccer a striker who is able to anticipate a cross and feint toward the far post before making a near-post run may be able to get in front of a defender who is theoretically faster but is less effective at perceiving key information and cognitively processing this information, all resulting in a slower response time and the loss of a first step to the attacker. This is a disadvantage that can prove critical given the short running distance involved. Importantly, this wider consideration of the constraints to speed outlines some of the challenges in using track ideas as the sole focus of consideration. Given the nature of track, speed analysis has almost solely focused on physical and motor control considerations and naturally excluded analysis of the other constraints (i.e., cognitive and motor). Unfortunately, this mindset, to an extent, has pervaded the field of speed development in other sports, and as a result many of the anomalies of faster athletes being outperformed by theoretically slower ones have defied explanation and been attributed either as contradictions or the result of vague concepts such as gamesense (8). However, when viewed from the perspective of gamespeed constraints, they are more effectively explained, with capacities across all constraints considered. From a speed development perspective, these additional considerations open up multiple opportunities to enhance speed, over and above those traditionally included in speed development programs. Later chapters in the book will apply these concepts to specific sports.

THE SKILLED NATURE OF SPEED

While linear speed and gamespeed share characteristics, they also differ. Gamespeed has a number of additional constraints, all of which can affect speed. When linear track speed is considered, it is important to remember that although force is important, sprinters cannot be built solely in the weight room. Instead, they need to ensure that the gains made in the weight room transfer onto the track, and this requires that the motor control constraints are also considered.

Here the view of speed as a coordinated motor action is important. Running speed and acceleration are skills and need to be trained in the same manner as other skills. In this way the coordinative elements of speed assume an important role. Athletes need to learn how to assume effective postures and how to use and coordinate arm and leg actions to maximize ground force and stride rate and, thus, maximize running speed and acceleration. Effective technique maximizes stride effectiveness through appropriate body alignments and maximal efficiency, thus conserving energy. (See chapters 3 and 4 for key technical areas to address.) This role of skill development becomes even more important when gamespeed is considered; not only is a greater range of movements required, but these movements themselves need to be adapted in response to the contextual challenges being faced by the athlete at any time.

PROCESS OF SKILL DEVELOPMENT

All athletes generally learn skills through three stages: the motor (cognitive) stage, the fixation (associative) stage, and the autonomous stage (10). Although running may seem a natural ability, a look at typical running actions on any playground or sport field demonstrates that it is anything but. Effective running actions need to be taught and practiced repeatedly if they are to become ingrained in the athlete. Chapter 4 focuses on the development of running actions.

To maximize the productivity of an exercise or practice, it is important to understand the characteristics and requirements of the athletes in each of the stages. In this way, training sessions and programs become learning opportunities in which technique is developed and constantly honed until it becomes a skilled act that can stand up under pressure (4).

In the motor stage, athletes are learning the skill. Here, their movements are often uncoordinated, jerky, and inconsistent. Their focus therefore needs to be almost totally on the task at hand. The challenge of the exercise should be limited, focusing on single tasks. Because the movements are unstable, they often break down, so a challenge such as a competitive run should be closely monitored and limited so it does not interfere with learning the skill.

Similarly, exercises to develop technique should emphasize the quality of performance and not just the speed of performance to ensure the development of appropriate technique. Coaches should limit the technical complexity of their feedback at this time. Guidelines for coaching athletes in the motor stage (3, 7) are summarized in table 1.1.

In the fixation stage, an athlete's performance shows much more coordination and consistency. At this time, exercises can be challenging in terms of their complexity, speed, and the level of competition. This progression should develop through the stage and should be guided by the athlete's performance. A coach should not worry about regressing an exercise if performance breaks down. As an athlete's movements become more automated, more challenging exercises can be introduced, which requires focus on both the speed of performance and additional considerations as they relate to the application of gamespeed. See table 1.1 for guidelines for coaching at the fixation stage (3, 7).

After considerable practice, some athletes will enter the autonomous stage, where movement patterns are of high quality and are consistent. At the autonomous stage, movement patterns are well developed, and the athletes' aim is to perfect these patterns while also ensuring that they can use them effectively and

consistently in intense sport-specific environments. This stage sees a predominance of high-intensity, highly complex drills. Coaching input is less frequent
but more detailed and includes precise feedback. Guidelines for coaching at the
autonomous stage are summarized in table 1.1 (3, 7).

Table 1.1 Guidelines for Coaching at Each Stage of Motor Development

Motor (cognitive) stage	Fixation (associative) stage	Autonomous stage
Focus on developing technique.	Continue to hone technique while increasing challenges.	Develop the ability to maintain technique in game-like situations.
Focus largely on general speed capabilities.	Continue to develop general capacities and also start to apply these to game conditions.	Focus on the application of speed while continuing to present general work to ensure these capacities are maintained.
Use selective drills to develop targeted technical capacities where required (e.g., arm-action drills, wall drills).	Continue to use drills and supplement them with more applied work.	Focus on applied work, with drills used in warm-ups and other situations to maintain technical capacities.
Focus on a few selective movements per session.	Increase the variety of exercises per session.	Provide a high degree of variation within and between sessions.
Use a great deal of noncompetitive work to focus on technique.	Add more competitive work, but not at the expense of technique.	Practice much of the work in competitive situations.
Practice in a non-fatigued state.	Practice in a non-fatigued state.	Practice predominantly in a non-fatigued state, but introduce challenges to develop the ability to run at speed under pressure.
Enhance learning through the use of demonstrations and develop key technical cues.	Use the key cues to reinforce technique as appropriate. Use demonstrations as required.	Use key cues to reinforce technique where breakdowns occur.
Use a great deal of simple feedback.	Reduce the quantity of feedback, but increase its precision.	Give feedback infrequently, and make sure it is precise.

Reprinted by permission from I. Jeffreys, *Total Soccer Fitness* (Monterey, CA: Coaches Choice, 2007).

KEY ELEMENTS OF SPEED TRAINING

This chapter has demonstrated that linear track speed relies on both motor skill development and the development of physical capacities to produce effective ground-reaction forces. When gamespeed is considered, the range of constraints is far greater, with the perceptual and cognitive requirements of the task providing additional organismic constraints while the task and environmental constraints also have to be taken into consideration. For these reasons, a speed development program should include three key elements:

► *Development of physical capacities.* An effective speed development program must develop an athlete's force production capacity in the musculature involved in sprinting. Each of the following is likely to play an important role in determining running speed:

- Maximal force capacity
- Rate of force development
- Optimal strength-to-weight ratio
- Stretch-shortening cycle ability

► *Technical development.* Development of sound running technique helps ensure that athletes can use their physical capacities to enhance their speed. Technical training should target areas of deficiency in the running action. This form of training starts with an analysis of performance and then addresses areas of deficiency such as posture arm action and leg action. Additional technical development should include considerations of how speed is used in context and use some of the key questions outlined in later chapters.

► *Application of speed.* The development of technique and the development of physical capacities are of no benefit unless they enhance running speed in the sport-specific context. Thus, the critical question is how to effectively transfer them to enhance gamespeed. This transfer requires an athlete to perform high-quality, contextually driven, and sport-specific bursts of speed. While this may seem obvious, much field sport training neglects contextually relevant high-speed running, and some even omits high-speed running of any type. Thus, a speed improvement program must involve speed application and address all elements that affect performance in a particular sport. Later chapters in the book outline methods of directly applying speed in sport-specific contexts.

These three elements should be integrated into a speed development program. The omission of any of these may result in suboptimal results. These elements also should be tailored to the individual athlete's characteristics. Some athletes use great technique but lack the physical capacities to maximize this technique, and others may possess excellent physical capacities but lack the required technique to optimize them. Therefore, the relative importance of each aspect of training should be different for each athlete. No speed development program will be universally optimal, so coaches need to adjust programs in response to these differences. Undoubtedly, the more knowledge a coach or athlete has regarding the scientific principles of program design, the more effectively they will be able to adapt programs to their specific needs.

CHAPTER 2

Factors Determining Linear Speed

Jean-Benoit Morin

Running and sprinting seem to be basic and simple tasks, and athletes produce linear speed naturally and repeatedly when practicing or playing their sport. However, generating linear speed is a very complex task from a neuromuscular and biomechanical standpoint; even the most advanced robots are still not able to stand still on two legs, accelerate up to human-like values, and decelerate back to the initial speed and position. This chapter will describe and comment on the determinants of linear speed, such as the laws and principles of physics that explain running speed production, the main mechanical and neuromuscular performance indicators, and how sprint mechanics can be assessed to better understand athletes' individual profiles and guide training.

SPEED AS PURE LINEAR SPEED

Moving—and especially running fast—are key in many sports. This fast running is termed *sprinting* when the highest possible levels of acceleration or speed are reached. As seen in the previous chapter, speed is the rate at which the position of the overall body changes over time (scalar value). It is synonymous with *velocity*, a vectorial quantity that also considers the direction of position change. In some languages, *speed* and *velocity* are used interchangeably (e.g., *vitesse* in French). In this chapter, we will consider linear speed as the rate of change in position in a forward linear movement. It characterizes sport actions such as track and field straight-line runs (e.g., 60 m or 100 m dash) or any type of field-based straight-line sprint (e.g., offensive or defensive actions in football, rugby, or soccer). Although many sport actions are not fully linear displacements, linear speed is a key factor in many decisive actions in sports and the main way sprint capabilities are tested. A linear sprint test allowing athletes to reach their top speed remains the best way to express and thus assess "pure speed" and an athlete's maximal acceleration (rate of speed increase) and speed capabilities.

During speed tasks, all body segments move, and the overall body displacement forward with a linear path results from joints' rotational movements. In this chapter, we will simplify the approach by considering the entire body as a single point: the center of mass (CoM). For example, as detailed later, when a force is acting on the athlete's body and the running speed of the athlete is 5.5 yards per second (5 m/sec), we will consider that the force is acting on the CoM and that the speed of 5.5 yards per second is the speed of the CoM. For simplicity, we also will consider that during linear running tasks (from a sprint start to the top speed phase), the position of the CoM is close to the center of the pelvis (figure 2.1).

During a maximal-intent run, linear speed systematically covers a spectrum of values that range from 0 yards per second (m/sec) to the maximal individual value of approximately 5.5 to 13 yards per second (5-12 m/sec) depending on the athlete's age, sex, and sprinting capabilities (16). Typical phases of a long sprint like the 100-meter dash include acceleration (increase in speed), a top speed plateau (constant speed), followed by a deceleration phase (decrease in speed). Since acceleration is the rate of change in speed, it is maximal at the beginning of a linear sprint and decreases as speed increases, down to a value of 0 yards per second squared (m/s²) when top speed is reached. At that point, the athlete runs very fast but does not accelerate anymore. This means that at any point in time during a linear sprint action in any sport, an athlete's CoM movement can be described by the combination of its speed and acceleration (see example in figure 2.2a). The neuromuscular system is also not able to produce high amounts of acceleration at high speeds, which is further described by the concept of the acceleration–speed relationship (figure 2.2b).

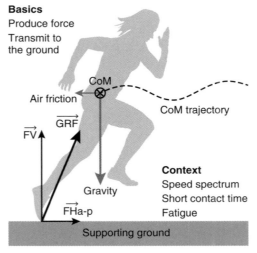

Figure 2.1 Two-dimensional schematic representation of the center of mass (CoM) and the ground reaction force (GRF) vector at a given moment of the sprint support phase.

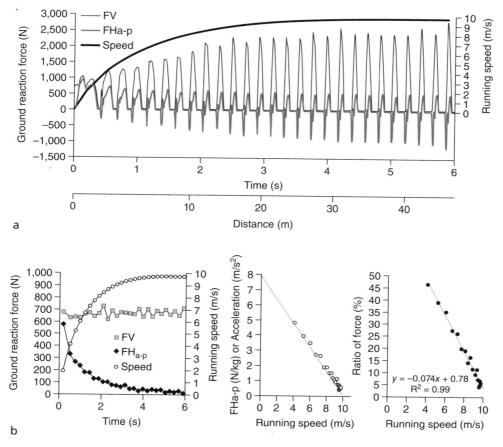

Figure 2.2 *(a)* Acceleration is maximal at the beginning of a linear sprint and decreases to zero when top speed is reached; *(b)* graphical representation of the of the acceleration–speed relationship.

Finally, when running at maximal intensity, athletes cover their individual 0-to-top speed spectrum in approximately 15 to 75 yards (or meters)—or about 2 to 8 seconds—depending on their age, sex, and overall sprinting skills. Also, faster runners generally reach their top speed later than slower ones (20). Note that the time or distance needed to reach top speed does not always depend on the level of practice; for example, some elite basketball centers or rugby forwards reach top speed early due to their body dimensions and overall lower maximal speed. In addition, linear speed sport actions are not always maximal, and beyond this all-out acceleration–speed spectrum, athletes often operate at submaximal levels of speed and acceleration. As for any movement and play in sports, the laws of physics explain performance, through the laws of motion applied to the human body or sports apparels (e.g., ball, discus, bobsleigh).

Linear Running Speed and the Laws of Motion

As explained in chapter 1, Newtonian *laws of motion* were formulated at the end of the seventeenth century by Isaac Newton and explain the causes of movement under the earth's gravity field. This is the mechanical reference framework in sports, explaining the causes of body and sports apparel (e.g. balls and projectiles) movements. In this chapter, we will focus on the motion of the athlete's CoM, which indirectly informs the motion of the entire body in this linear speed context.

The second fundamental law of motion states that the acceleration (change in speed over time) of a body in a given direction is directly proportional to the net force applied to this body and is made in the direction of the straight line in which this net force is applied. The acceleration is also inversely proportional to the mass of the body. In practice, for example, a 70-kilogram body onto which an external net force of 200 newtons is applied in a given direction at a given time point will accelerate by 2.86 meters per second squared in that direction (i.e., 200 N/70 kg). Should this force be constant in magnitude and direction over a second, and the movement starts at a speed of 0 meters per second, the speed of the body after one second will be 2.86 meters per second. This basic example shows that speed directly depends on acceleration but also on the mass of the moving body. The heavier the athlete, the lower the acceleration for a given external net force, and vice versa. In sports where body mass and *momentum* (mass multiplied by velocity) are not key to collision actions, regulating body mass and composition may be an important factor to avoid unnecessary excess of body mass altering acceleration and in turn speed-production capability.

Based on these laws, it could be suggested that more force equals more acceleration; unfortunately, it is not that simple. The second part of the fundamental law of motion states that the *direction* of the acceleration (and in turn of the CoM motion) follows the same line as the net external force applied to the body. This suggests that in order to accelerate the CoM forward and increase running speed in that direction, both the magnitude and the direction of the motive force produced are important. As we will see in the next part, the CoM shows an undulatory movement during acceleration to top-speed running, which means that the net external force acting on the CoM has both a vertical and a horizontal (anteroposterior) component. It is important to note here that, despite its importance in sport actions, deceleration (i.e., speed decrease) will not be the focus of this chapter.

So where do the external forces acting on the CoM (and causing its motion) come from? They initially come from the body's physiological motor: the neuromuscular system. Muscles, especially lower limb muscles, produce force, and muscle contractions, coordination, and synergies eventually make the body move and run—but not directly. What is not shown in figure 2.1 is the force vector representing the athlete's pushing actions into the ground (directed along the same line as the *ground reaction force* [GRF] vector, but downward and backward with the same magnitude). The third law of motion explains how the athlete's muscle actions cause the CoM and overall body movements: action–reaction. It is in fact the GRF that causes the CoM motion. Since there is currently no way to measure individual muscles or even groups of muscles force output directly during running, measuring and analyzing the GRF is the gold standard in sprint biomechanics. It is assumed that should a GRF of 1,000 newtons be measured at a given time point, it is the result of all muscular actions of the athlete producing force into the ground and the ground, in turn, reacting with a force vector that has the same magnitude in the opposite direction.

As shown in figure 2.1, the orientation angle of the GRF vector at a given instant directly explains the relative magnitude of the vertical (FV) and horizontal (FHa-p) components of the GRF vector and, in turn, the acceleration of the CoM they induce in the vertical and forward directions. To directly describe this GRF orientation and the induced ratio between FHa-p and FV components, we proposed the simple computation of the *ratio of force* (RF) as the ratio of FHa-p divided by GRF (10). For example, in figure 2.1, this RF is about 40% (FHa-p divided by GRF magnitude), which means that about 40% of the total GRF produced at that point in time is directed forward and will induce a forward acceleration of the CoM. This percentage is directly proportional to the angle of the GRF vector with the supporting ground: the higher the RF, the more forward the GRF angle and vice versa.

The two other external forces acting on the athlete's CoM are gravity (directed overall vertically) and air friction (directed overall parallel to the supporting ground and CoM trajectory). In the absence of significant wind conditions, the latter is estimated to a couple of newtons and approximately 50 newtons at most for tall and elite sprinters. Note that GRF measurements actually take these two external forces into account since the athletes' propulsion into the ground represents their actions aiming at accelerating or maintaining speed within and between steps, which includes acting against the effects of both gravity (vertical) and air friction (horizontal).

In summary, the laws of motion explain that generating and maintaining linear speed is about generating a pushing force via the neuromuscular system and applying it to the supporting ground so that the GRF magnitude and orientation will cause the CoM (and by extension full body) motion. The following section includes these basics within the context of sprinting, during which actions (1) are not instantaneous (force production into the ground occurs during the entire support phase), (2) occur at a very high speed and rate of movement, and (3) are often produced in fatigue conditions (e.g., in field-based sports).

A Functional Model of Linear Speed

The basics discussed in the previous section are described within an "instantaneous" framework, illustrated in the screenshot of an instant in figure 2.1. These basic components of sprint mechanics state that linear speed is mainly caused by athletes producing force and applying it to the supporting ground.

However, sprinting is in fact a continuous series of actions, and if one considers a 5-second acceleration or top-speed movement, athletes usually operate at 4 or more steps per second, during which GRF varies constantly in both magnitude and orientation over the support (or ground contact) phase.

To better understand and capture the temporal dimension and complexity of speed GRF application during running (beyond illustrative instantaneous pictures), it is necessary to use and study the *impulse* associated with the GRF. This mechanical variable is defined as the product of the force by its time of application. In sprinting, impulse is equal to average GRF multiplied by contact time. In each direction, the impulse associated with vertical force (FV) and FHa-p components of the GRF will be equal to average FV times contact time and average FHa-p times contact time, respectively. As shown in figure 2.3, the impulse associated with each GRF component is graphically represented by the area under the force curve. The larger the area, the larger the impulse. In turn, following the impulse–momentum law of mechanics, the change in velocity of the CoM in a given direction during the support phase will be equal to the impulse divided by the body mass of the athlete.

Beyond these basics of linear speed (produce force and transmit it to the ground), some context is needed to understand linear speed and in turn how it should be trained.

First, generating as much GRF impulse as possible should be done within a high to very high movement speed context. As suggested by the previous example, speed increases very rapidly during a sprint acceleration: athletes generally reach 50% of their top speed within less than 2 seconds (20). At the end of an elite sprinter's starting-block initial push, the CoM speed in the horizontal direction can be close to one-third of their top end speed (16). This implies that what matters is not exactly the ability to generate and apply high amounts of impulse (especially in the horizontal direction in the acceleration phase); instead the key to sprint performance is the ability to do so at a high to very high running speed and within short to very short contact times. Typically, after a couple of steps, the time and speed context of GRF impulse production is a movement speed above 3 to 4 meters (about 3-4 yards) per second, contact times below 0.2 to 0.15 second, and step rate above 4 steps per second (16, 20). The fastest athletes are not those able to generate the highest absolute GRF impulses, but those who are able to do so in this constrained linear speed context. The duration of the support phase is so short that it is necessary to prepare

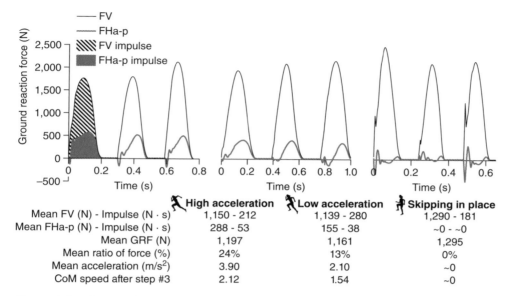

	High acceleration	Low acceleration	Skipping in place
Mean FV (N) - Impulse (N · s)	1,150 - 212	1,139 - 280	1,290 - 181
Mean FHa-p (N) - Impulse (N · s)	288 - 53	155 - 38	~0 - ~0
Mean GRF (N)	1,197	1,161	1,295
Mean ratio of force (%)	24%	13%	0%
Mean acceleration (m/s^2)	3.90	2.10	~0
CoM speed after step #3	2.12	1.54	~0

Figure 2.3 The impulse associated with each GRF component is graphically represented by the area under the force curve. For example, during the first step of a high-acceleration linear sprint (the shadowed area), a 74-kilogram athlete applying an average FHa-p of 400 newtons during a contact time of 0.19 seconds will generate an impulse of 400 × 0.19 = 76 N/s in the horizontal direction. This will correspond to an increase in running speed of approximately 1 meter per second during this contact phase (as explained, the change in velocity is equal to the impulse divided by body mass: i.e., 76 ₍ 74, or about 1). So, the magnitude of the GRF and the associated impulse will directly influence CoM speed production, and the ratio of forces (or the mechanically equivalent ratio of impulses) will directly influence the orientation of the CoM motion.

ground contact with very intense leg actions toward the ground to ensure an efficient GRF impulse production during the support phase, as well as linear speed production or maintenance (3, 4).

Finally, most of the time in team sports, field-based sports that include sprint movements, and even by the end of the 100-meter dash, fatigue induces an inability to maintain linear top-speed levels over time. All 100-meter runners face a decrease in running speed (albeit very small for some athletes), and all team sport athletes face a decrease in their linear sprint capabilities with repeated sprints over a game or a training session. This decrease in performance is an observable consequence of the fatigue phenomenon, and thus linear speed performance should also be considered within this context. The best athletes are not only those able to perform better in fresh conditions, but also those who are able to maintain the highest level of performance under fatigue. As we will see later, there is a large interindividual variability in the effects of fatigue on linear speed mechanics and performance.

In summary, previous models of linear speed performance stated that linear speed was the product of step rate (i.e., steps per second) by step length (i.e., meters per step). While this is a correct description from a spatiotemporal standpoint, the functional model proposed here focuses on the causes of motion: GRF and the associated impulse, and their orientation in space. Since you can only understand and develop what you measure correctly, the next part will address force measurements during sprinting.

FORCE PLATE ANALYSES

In human movement studies, a force plate system consists of one or several plates—typically about 1.6 feet (0.5 m) wide, 2.6 feet (0.8 m) long and 0.3 feet (0.1 m) high—installed in series onto the running ground or, better, embedded into the running ground or track. Historically, pioneers of movement and exercise biomechanics such as Étienne-Jules Marey performed the first ground reaction force estimations via pressure systems in the end of the nineteenth century. Then, running dynamics were estimated based on running speed measurements and the laws of motion described earlier (1, 7), and the first use of force plates for sprint analysis was reported in the seminal work of Giovanni Cavagna and colleagues in 1972. In this study, several sprints were necessary to study GRF at different time points and to reconstruct an entire sprint acceleration data with a shorter (approximately 5.5 yards [5 m]) system (2). Force plates are usually stiff and allow a wide range of forces to be recorded in three dimensions via calibrated force sensors at a high sampling rate (typically >500 Hz). Therefore, this method is considered the gold standard for locomotion mechanics measurements. The most advanced systems are directly installed into a synthetic running track and allow 55- to 66-yard (50-60 m) continuous measurements, thus capturing an entire linear sprint acceleration over a single trial (5).

We will use a trained sprinter's linear sprint data to describe the main sprint mechanics throughout the entire spectrum of linear speed, from a starting-block push to the top-speed plateau (figure 2.2) (15). This example clearly shows the high-speed and short contact time context of GRF and impulse production: the rapid early increase in running speed (more than 70% of top-end speed reached in approximately 2 seconds) is associated with a decrease in acceleration and FHa-p averaged over each contact phase, while average FV is approximately constant throughout the sprint. On the instantaneous (1000 Hz) traces presented in figure 2.2, it is clear that FHa-p over the first steps shows a predominance of propulsive (i.e., positive) force and associated impulse, while braking (i.e., negative) phases appear and increase in the late acceleration and top-speed phases. The braking and propulsive phases and impulses characterize the running support phase in the horizontal direction, and their overall sum indicates linear speed increase (positive net FHa-p and impulse), maintenance (net

FHa-p or impulse close to zero), or decrease (negative net FHa-p and impulse). In addition, as mentioned earlier, the magnitude of this net FHa-p and impulse is directly proportional to the speed increase or decrease.

Additional analyses include the linear relationship between acceleration or FHa-p and speed and the linear decrease in RF at each step with increasing speed. The latter relationship shows that GRF orientation is overall becoming more vertical as speed increases toward top speed. The rate of decrease in RF with increasing speed (slope of the linear RF–speed relationship) is 7.4% in the example presented in figure 2.2 and will be further discussed as the D_{RF} variable.

Since force plate measurements are only possible in a very limited number of laboratories, two alternative approaches have been developed to assess sprint kinetics. First, instrumented sprint treadmills have been developed since the 1990s, but they are also rare and expensive and suffer several experimental limitations. Second, a field computation method was proposed in 2013 and later validated against force plate measurements (15). Based around the early-twentieth-century works by exercise physiology pioneer Sir Archibald V. Hill, this method is constructed around running speed or position measurement over time and the application of basic laws of motion (7). The most recent works using this method show that it is possible to estimate most GRF variables described in this part from accurate speed measurements performed during a complete acceleration trial.

In summary, force plate analyses allow accurate measurements of sprint spatiotemporal and GRF variables and give a clear individual picture of the mechanical underpinnings of linear speed. The next part of this chapter will address the main key performance indicators within this set of biomechanical variables and introduce associated training frameworks.

FROM GROUND REACTION FORCE ANALYSIS TO LINEAR SPEED PERFORMANCE

Among the numerous mechanical variables that can be measured during a sprint trial, some influence more speed production than others. For these key performance indicators, faster athletes show different values than slower ones, and research has shown these differences in testing and by comparing athletes of leisure to elite level.

Main Mechanical Key Performance Indicators

Laws of mechanics explain that GRF impulse in a given direction (or average GRF over a given contact time) is proportional to the acceleration of the CoM in that direction. Therefore, the main mechanical variable associated with linear acceleration performance (the ability to increase speed in the forward direction) is FHa-p and the associated net (propulsive plus braking) impulse. For a same given magnitude (e.g., 1000 N), if the athlete's push onto the ground be directed more horizontally backward, the GRF vector will be directed more forward and the FHa-p will be greater while FV will be smaller, resulting in a more forward-oriented acceleration of the CoM at that time point, all other things equal. Additional research has shown that heavy resistance sprint training, for example, is a good way to improve these key performance indicators of sprint acceleration (8).

This mechanical logic was verified experimentally, with studies consistently showing that faster athletes were able to accelerate more because of their ability to produce more FHa-p during acceleration (5, 11, 13, 16). This was due mainly to their ability to produce high RF values and to limit the decrease in RF with increasing speed (i.e., a more forward-oriented application of the force onto the ground rather than higher GRF magnitudes). This was observed over a wide range of speed capabilities in athletes (leisure to world class) from various sports including track and field and team sports. For example, Colyer and Nagahara compared football athletes and sprinters at the same speed (around the top-speed value of the football athletes) (5). At that point, football athletes could not generate more speed, while sprinters were still able to accelerate toward higher linear speed. At that top-speed limit of approximately 9 yards per second (8.0 m/sec) for football athletes, the athletes who could run faster produced on average about the same GRF (20.5 N/kg body mass for sprinters versus 19.2 N/kg for soccer athletes), but the FHa-p component was 50% greater in sprinters (2.5 versus 1.7 N/kg) and the FV component was only 6% greater (19.6 N/kg for sprinters versus 18.4 N/kg for football athletes) for overall similar contact times of approximately 0.1 second in both populations. One of the conclusions of this study was that the higher linear speed reached by sprinters was mechanically related to their ability to produce greater GRF at high speed and, more importantly, transmit the force with a more forward orientation to accelerate longer and thus reach a higher top speed.

Similar results were found when comparing elite (including sub-10-sec 100-m specialists) to subelite sprinters acceleration capabilities: Rabita and colleagues and Morin and colleagues overall found that the main differences in sprint mechanics were in the FHa-p component and in RF and D_{RF} rather than FV or resultant GRF magnitude when averaged over the entire 40-meter test and speed spectrum (13, 16). These results collectively suggest that generating linear speed depends mainly on the FHa-p impulse and the ability to orient the GRF forward (while maintaining enough FV to keep balance and running stance) especially as speed increases.

A typical example is shown in figure 2.3 to understand that even if the magnitude of FV is greater than the magnitude of FHa-p, the latter is more important mechanically to generate forward motion. In all three movements compared (three first steps of a high acceleration, low acceleration, and skipping in place), the mean FV was almost equal between the three actions, and the associated impulse was even greater during low acceleration compared to high acceleration. It is the FHa-p mean force and impulse and the ratio of force that differed between skipping in place (no forward movement, null linear speed produced after three skips), low acceleration (intermediate FHa-p, RF, and speed eventually produced), and high acceleration (highest FHa-p, RF, and speed eventually produced).

Another illustration that FHa-p is a limiting factor for linear speed is the fact that when pulled horizontally (e.g., by pulley system or robotic assistance device), athletes almost systematically reach a higher top speed than without this additional source of FHa-p. However, the extent of this speed increase under external assistance is usually limited to 5 to 10%, which suggests that other mechanical factors limit top-speed performance.

Indeed, once top speed is reached, the support phase is divided into braking and propulsion phases, and the mean FHa-p or impulse are close to zero (braking and propulsive FHa-p impulses are equal in magnitude but cancel out due to one being positive and the other being negative). Thus, the GRF is overall directed vertically (RF is zero, figure 2.2), and the key performance indicator is the ability to generate high amounts of GRF and FV within a short time (3). This ability to produce high FV per unit body mass and apply it to the ground within a short (typically 100 to 150 ms) time is related to lower limb and especially ankle stiffness and bouncing capability, and to the intense actions performed during the swing phase (prior to contact) to attack the ground forcefully and "whip from the hip" (4).

Finally, in the context of fatigue induced by repeated linear sprints, an instrumented treadmill study in trained athletes showed that in addition to the decrease in GRF production, the effectiveness of the GRF orientation was impaired to an even greater extent (12). In another study in elite rugby sevens athletes, the variables describing the forward orientation capability throughout the sprint acceleration (RF during the first steps and D_{RF}) were also clearly altered after a 10×40-meter repeated sprint exercise, while the GRF production remained almost unchanged (9).

The functional model proposed in this chapter explains the main mechanical factors underpinning linear speed and builds a framework to design and orient training to develop linear speed performance. The next section discusses the most recent research and practice evidence connecting key mechanical factors or propulsion and linear speed to the underlying trainable motors of speed performance.

From Mechanics to Muscles: Introducing a Training Framework

From a basic functional anatomy standpoint, pushing the body CoM in the direction of running and accelerating it forward in an overall standing posture (as in figure 2.1) requires backward and downward actions of the lower limbs onto the ground. This is mainly done through an overall lower limb and hip extension, and the GRF is eventually transmitted to the ground via a plantar-flexion motion, within the context of a very high force in a short amount of time. Based on this, research and training practice have centered on the potential role of hip, knee, and ankle flexion and extension actions and the associated muscle groups.

The most recent experimental studies on linear acceleration performance executed on instrumented treadmills and tracks tend to show that FHa-p and overall mechanical work production are mainly associated with hip extensors (e.g., gluteus and hamstring muscles) and ankle plantar flexors (e.g., triceps surae) contribution (14, 18, 19). For example, the reference study on the topic (19) shows that during high acceleration runs, more than 80% of the negative and positive work during the support phase is generated at the hip (extension) and ankle (plantarflexion). This suggests that improving hip extension and plantarflexion strength and power as well as the ability to perform these actions and switch legs at a high speed and step rate is key to improving acceleration and thus speed performance.

At high speed (low acceleration), the latter study shows about the same result, yet the relative contribution of the ankle is greater than in the low-speed and high-acceleration condition (more than half of the total mechanical work generated). This predominance of ankle plantarflexion work and power is in line with the modeling study of Dorn and colleagues showing that when linear running speed increases toward top speed values (i.e., from 4 to 8 yards/sec [3.5-7.0 m/sec]), the plantar flexors are mainly responsible for increasing stride length by generating higher support forces during ground contact (6).

In this summary of the main muscular groups explaining propulsion and linear speed production, the focus has been on the lower limb. However, the entire body is expected to move under the effects of GRF impulse mainly driven by lower limb actions. This means that the high GRF that crosses the entire body during the support phase requires the pelvis, trunk, and upper limbs to control actions to limit mechanical energy dissipation and ensure a good transmission of GRF to the CoM forward motion. In other words, should the high amounts of GRF during the support phase result in too many uncontrolled deformation movements at the pelvis and trunk (drop, rotations, lateral or sagittal flexions), the conversion of GRF into CoM linear speed may be altered. This likely justifies improving the lumbopelvic and trunk control to improve the overall force transmission effectiveness during sprinting and the transmit part of the functional model proposed in this chapter. Although more research is needed on this topic, emerging evidence tends to support this functional link between lumbopelvic control and trunk muscles training and performance in linear speed and other sport-specific power tasks (9, 17).

These results do not suggest that only the muscles and actions discussed should be trained and developed but that comprehensive training for linear speed performance should prioritize these actions that are fundamental to the key mechanical performance indicators identified in this chapter. Further developments and applications of this biomechanical analysis of the determinants of linear speed also support the regular monitoring of individual sprint mechanics to both guide and regulate training interventions.

CHAPTER 3

Technical Aspects of Speed

Dana Agar-Newman
Matthew Barr

As discussed in preceding chapters, coaching the technical aspects of speed represents a unique challenge, because it is a cyclical activity with unique biomechanical differences from the initiation of a sprint up to when an athlete achieves maximal velocity. Although there is some debate about the relevance of applying technical models of sprinting to more open-field sport situations, these models are still a relevant place to begin because of the following:

1. Better performers in some sports achieve higher speeds (1).
2. A faster maximal velocity increases the athlete's anaerobic speed reserve (6).
3. Better technique could reduce the risk of injury (9).
4. Sprinting technique should be viewed from a general stance in that good technique affords the opportunity for strength training at high velocities, which cannot be achieved in a weight room setting.

Coaches would not allow athletes to power clean with a technique that limits the load they can lift, so why would coaches allow athletes to run with a technique that limits their speed and therefore the force they can impart into the ground? However, it is important to note that biomechanical differences exist between sprinters and field sport athletes that are affected by a multitude of factors including the individual constraints of the athlete, the constraints of the task, and the constraints of the environment (23). It is important that a coach recognizes that the movement outcome, the athlete's speed, is the result of the interaction of these factors and not purely the result of conforming to a technical model.

When examining an athlete's acceleration technique, evaluating a single stride will result in unique biomechanics that will differ from each preceding and succeeding strides, making developing a model a challenge, because athletes may take 14 or more strides to reach maximal velocity (16). However, the final strides of acceleration will have nearly indistinguishable biomechanics to those at maximal velocity (16). Developing a technical model for maximal velocity is simpler in that each stride's kinematics and kinetics are relatively stable. Due to the uniqueness of acceleration technique and the stability of maximal velocity technique a coach may wonder how many phases they should use in their technical model. While a case could be made to use several, a simple way of thinking of acceleration and maximal velocity would be to split into the following phases:

1. In the *initial acceleration phase*, the first few strides from a stationary (or near-stationary start) characterized by relatively (to later strides) longer ground contact times, shorter flight times, and increased trunk and shin angles. The key technical aspects for coaching are (1) at touchdown the center of mass will be ahead of the support foot and (2) at toe-off athletes will have optimized the horizontal and vertical projection of their center of mass to maximize horizontal velocity while maintaining balance in subsequent steps.

2. The *mid- to late acceleration phase* (roughly stride 4 up until approximately stride 15) is characterized by decreasing ground contact times, longer flight times, and decreased trunk and negative shin angles at touchdown. The key technical aspect for coaching is that the foot contacts slightly ahead of the center of mass and the shin and trunk angles will both gradually change from forward oriented to more upright.

3. The *maximal velocity phase* is somewhat nebulous, when foot strike happens with a negative shin angle and when most biomechanical parameters such as trunk and head angle will be relatively stable as horizontal velocity approaches (>95%) and is maintained at maximal velocity. The key technical aspect for coaching is the slightly forward-oriented trunk position and slight negative shin angle and the lack of stride-to-stride change in kinematics.

Using a simple model like this narrows down the areas to focus on, because the key technical aspects that differentiate the phases are distinct. However, when observing athletes, each phase should bleed into the subsequent phase without abrupt changes in positioning. Simply put, coaches should see athletes initially pushing themselves forward from a crouched position at the start of the sprint, with their shin angles gradually becoming more vertical at initial ground contact and the torso angle doing the same, albeit at a slightly delayed rate until they achieve an upright balanced position at maximal velocity (see figure 3.1). Typically, sprinters will increase speed through an increase in stride rate (frequency) in the initial acceleration, an increase in stride length during the mid- to late acceleration, and a change in the individual stride length or stride rate during the maximal velocity phase (20). However, every athlete and sport will have subtly different solutions or styles to impart the necessary forces in the proper direction and time to run fast (29). Therefore, when evaluating technique, it is important that coaches consider multiple trials, examining the critical differences and similarities in relation to how they affect the individual's ability to change velocity over time and achieve a high maximal velocity.

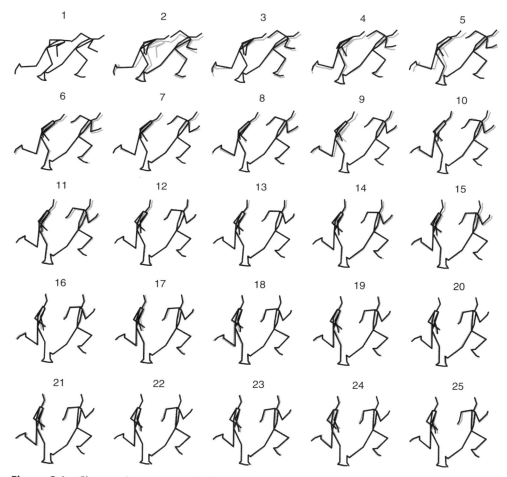

Figure 3.1 Changes in average sprinting motion during the entire acceleration phase. The stick figures illustrate the body segment positions at the foot-strike and just before the toe-off from the 1st to 25th step. Numbers in the figure indicate the respective steps. The gray figures overlapping the black figures are those immediately before the respective steps. The MP joint was used as a reference to adjust the horizontal positions of the stick figures of adjacent steps.

TECHNICAL MODEL OF SPRINTING

When building acceleration and maximal velocity technical models for team sport athletes, the technical models developed for elite sprinters is an obvious starting point. However, the study of elite sprinters is unique compared to team sport athletes in that sprinters represent a relatively physically homogenous population sample competing on standardized surfaces without external implements or the direct interaction of opponents and teammates under unique time and space constraints (i.e., different individual, environmental, and task constraints). Consequently, the technical aspects unique to the sport are critical to evaluate when improving sprinting ability in field and court sport athletes. Nevertheless, elite sprinters provide a starting point, and as more sport-specific sprinting research becomes available, technical models can be modified for each sport and positional subgroups. Ultimately, the holy grail for coaching speed is to focus on the most important modifiable technical aspects, coached in a concise manner within the small amount of time that is often afforded to speed training by technical and tactical coaches. The next sections will address the key technical aspects of the initial acceleration, mid- to- late acceleration, and maximal velocity phases of sprinting.

Initial Acceleration

Initial acceleration positions the athlete to maximize horizontal forces while maintaining balance in subsequent steps. The key characteristic of the initial acceleration phase is an aggressive forward lean that places the center of mass ahead of the foot at touchdown (figure 3.2). This removes the braking phase and will give an athlete the sensation of pushing throughout the stride, which is unique to this phase and done for the benefit of rapidly increasing speed by maximizing propulsive forces and increasing stride length (12). To maximize the propulsive forces, coaches may cue and look for triple extension of the ankle, knee, and hip joint during initial acceleration; while this demonstrates the correct intent of maximizing the push through the ground by the athlete and may be useful in teaching beginning athletes the correct intent, it is likely that the force generated through the last few degrees of knee extension is not worth the increased time on the ground. Top-level sprinters are often observed extending through the hip and ankle while leaving a subtle bend in the knee prior to toe-off. To further emphasize the position at toe-off, a stance foot position more posterior relative to the center of mass at toe-off is associated with better sprint performance and appears to be a critical difference between sprinters (fastest), rugby union backs, and rugby union forwards (slowest) (29). Initial ground contact times are long with negligible flight times; as speed increases the ground contact times become shorter and the flight times become longer. An initial large forward lean is followed by a gradual step-by-step increase in trunk angle, hip height, and a less forward-oriented shin at touchdown. An athlete needs to push vertically just enough to elevate the center of mass and forward as much as possible to maximize stride length. The first step may start quite wide (1.0-1.3 ft [0.3-0.4 m]) and get progressively narrower (19), and coaches may also note a forward-tilted pelvis relative to the ground and larger amounts of thoracic obliquity with little pelvic or shoulder rotation (compared to maximum velocity) (21), both of which likely help contribute to greater horizontal propulsive forces.

Actively focusing on a forward lean will help to optimally orient force and reduce braking time (14). However, this lean is a balancing act. If a coach observes an abrupt change in shin or torso angles during initial acceleration (e.g., the athlete stumbles or stands upright), this likely can be traced back to an improper balance of horizontal and vertical forces in the prior steps and likely is the result of the athlete trying to project too horizontally for his or her physical ability. Related to this, athletes without well-developed strength qualities may be limited in the amount of forward lean they can adopt. This balance of vertical and horizontal forces is how stride rate and stride length are developed, with propulsive vertical impulse in early acceleration the key factor for determining the stride length–to–stride rate ratio (21). Actively cueing athletes to focus on not collapsing the ankle on foot contact and plantarflexing can increase speed, because the ankle joint plays a critical role during this phase in transferring force into the surface (24), although coaches may want to be cognitive of the

Figure 3.2 Initial acceleration positions with forward-oriented trunk and shin angles and relatively short flights times.

potential downsides of internal cues. This rigid foot contact will shorten the time spent on the ground, which is critical for speed, but here again this is a balancing act: There likely is an optimal level of tension present in the foot and ankle joint, because some absorption does happen even during maximal effort acceleration (24). The short flight time is unique in this phase, and cueing athletes to actively drive the swing leg back into the ground to minimize time in the air and optimize push time can be a valuable coaching tool. Recently, it has been suggested that the toe should drag along the ground to minimize or eliminate flight time over the first step, but care should be taken in advising this because the retardant drag forces likely outweigh any advantage of this technique. Simply maintaining a recovery position low to the ground ("drag through the tops of the blades of grass" rather than ground) without touching would accomplish the intended outcome of minimizing flight time and getting the foot back on the ground for the next propulsion.

When beginning from a static start, the initial acceleration phase ends when the foot strikes slightly in front of the center of mass, which typically would be after three or four strides (around 4 or 5 yards or meters) (18), whereas an athlete beginning a sprint from a jog or run hypothetically could perform the initial acceleration phase in one stride (or skip it altogether if the velocity is high enough) and move directly to the mid- to late acceleration phase.

Mid- to Late Acceleration

The mid- to late acceleration (figures 3.3-3.4) begins when the foot strikes slightly in front of the center of mass (13) after three or four strides (around 4 or 5 yards or meters) (16). Mid- to late acceleration can be thought of as solving the problem of continuing to maximize horizontal forces while maintaining balance with the additional restriction of a decreasing ground contact time (e.g., time to produce force). This increase in speed shifts the importance from initially maximizing propulsive work to reducing braking forces later in acceleration (5, 8).

Quickly developing force as the foot strikes ahead of the center of mass and redirecting the body upward the optimal amount is key to shortening time on the ground; vertical impulse in the braking phase now becomes highly important (13). The slight forward lean (which decreases with each stride throughout this phase) and forward-oriented shin angle will help increase stride length as the athlete accumulates forward momentum. Minimizing the braking forces through a touchdown as close as possible to a point under the center of mass, negative footspeed prior to contact and maximizing horizontal propulsive forces are key. Knee extension velocity increases until about halfway through the phase, while hip extension velocity continues to increase (16). As an athlete progresses through the mid- to late acceleration phase, the knee joint at touchdown becomes more extended and a more upright posture is adopted,

Figure 3.3 As the athlete progresses out of early acceleration, the foot will contact the ground slightly ahead of the center of gravity with a forward oriented shin angle at touchdown with a stiff ankle at contact.

Figure 3.4 Throughout acceleration, trunk angle continues to become slightly more upright through each stride.

which means the hip extensors become the largest contributors to speed (16). The arm action should be aggressive, driving the arm down and backward, with the elbow opening slightly during the back stroke of the arms and then returning toward the midline of the athlete (but not across) and with less of an angle at the elbow. As outlined in the previous chapter, mean propulsive force relative to body weight and applied in the correct directions is the key variable for acceleration (15). As in the initial acceleration phase, a forward orientation of the pelvis (i.e., anterior pelvic rotation) during the mid- to late acceleration phase, and with decreasing trunk rotation and thorax obliquity during the final section in the entire acceleration phase of sprinting, are consistent with effective acceleration (17). This pelvic orientation may be helpful for increasing backward leg swing to increase propulsive forces during acceleration (17).

Increases in speed during this phase can be cued by focusing on an active, fast foot strike, which likely will result in shorter ground contact times (18). Encouraging a neutral pelvis position neutral that allows the athlete to use the stretch-shortening cycle and building up eccentric strength in the hip flexors are key for quickly getting the foot back in front of the body for the fast foot strike and minimizing time on the ground. As such, coaches should observe the athlete's knee moving forward soon after toe-off when viewed from the side, or the bottom of the foot should disappear quickly after toe-off when viewed from behind the athlete. Interestingly, elite sprinters have better-developed hip flexors than their subelite counterparts (10). This is likely from the large forces required for a fast recovery of the swing leg back in front of the body. The mid- to late acceleration phase ends with the trunk in its most upright position (figure 3.5) and the shin with a slightly backward angle at foot strike (typically ends at about 14th stride, or 22-27 yards [20-25 m]) (16).

Dan Mullan/Getty Images

Figure 3.5 The mid- to late acceleration phase will still be characterized by a more forward oriented trunk angle than the maximal velocity phase.

Maximal Velocity

The maximal velocity phase happens when an athlete's horizontal velocity stabilizes and may occur at 33 to 44 yards (30-40 m) in most field sport athletes (2) but can extend up to 66 yards (60 m) in in track athletes (26) and is dependent on the athlete's acceleration ability. Therefore, the problem a coach is trying to solve is how to best position the sprinter to maintain maximal velocity; this requires a position that allows the sprinter to effectively apply vertical force into the ground while minimizing braking forces. Maximal possible horizontal velocity is limited by how quickly force can be developed during the initial part of the ground contact, with better sprinters putting more force into the ground during the first half of ground contact (4). It is important to emphasize that quickly applying force as the foot strikes slightly ahead of center of mass and redirecting the body upward the optimal amount is key to shortening time on the ground. Optimizing vertical push to find the balance between shortening time on the ground and maximizing stride length is critical to finding the individual solution to the fastest possible maximal velocity (21). Another factor affecting the ground contact time is the athlete's *contact length* (i.e., the distance the hip travels from touchdown to toe-off). Coaches should be aware that taller athletes naturally will have a slightly longer ground contact time due to this increased distance and should not chase an arbitrary ground contact time. An upright posture will allow an optimal eccentric contraction in the hip flexors (before and as the foot leaves the ground) and quads (the instant before the foot contact the ground), which facilitates force application.

Pelvic tilt becomes consistent once an athlete reaches the maximal velocity phase, with less movement of the trunk compared to the earlier acceleration phase (17). Maintaining posture with high hips, a neutral pelvis, and a slight forward lean will allow hip flexors to perform their critical role of getting the foot in front of the body for optimal foot strike. As in the mid- to late acceleration phase, coaches should observe the knee advancing forward soon after toe-off. An active, fast foot strike with tension in both the plantar flexors and dorsiflexors as well as building reactive quadricep muscles and calf muscles that can rapidly apply forces are important training adaptation (22). The faster the running speed, the closer the knee of the swing leg needs to be rotated through to the midline of the body at stance leg touchdown (11). Good sprinters will have the swing leg knee beside or slightly in front of the support leg knee at touchdown. Mirroring the action of the lower body are the arms. The hand should be driven down aggressively, with the arm opening slightly on the downstroke; this angle of opening at the elbow joint is a function of the athlete's forward velocity and is necessary to counter the rotational forces on the trunk produced by the legs. The downward action of the hand and arm will allow the athlete to use the stretch-shortening cycle and naturally return the arm to the midline (but not across), encouraging a rapid stretching of the muscles of the shoulder and across the anterior sling to the opposite hip. While it is a myth that the arms should stay at 90 degrees during sprinting, the arm will shorten to an angle of approximately 90 degrees on the return to the midline, mirroring the contralateral leg that will be shortening to assist in its recovery.

When examining sprinting technique (figure 3.6), it is useful to address it through the PAL (posture, arms, legs) framework popularized by Vern Gambetta (7). In this framework technical issues are typically corrected in the previously mentioned order (e.g., postural issues prior to legs).

Figure 3.6 Technical Cues for Each Phase of Sprinting

INITIAL ACCELERATION

- Each stride becomes longer, with less time on the ground as the athlete accelerates. The hips rise with the less acute torso angle, and there is a higher knee lift relative to the hip, with the foot of the recovering leg gaining height with each stride.

Posture

- Greatest magnitude of forward lean which is subtly reduced with each step.
- Center of mass is in front of the foot at touchdown.
- Pelvis is held in a neutral position relative to the torso.
- Hips rise higher with each step.

Arms

- Large ranges of motion in the arms to match the ranges of motion in the lower body on the contralateral side (e.g., as knee travels forward, opposite arm is travelling forward).
- The arms are driven aggressively backwards.
- May see the humerus (upper arm) internally rotate to allow for a greater range of motion during the first step if starting from a stand still.

Legs

- Piston action in the legs which is backward and downward.
- Lower heel recovery relative to the ground.
- Forward orientated shin angles at contact.
- Optimal stiffness in the foot and ankle (ankle does not collapse at strike).
- Knee travels forward soon after toe-off.

MID-TO LATE ACCELERATION

Posture

- Forward lean is reduced each step gradually assuming an upright position.
- The pelvis is held in a neutral position relative to the torso.
- Foot gradually begins to contact closer to underneath the center of mass.
- Hips continue to rise higher with each step.

Arms

- Arm action continues to match the ranges of motion in the lower body on the contralateral side (e.g., as knee travels forward, opposite arm is travelling forward).
- The arm is driven aggressively backwards while the opposite arm moves towards the midline of the body.

Reprinted by permission from V. *Gambetta, Athletic Development*, 1st ed. (Champaign, IL: Human Kinetics, 2007).

Legs

- Piston action in the legs gradually transitions to a more circular heel recovery.
- Heel recovery becomes higher each step.
- Forward orientated shin angles gradually becoming more vertical.
- Optimal stiffness in the foot and ankle.
- Knee travels forward soon after toe-off.

MAXIMAL VELOCITY

Posture

- Subtle forward lean in the torso.
- The athlete is looking down the playing surface with a neutral head position.
- The pelvis is held in a high neutral position and may have a slight posterior tilt.

Arms

- Arm action continues to mirror the contralateral limb (i.e., when the touchdown leg is in its longest position the opposite arm will be in its most open position to balance the body).
- The hand is driven hard down below the waist on the downstroke and returns to the lip in with a more acute angle at the elbow (approximately 90 degrees on the return).
- Arms move to the midline of the body but not across.

Legs

- Slight knee bend at toe-off.
- The knee travels forward soon after toe-off with the shank folding up against the upper leg.
- High heel recovery with the foot stepping over the opposite knee.
- Knees rising high enough in front of the body for an aggressive strike down and back into the track.
- Foot should be travelling down and backwards (negative foot speed) prior to foot strike.
- Foot striking close to underneath the center of mass (will be slightly in front). At touchdown the opposite knee should be beside or slightly in front of the knee on the touchdown leg.
- Optimal stiffness in the knee, ankle, and foot at touchdown.

SPORT-SPECIFIC CONSIDERATIONS FOR TECHNICAL COACHING

The standardized environments in which sprinters compete and their relatively homogenous body types mean that technical models developed for sprinters will not completely apply to field sport athletes, and differences in technique have been noted (29). Compared to specialist sprinters, field and court sport athletes have some small to large differences based on the following:

1. Individual constraints (e.g., body mass, strength qualities, limb length)
2. Environmental constraints (e.g., playing surface and footwear friction)
3. Task constraints (e.g., interaction with implements or balls being carried, interactions with other athletes, starting position)

Body Mass and Momentum

One of the single biggest trade-offs that team sport athletes, especially in the contact football codes, must consider is the optimal body mass required for different sports. Elite sprinters have a typical narrow cluster of body masses (27) because maximal velocity is constrained by the ability to rapidly produce mass-specific forces that favors lighter athletes (28). This is combined with a typical range of heights that optimizes stride length. Sprinters who deviate from this narrow range (i.e., Usain Bolt) gain the benefit of a longer contact length from greater stature but with the negative trade-off of heavier body mass (figure 3.7). However, collision sport athletes require *momentum* (mass × velocity). This increased momentum is achieved through a compromise of body mass and speed and may be a key factor to success in both offense and defense.

It is not difficult to imagine that the mass of an American football offensive lineman or a rugby union prop may not be optimal to maximize their sprinting capabilities. The body masses of contact football code athletes usually fall in line to meet a profile of speed and the momentum they require in collision situations. American football linemen and rugby union props are in collisions where the mass part of the momentum equation plays a more important role for their positional demands as opposed to an American football wide receiver or rugby union winger for whom the velocity component of the momentum equation is more important. This is an important aspect to consider when thinking of the overall physical preparation of an athlete and the impact this has on technique. Further, this increase in mass and therefore decrease in relative strength may require the athlete and coach to seek unique ways to increase the contact length to buy more time to apply the necessary forces into the ground.

Figure 3.7 Sprinters with varying heights, mass and contact lengths.

Height, Stride Length, and Contact Length

An interesting relationship exists between an athlete's height, stride length, and the distance the center of mass covers while on the ground (contact length). It is intuitively apparent that a taller athlete with a higher center of mass will see the center of mass move through a longer horizontal distance (contact length) between foot strike and the toe-off even though the degrees of hip extension are identical (21). The trade-off is that ground contact time becomes longer. A taller athlete may run at identical speeds as a shorter athlete, but longer-legged athletes will have more knee flexion as their foot touches down (11) and less extension through the hip, knee, and ankle at toe-off than shorter athletes. This means that longer-legged athletes will cover more distance on the ground but at the expense of an increased ground contact time. Optimizing vertical push to find the balance between shortening time on the ground and maximizing stride length is a key to finding the individual solution to the fastest possible top speed. While height determines contact length, vertical impulse determines flight length and the ratio of stride rate to stride length (21).

When using technical speed models to coach athletes it is useful to consider whether athletes are physically capable of achieving the positions or timing compared to a model. A coach may cue athletes to direct force more horizontally because they are relatively inefficient at applying forces in the appropriate vectors, but on the other hand their technique may be limited by physical constraints. In this example, the vertical forces that the athletes are required to overcome may take up a relatively large share of their physical capabilities and they may be applying forces in the most optimal manner for their capabilities. Strength, power, and plyometric training may provide the necessary training adaptations that allow for the capability to achieve optimal technique that cannot be cued.

Environmental Constraints

Track and field sprinters typically compete in a standardized environment on a synthetic surface designed to maximize sprinting speed, with footwear designed to maximize friction between the foot and the track for linear sprinting. Across multiple court and field sports, the shoe and surface interactions vary from each other and the conditions in which track athletes train and perform. For example, a basketball shoe's sole and a hard court may result in different friction and some different kinematics than a football shoe's cleats on soft, wet ground. Football codes may be played on dry field turf or wet grass from game to game, requiring different footwear. Generally, when the coefficient of friction is reduced, a more upright position needs to be adopted for acceleration due to the need to maintain balance, and this must be accounted for when coaching. In these cases, coaches and athletes may want to consider changing into footwear that allows for better traction and more similar technique to dry conditions. In addition, softer surfaces can affect technique, leading to longer ground contact times than on harder surfaces and need to be factored in when building a sport-specific technical model.

Starting Position

One of the largest differences between coaching field and court sport athletes is that sprinters start out of the blocks. Field sport athletes vary between transitioning from jogging or rolling starts, standing starts, and different positional starts (e.g., in American football where athletes may start with a hand on the ground like sprinters). In addition, cutting and lateral movement actions may precede the linear sprint, or an athlete may begin a sprint after back pedaling. The critical question when adapting acceleration technique is, "What horizontal velocity is the athlete at when they begin the sprint?" This will dictate what the acceleration technique should look like. A start out of the blocks by a sprinter or an American football wide receiver in a standing crouch may have a full initial acceleration phase with three strides and no braking phase, whereas a soccer athlete initiating a sprint may only have a single stride in the acceleration phase before the foot strikes ahead of the center of mass. Speed training programs should consist of starting sprints from all the different positions and at speeds an athlete will experience on the field or court. For example, a baseball athlete would adopt a starting position sideways to the direction of travel, and the first step would aim to drive the center of mass outside of the base of support to be in a position where effective horizontal and vertical forces can be applied. An understanding of the biomechanics governing speed, covered in previous chapters, will help inform the technique to put the athlete in a position to maximize horizontal forces while maintaining balance in subsequent steps.

Interactions With Teammates and Opponents

Another common technique characteristic of sprinters is the head position while accelerating. A sprinter's gaze may be at the ground during acceleration, which may be optimal for acceleration in track or testing scenarios; however, it can be counterproductive for team sport athletes who must scan the field or court and make decisions on what they see. Speed training programs should coach athletes to maintain a neutral head and look up through their eyebrows during the first initial steps. Further, in certain situations coaches may ask for athletes to adopt a more upright and balanced position during acceleration to allow them to effectively change directions, which creates time and space between their opponents. When at maximum velocity a contact sport athlete may assume a slightly more forward lean of the torso prior to running into a potential contact situation or a lower heel recovery to better allow change in direction.

Ball and Implement Carrying

Possibly the largest difference in how field sport athletes sprint compared to sprinters is the use of implements (carry or dribble a ball, carry sticks, or wear equipment). For example, rugby league and rugby union athletes must carry a ball in either hand or both hands. If athletes are completely comfortable sprinting with a ball in two hands, they are now a passing or kicking threat that defenders must consider. If athletes can carry the ball comfortably in either hand, their evasive skills are strengthened because the free hand now becomes available to fend off opponents. A speed training program that improves effective ball-carrying speed could be considered a success, even if it does not enhance the standard 40-yard or 40-meter sprint test (3, 25). Introducing ball control or implement carrying becomes an important consideration of the role of the arms in sprinting. The arms are important for balancing the torques produced by the lower limbs, and they do assist in applying some vertical force. This is typically done by moving in the sagittal plane with the contralateral upper limb mirroring the lower limb. However, carrying a rugby ball with two hands makes it impossible for the arms to move in this fashion, and instead an athlete will move the ball laterally across the chest to balance and control the trunk. Small additions of ball or carrying drills during speed training could be effective at fixing gaps in individual sport-specific speed model. A suggestion to coaches is to profile their teams' speeds with and without an implement and to look for technical commonalities in the athletes who do or do not decrease their speed while using an implement. Further, when devoting time to technical speed training it is important to remember that in most sports (with some notable exceptions) most athletes are performing locomotion without an implement or ball at any time during the game.

CHAPTER 4

Universal Technical Development of Linear Speed

Boo Schexnayder

The development of speed is often the most critical piece of a sport performance program. In this chapter we will examine some fundamental premises that govern the design of speed development programming and the teaching of speed-related skills. We will then review those skills and specific drills, exercises, and training constructs that will provide the best environments for the development of speed and the teaching of those skills.

MOVEMENT ORGANIZATION AND IMPLICATIONS FOR SPRINT TEACHING

Movement organization is a term used to describe the way humans initiate and control their movements. Each day we perform thousands of movements—some simple, some complex—and these all must be managed carefully if movements are to be smooth, accurate, and effective. Many different biological processes, many of which are still not completely understood, are at work any time human movement takes place.

Some movement is controlled by human cognitive processes. In these cases, the brain is in charge as our thought processes control the appearance of the movement. However, humans perform thousands of movements daily that require practically no thought at all. This means that much of the appearance of the movement is controlled elsewhere.

Some movements are controlled *subcortically*. This means that rather than the brain being in control, other parts of the nervous system are governing the appearance of the movement (3). This explains how we can go about performing simple primal movements such as walking and running without any thought at all.

Environmental factors come into play as well. For example, if we decide to take a sip of water from a nearby cup, the position of the cup will likely determine which hand we choose to use. A soccer athlete may change direction in reaction to the ball's movement without any thought of the technique involved. This decision is made without a lot of thought and cognition. We have the ability to take our surroundings into account as we move, with minimal cognitive involvement.

Certain reflexes are hardwired into the human nervous system, which may elicit or affect movements as well (2). Anyone who has touched a hot stove knows that a series of reflexes cause the hand to pull away, even before the victim realizes what has happened. A person who is pushed in the back and about to fall will instinctively reach out with a hand or foot to regain balance without any thought at all. Many of these reflexes are rooted in self-preservation and safety, and they take precedence over other movement-altering processes.

Movement organization is a catch-all term that refers to all of these factors that control the appearance of movement. Cognition, subcortical neural processes, environment, and reflexes all play a role in determining the appearance of movement. At the high intensities involved in sprinting, the subcortical processes and reflexes are highly involved, and cognitive processes play a very small role. Sprinting, like many other primal movement patterns, is predominantly organized subcortically and is highly dependent on reflexes. After all, an athlete would never think, "Left-right-left-right," while performing a sprint! The fact that cognitive processes play such a small role in high-speed movements presents some important governing principles for how sprinting skills are taught.

Many traditional drills have been regarded as key components of sprint teaching for many years. These drills may play a role in the acquisition of sprint skill and assist in developing many other useful athletic abilities. However, these drills require intensity levels far below those demonstrated in sprint performances. The movements are mainly organized cognitively and do not involve high levels of subcortical or reflexive activity. As a result, skill transfer from the drills to sprint performance is very low. Every coach who has experience teaching sprint skills has experienced the athlete who does all the drills perfectly but still has serious flaws in her sprinting mechanics.

This does not mean that time spent on these drills is wasted. They do provide an opportunity to develop mobility and coordination, as well as a chance to teach conceptually many fundamental sprint positions and movement patterns. The teaching of these skills is critical to improving performances and closing the gap between present levels of performance and one's genetic ceiling. Yet the limitations of these drills demonstrate the need to teach sprint skills within the context of the sprint itself. Technical improvements in sprinting come about primarily as a result of the coaching that takes place inside of the sprint sessions themselves, and a reliance on skill transfer from drills to make the needed improvements in sprinting is likely to result in failure. It is important to realize that the drill itself is not a teacher. The drill provides an environment in which to teach.

SPEED TRAINING AS PART OF THE TRAINING PROGRAM

Significant speed improvements result from a wide variety of training components. The speed improvements we hope to gain depend on many forms of training, including many that we would normally classify as lying outside the boundaries of speed development programming. Effective resistance training, mobility training, restorative training, and fitness work all contribute to the effectiveness of the speed development program.

Even the best speed development training will fail if these other components of the athlete's training program are programmed poorly. These other forms of training may impair and inhibit the acquisition of speed if omitted or programmed in a way that is not compatible with the speed development program. For example, the short-term fatigue that results from typical squat work can result in decreased rates of speed acquisition, so placement of this type of work with respect to critical speed sessions must be exact. Additionally, extremely high-level glycolytic fitness training may interfere with speed acquisition if scheduled arbitrarily.

It is difficult to identify and classify certain exercises as speed development exercises, since nearly every component of a good training program contributes to speed acquisition in some way. Resistance training, plyometrics, and mobility work all contribute greatly to speed acquisition. Restoration training accelerates recovery, permitting higher quality speed training on a more frequent basis. This type of training also alleviates potential overuse or repetitive movement syndromes, improves general coordination, and is an important part of injury prevention. Nearly every component of a good training program assists in improving the athlete's general quality of movement and therefore speed skill.

SPEED AND STRENGTH

Speed and strength share a unique relationship. We commonly think of speed training as a way to improve running speed or speed of movement. This is obviously true, but type of training results in other benefits as well:

- ▶ Speed-based training improves the nervous system's ability to activate muscle tissue through improvements in recruitment and rate coding.

These neural adaptations develop speed but also result in increased power and strength levels (1).

▶ Speed training produces very high levels of tension in muscles, tendons, and other tissues. The level of load applied to these tissues is high, often exceeding those that are achieved (or can be achieved) in a resistance training program. Many coaches and athletes engaged in regular resistance training have experienced the soreness that results from a sprint session. This is because the levels of tension and tissue load experienced in the sprint are sometimes greater than those experienced in the resistance training program. Speed training, in this way, drives strength improvements and may even result in levels of tissue load unreachable in a traditional resistance training program.

For these reasons, speed training should be viewed not only as a way to get faster but as a critical exercise that increases the effectiveness of other areas of the training program and reaches distant corners of strength development that cannot be reached otherwise. Coaching cultures have commonly viewed strength improvements as a route to speed acquisition, but the reverse is also true. These reasons also explain why speed development training could be very helpful to athletes in many sports, even those sports that do not contain a significant sprinting component.

CHARACTERISTICS OF GOOD SPEED TRAINING

When we examine effective speed development programs, we see a variety of methodologies employed. However, any successful methodology will, at its core, demonstrate an adherence to the following three key tenets.

High Intensity

The achievement of high intensities in training is essential to develop any type of speed. The high levels of motor unit recruitment, rate coding, and tissue loading needed in speed training simply are not present in submaximal-intensity training situations. While some drills and exercises of submaximal intensity may play a supporting role in developing related qualities and providing teaching opportunities, they alone will not drive improvements in speed-related qualities. The most critical elements of speed training are high-intensity sprint sessions. These sessions must achieve maximal intensities, maximal levels of power output, and, at times, maximal velocities. The value we place on these intensities dictates other aspects of a good speed training philosophy.

Sufficient Recovery

Since the achievement of high intensity in speed training is critical, the length of the rest intervals between the repetitions in high-intensity speed training should be significant. If rest intervals are too short, fatigue accumulates throughout the workout, resulting in a decrease in intensity, velocity, and power output. While work is being done (and possibly fitness-related qualities are being trained), the program in this case will fail to achieve speed improvements. Many coaches fall victim to haste and mistaken applications of work ethic shorten these recovery times. Failure at speed development results.

Manageable Volumes

Since the maintenance of high intensities throughout a speed training session is critical, session volumes should be chosen carefully. Session volumes should permit the maintenance of high levels of intensity, velocity, and power output throughout the entire session, from beginning to end. In many cases, total session volumes or numbers of repetitions are excessive, resulting in decreasing quality as the session progresses. Good speed development models favor quality over quantity, and at times it is striking to see how little volume is needed to create substantial gains.

SPEED TRAINING AND SPORT SPECIFICITY

Various sports show the need for many different types of starts and variations of acceleration and sprint skills. In spite of this fact, it is important to note that the achievement of the highest velocities and power outputs are critical to success in speed programming. In most cases sport-specific variations of starts and acceleration skills, while undoubtedly essential to success in the sport, do not allow for the achievement of these high intensity levels.

For example, a baseball athlete, in a game, typically accelerates from a bilateral stance, often in a lateral direction. This means the baseball athlete should, at some point in the program, rehearse these movements. However, if these starts would be employed in the speed development program, it would be difficult to achieve the highest levels of intensity, power output, and velocity. For this reason, despite the nature of the sport of baseball, the starting, acceleration, and speed skills the baseball athlete uses in training speed should resemble those a track sprinter may use. They best enable the accomplishment of the intensities and velocities needed.

Attempting to use high levels of sport specificity in the speed development program often brings less than optimal results, and sticking with traditional sprint training skills and methods is a better strategy. Sport specific variations should be trained, but elsewhere in the program and typically later in the training calendar.

SPRINT START SKILLS

The primary purpose of the sprint start is to overcome inertia and to position the body to enter an effective acceleration pattern. Start training provides an opportunity for the technical teaching and rehearsal of these movements. In addition, the sprint start itself is an excellent power development exercise and has use outside of the speed program, even with athletes in sports that do not contain a significant sprinting component.

Sprint Start Drills and Exercises

Start training consists of two main categories of work. The first is rehearsal of the start itself, with strict adherence to the technical features of starting. The other is starts from compromised positions, developing the ability to start and accelerate in a variety of sport-related situations.

Wall Start

The wall start drill is a good way to rehearse the start in a remedial format. In the wall start drill, the athlete assumes a two-point starting stance with the toe of the front foot located 4 to 5 feet (1.2-1.5 m) from a (preferably padded) wall, facing the wall. The athlete then executes a start, pushing off in an upward and outward direction using a complete extension of the front leg. As the athlete extends the front leg explosively, the rear leg moves forward and the arms extend outward, catching the wall and finishing the start in a position of forward lean, braced against the wall. The drill finishes with the forward thigh nearly parallel to the ground so that the angle between the thighs at the drill's completion is large. After checking the finishing position, the athlete resets for the next repetition. Details of the starting technique are presented shortly. The wall start drill is helpful primarily because of its efficient use of time, permitting large numbers of repetitions to be done in a short period of time.

Crouch Start

The crouch start is a simple start, initiated from a standing position without contact between the hand(s) and the ground. The stance shows the feet directed forward, with a distance of 6-12 inches (15-30 cm) between the heel of the front foot and the toe of the rear foot. Achieving sufficient height of the hips in the set position is an important factor, and a stance that is too wide reduces that height. The shins should be inclined forward, tilting to an angle of 45 to 60 degrees with respect to the ground in most cases. The position of the front shin is of particular importance because it ultimately determines the angle of projection achieved at the start. A smaller shin angle (the front knee pushed farther beyond the front toe) results in a lower angle of projection. Higher shin angles produce higher projection angles. The torso should be lowered so that the back is roughly parallel to the ground, and many good starters actually show the hips a little higher than the shoulders in the set position. This brings the chest close to the front thigh. This folding of the body allows the hips to apply force through a larger range of motion as they extend, and it helps to prevent premature extension in the knee and ankle. The arms are bent slightly at the elbow, alternated so that the arm on the side of the front leg is back, and the other forward. The front arm should be positioned so that the elbow is slightly lower than the shoulders; the rear elbow should be slightly higher than the shoulders. Both elbows should be positioned a few inches wider than the shoulders. This slightly widened position allows the arms to counter rotational forces in the start. The weight distribution in the stance means that the majority of body weight is placed on the front foot, but a small amount of weight is placed on, and pressure against the ground maintained by, the back foot. Failure to maintain a small amount of body weight on the rear foot prevents it from contributing to the start. It also usually results in an excessively low projection angle, resulting in stumbling and the inability to assume good posture later in the sprint.

There are two key simultaneous movements that initiate the crouch start. The first of these is a quick push against the surface in a downward and backward direction with the back foot, which precedes the forward movement of that leg. This quick push comprises the rear leg's contribution to the start. At the same time, the frontside shin rotates approximately 10 degrees, moving the knee forward and downward. This loads the quadriceps muscle group in preparation for the subsequent push of the front leg, as noted by A.L. Eggerth (verbal communication, July 2016). It is important to note that the alternating, swinging movement of the arms does not yet begin and is delayed until these movements are complete. The arms do not begin to move until the thighs do. Once these movements are complete, the front leg performs a powerful and complete extension, applying force to the ground in a downward and backward direction. This push should show complete extension of the hip, knee, and ankle at its completion. The rear leg swings forward simultaneously, finishing in a position with the thigh nearly parallel to the ground. As the front leg extends, the arms alternate powerfully. In a good start, the arms alternate and thighs open simultaneously and at the same rates, so that arms and legs both reach their positions of maximal split simultaneously.

Of particular importance is the trajectory of the athlete's center of mass that is established in the start. The athlete's body should displace significantly in a forward and upward direction. The horizontal and vertical components of the start are both critical to successful sprinting. The horizontal component obviously results in greater horizontal displacement and faster performances. However, the vertical component supplies the flight time needed for proper ground preparation, and it enhances stride length. The vertical component also begins the process of progressing body angles and the establishment of good pelvic alignment as high velocities are reached. Excessively horizontal starts cause several problems including stumbling, deceleration, and the inability to achieve good posture later in the run, as noted by D.A. Pfaff (personal conversations, April 1995).

Also of importance are the ranges of motion achieved in the crouch start. As the front leg completes its extension, the rear leg swings forward, finishing in a position showing the thigh nearly parallel to the surface. The angle between the thighs at the completion of the push-off should be large, establishing the large ranges of motion needed in the remainder of the sprint. Many sprint coaches remind athletes to keep a sprint "open," referring to the need to keep the split of the thighs large at the completion of each step.

Three-Point Start

The three-point start is a simple start, initiated from a standing position with one hand touching the ground. Many technical aspects of the crouch start apply here. The stance, shin positions, and torso positions are the same as those we saw in the crouch start. The hand on the same side as the rear leg is placed on the ground so that the arm is extended and the shoulder is directly over the hand, with only the fingertips touching the surface. The opposite arm is positioned with the elbow slightly bent, slightly higher than the shoulders, and slightly wider than the shoulder. Most body weight is equally distributed and supported between the grounded

hand and front foot, but some pressure against the surface should be maintained by the rear foot. The movements of the start are similar to those used in the crouch start. The three-point start, when compared to the two-point start, provides greater ease in creating horizontal forces. However, the previous cautions regarding insufficient vertical forces in the start are still valid here.

Four-Point Start

The four-point start is another simple start, initiated with both hands touching the ground. Aside from the grounded position of the other hand, the positions and movements of the four-point start are similar to those seen in the three-point start. The four-point start does represent an additional increase in horizontal emphasis over the three-point start, potentially improving sprint performance while creating an increased degree of difficulty in executing the remainder of the sprint.

Rollover Start

Unlike most starts that begin from a stationary position, the rollover start uses a preliminary rocking-type motion to build momentum before the actual start takes place. The rollover start is initiated in an upright, standing position. It is a convenient start to use in many training situations because the upright, standing position enables the athlete to visually locate some marker prior to the start's initiation. The stance shows the feet directed forward, with a distance of 6 to 12 inches (15-30 cm) between the heel of the front foot and the toe of the rear foot. The athlete stands upright, with the arm on the rear leg side slightly raised. To initiate the start, the athlete rocks back slightly, lifting the frontside toe in order to establish dorsiflexion in the ankle. Next, the athlete shifts the weight forward slightly and bends at the waist significantly. This movement loads the front leg for a strong push-off and brings the athlete into the same positions as discussed in the crouch start. From this point forward, the movements of the start are identical to those employed in the previously discussed starts.

Scramble Starts

Scramble starts are starts (combined with short accelerations) done from unusual positions and movement patterns. In addition to being a good starting and acceleration exercise, scramble starts drive coordination improvements and challenge the body's movement organization processes. They can be done in a variety of ways. For example, an athlete can be placed in a prone position. On a signal, the athlete must scramble to his feet, start, and perform a short (10-20 yards or meters) acceleration as quickly as possible. These can be done from a variety of different positions. A particularly effective use of scramble starts is to perform them at the end of a set of bodyweight exercises. For example, an athlete might be performing a set of push-ups. At the completion of the set, on a signal, the athlete scrambles to his feet and accelerates. Choosing multiple bodyweight exercises, combining them with scramble starts, and assembling them into circuits are a good way of training fitness and coordination as well as starting skills. Scramble starts can be done in combination with any bodyweight exercise and, in addition to the start improvements they produce, are particularly effective at driving coordination and agility improvements.

Key Technical Factors for Start Training

Certain key technical factors are common to all types of starts. Just prior to the start, the set position should show a conservatively spaced stance, tilted shins, flexed hips, arms alternated appropriately, and body weight distributed primarily (but not completely) on the front foot. The stance must be stable, but the center of mass should lie near the boundaries of the base of support in order to quickly initiate the instability needed to begin the starting movements. Upon starting, the initial movements are a short, quick force application of the rear leg and a forward rotation of the front shin to load the front leg. These preliminary movements are followed by a complete extension of the front leg and a powerful recovery of the rear leg through a large range of motion as the athlete's center of mass displaces significantly. Of particular importance is the trajectory of the athlete's center of mass, establishing proper balance between vertical and horizontal displacement.

ACCELERATION SKILLS

The primary purpose of acceleration work is to improve the athlete's ability to overcome inertia, develop momentum, and approach high velocities quickly. Momentum development goals are met by applying large forces over longer periods of time. These longer force application times dictate the use of longer contact times and slower stride frequencies early in the acceleration. A sound acceleration then displays a progressive decrease in contact times and patient increases in stride frequency as maximal velocity nears. Most acceleration training constructs consist of high-intensity sprinting, with distances chosen to isolate the acceleration component. A good rule of thumb is that most athletes, when accelerating maximally, reach their maximal velocity around the 40-meter (44 yards) mark. For this reason, most acceleration development sessions use sprints that do not exceed 40 meters in length. However, as covered in the previous chapters, this might not be the case for all athletes. Developmental athletes or athletes who are not proficient at sprinting will likely achieve maximal velocity in a distance shorter than 40 meters, and acceleration work should be planned accordingly. Elite athletes who are very proficient in sprinting might achieve maximal velocity well past the 40 meter mark, meaning acceleration work in these cases might extend beyond 40 meters.

Acceleration Drills and Exercises

Acceleration work has a purpose in addition to the improvement of an athlete's acceleration abilities. Acceleration work (as well as certain other forms of training) is stimulating to the nervous system. This stimulation often results in improved power output in work that immediately follows. Many good training setups use acceleration work to stimulate an athlete in advance of a weight training session, as well as on the first day of the week, after an off-day, or to restimulate the athlete, and can result in better training quality for the remainder of the week.

Wall Accelerations

The wall acceleration drill begins in the same way as the wall start drill discussed previously. In the wall acceleration drill, the athlete assumes a two-point starting stance 4 to 5 feet (1.2-1.5 m) from a wall. To initiate the drill, the athlete executes a start and extends the arms toward the wall, catching the wall and finishing the start in a position of forward lean, braced against the wall. Next, the athlete takes small steps, each contacting the ground a few inches (cm) in front of the other foot, pushing at a downward and backward angle. This moves the torso upward and toward the wall. The sequence of steps results in a progressive increase in the angle of the head, spine, and pelvis with respect to the ground. Once a vertical position is achieved, the athlete marches in place for a few steps, pushing directly downward against the ground in a vertical direction. The initial portion of the drill develops the concept of using the vertical portion of the push-off from each step to increase the body angle, attain upright posture, and bring the pelvis into a neutral position. If done correctly, the athlete experiences a climbing sensation, not unlike climbing stairs. The vertically directed steps at the drill's conclusion develop the concept of vertical pushing, which is critical in sprinting on reaching maximal velocity.

Acceleration Ladders

Acceleration ladders are an effective means of developing acceleration capabilities in addition to serving as an excellent power development exercise. From some predetermined type of start, a series of maximal-intensity accelerations are performed. Recovery times between runs are usually 2 to 3 minutes in length, long enough to ensure that fatigue will not affect intensities negatively as the session progresses. Typically, they are done in sets, with each set employing a longer sprint distance than the previous. For example, in a session an athlete might run 4 × 10 meters, then 4 × 20 meters, then 4 × 30 meters. The session is arranged this way so that shorter runs serve to potentiate and stimulate in advance of the longer ones. Also, since in acceleration work longer distances result in higher terminal velocities, the ladder construct results in predictable, periodic increases in tissue load, thus minimizing injury risk. Regardless of the specific arrangement, total session volumes range between 200 and 400 meters (219-437 yards) and sprint distances are no longer than 40 meters in length (5).

Resisted Accelerations

Resisted sprinting inherently increases or emphasizes the presence of many of the technical features associated with acceleration (e.g., body lean, ground contact times, triple extension, and patient development of stride frequency). For this reason, high-intensity resisted sprinting sessions fall into the acceleration development training category. The presence of resistance prevents the genuine achievement of maximal velocity, so at times sprints used in resisted sprinting work for acceleration development might exceed the 40 meter limit discussed earlier. While this is accepted practice, it is not often necessary, and the sprints, regardless of distance, must be performed at the highest levels of intensity and effort.

Modest levels of resistance accentuate many mechanical aspects of acceleration mechanics. For this reason, they serve as a good technical exercise for improving acceleration mechanics. They also serve as a good power development exercise. Resisted sprinting also provides a measure of safety, since the athlete can train at maximal intensity while the resistance limits the velocities achieved and angular velocities in the joints.

From some predetermined type of start, a series of maximal-intensity accelerations are performed. Simple constructs like 10-12 × 30 meters are commonly used, but ladder constructs can be used as well. Recovery times between runs are typically 2 to 3 minutes in length, long enough to ensure that fatigue will not affect intensities negatively as the session progresses. Typically, runs range in length from 20 to 60 meters. Regardless of the specific arrangement, total session volumes range between 250 and 400 meters (273-437 yards).

Some consideration should be given to the resistance mode employed. Many programs use uphill running to provide resistance. Other options involve various types of sleds and other resistance-producing devices. Generally speaking, some resistance apparatus attached to the waist or shoulders is superior to hills. The waist attachment allows the athlete to progress body angles properly while accelerating, while hills and shoulder placement require extended maintenance of a forward lean. To genuinely affect speed levels positively and for maximal skill transfer into the sprint, resistances should be chosen so that the sprints show subtle decreases in velocity. It is a commonly accepted coaching practice to limit resistance so that the athlete's performance shows no more than a 10% increase in elapsed time when compared to unresisted performance at any given distance. This is because this resistance serves as a subtle variation in the sprint training practice environment, and these variations result in accelerated rates of skill acquisition (4). Heavier loads might play a role in a training program but should be regarded as more of a power and strength development exercise than an acceleration skill-building one.

Contrast Training

Contrast sessions for acceleration development are sessions that combine resisted and unresisted accelerations into the session. This combination in a session can be an effective acceleration development tool, providing a diverse and complex training stimulus. This may enhance rates of adaptation and skill acquisition. Many programs use contrast work in the latter stages of training, after simpler acceleration development methods have been employed for a while. The nuance of the contrast sessions brings a new training stimulus at a time when athletes may be experiencing the staleness associated with overly repetitive training. Many programs use contrast training during critical competition or peaking times for the same reasons. Most workout structures involve sets of resisted and unresisted accelerations in some predetermined sequence. Sometimes the resisted components of the session might involve varying loads. The number of possible arrangements and formats used in contrast training is infinite, and nearly every imaginable combination is likely being used by some coach with some success.

Key Technical Factors for Acceleration Training

Regardless of the type of sprint-based acceleration training used, certain key technical factors must be addressed. Ranges of motion, particularly in the hip, should remain large so that the split position achieved between the thighs at the completion of each step shows a large angle. Good sprinters during acceleration routinely show an angle between the thighs of 120 degrees or more when one hip achieves maximal flexion and the other reaches maximal extension. A consistent progression of torso angles, from a position of forward lean to an upright posture, should be seen throughout the acceleration. The direction of force application changes consistently throughout the acceleration as well, beginning in a downward and backward direction but progressing to a nearly vertical, downward direction as maximal velocity is achieved. Observations of the angle of the shin when the foot touches down on each step show this progression, because shin angles progressively increase in a good acceleration pattern. It is important to note that the rates of progression of torso and force application angles is individualistic and based on ability levels. Elite athletes might require 45-50 meters to achieve upright postures and vertical pushing, while a developmental athlete might require as little as half that distance. Improved power levels result in the ability to accelerate over longer distances and thus achieve higher maximal velocities. Finally, good accelerations favor strong, forceful strides over the quick development of stride frequency. This strategy results in better momentum development and, as a result, more efficient sprinting later when maximal velocity is achieved.

MAXIMAL VELOCITY SKILLS

Maximal velocity training is training designed primarily to improve an athlete's top-end speed. Maximal velocity training may involve exercises that address and improve maximal velocity mechanics, but the most important type of maximal velocity training involves sprint work that places the athlete in high-intensity, maximal-velocity sprinting situations. These situations must permit athletes to sprint maximally in a manner that allows predictable and consistent force application. This is why genuine speed development is impossible on irregular surfaces or even on the finest high-speed treadmills.

In addition to improving maximal velocity performance and mechanical improvements, maximal velocity training accomplishes other goals as well. Maximal-velocity sprinting is stimulating to the nervous system and improves the nervous system's ability to stimulate muscle tissue through improvements in motor unit recruitment and rate coding. Maximal-velocity sprinting also results in high levels of tissue tension and load. In many cases the tension applied to muscles and tendons actually exceeds the tissue load, which can be achieved in resistance training. For these reasons, maximal velocity training assists in increasing the effectiveness of the resistance training program and actually operates as a strength development exercise in addition to a valuable speed development tool. Not only will an athlete improve maximal velocity as a result of this type of work but also experience improvements in strength and power.

Maximal Velocity Drills and Exercises

Nearly all athletes, having accelerated to maximal velocity, are capable of sustaining that velocity for approximately 3 seconds. This is true for athletes of all levels. Once this 3-second threshold is crossed, deceleration begins to take place regardless of the effort level. Good maximal velocity training involves bringing an athlete to maximal velocity, allowing he- to experience maximal velocity sprinting, yet ending the maximal velocity sprinting before the inevitable deceleration takes place. All effective maximal velocity training constructs are based on having the athlete accelerate to maximal velocity, then maintaining maximal-velocity sprinting for a period of time that does not exceed 3 seconds. More is not necessarily better, and many good programs use 1- to 2-second windows of exposure to maximal velocity. The sprint distances chosen should be designed to place the athlete in these brief windows of maximal performance.

Readiness is an important part of planning maximal velocity work. While maximal velocity work is neurally stimulating, high levels of stimulation are needed before entering the session. For this reason, many good programming plans do maximal velocity work later in a week after neural stimulation levels have been elevated through more remedial forms of speed and power work earlier in the week. Effective programs seldom do maximal velocity training after an off-day because of the potential absence of this stimulation. For example, many programs would use acceleration development training on a Monday after an off-day on Sunday, and schedule maximal velocity training on a Thursday or

Friday. The Monday session stimulates the athlete neurally. This stimulation is maintained throughout the week by the other types of training done, and the maximal velocity session is scheduled in a spot that has allowed recovery from Monday's sprint.

Stair Running

Stairs can provide an effective environment for teaching many of the critical technical features of maximal-velocity sprinting. The athlete runs 15 to 25 stair steps, hitting every step along the way. In maximal-velocity sprinting, the direction of the resultant ground reaction force applied is predominantly vertical. Hitting every step puts the athlete in an upright position but, more importantly, allows the athlete to push against the step in a downward, vertical direction and accumulate large numbers of repetitions of vertical, downward force application. The athlete should not try to maximize stride frequency but maintain a tall, upright posture. Excessive knee lift will place the athlete in an unwanted seated position and compromise posture, so knee lift should not be overemphasized in this drill.

Fly Work

Fly work consists of sprint efforts that have the athlete accelerate, achieve maximal velocity, and maintain maximal velocity over a certain distance or period of time. The sprint course consists of two parts: the acceleration zone, where the athlete accelerates to maximal velocity, and the fly zone, in which the athlete is sprinting at top speed.

In adherence to the basic principles of maximal velocity previously discussed, the distance sprinted at maximal velocity should be chosen so that it can be covered in less than 3 seconds. It is important that the athlete accelerate maximally and that the distances employed during the acceleration phase allow enough distance for the athlete to achieve maximal velocity. Most athletes, when accelerating maximally, need an acceleration zone of 40 meters to achieve maximal velocity. Also, most athletes at top speed cover approximately 10 meters in a second. This means that in most cases the acceleration zone provided must be at least 40 meters in length, and the additional maximal velocity zone can range from 10 to 30 meters. Distances of 50-60 meters are most typically used. Total volumes usually range from 350-500 meters (383-547 yards). Rest intervals range from 3 to 5 minutes, long enough to assure quality as the session progresses (5).

It is important to note, though, that the distances and setups chosen in fly work must be individualized. Developmental athletes or athletes who are not proficient in sprinting, when accelerating maximally, may achieve maximal velocity in distances less than 40 meters. This would indicate the need for a shorter acceleration zone. Elite sprint types take considerably more distance to reach top speed. In this case, a much longer acceleration zone (possibly as long as 55 meters) may be needed.

A common mistake in planning fly work is not providing enough distance for the athlete to achieve maximal velocity. In these cases the athlete might be exhibiting maximal intensity and effort levels in the fly zone, but genuine maximal velocity has not been achieved. Another common error occurs when the athlete fails to accelerate maximally and, as a result has not reached maximal velocity on entering the fly zone.

Variable Speed Sprinting

In variable speed sprinting, the athlete accelerates to maximal velocity and then goes through alternating phases of maximal-velocity sprinting and relaxed, slightly submaximal sprinting, within the context of a single running repetition.

Sprint-float-sprints are highly effective and are possibly the most commonly used variation of variable speed sprinting. In a sprint-float-sprint effort, the athlete accelerates maximally, achieving maximal velocity and maintaining it for a short distance. The athlete then relaxes slightly, sprinting at slightly submaximal effort (approximately 95% intensity) for a prescribed distance. The athlete then resumes maximal-velocity sprinting and maintains it until the end of the effort.

Sprint-float-sprint courses are typically set up so that the maximal-velocity sprinting windows of time range from 1 to 2.5 seconds. For example, an athlete who can achieve maximal velocity in 40 meters might be asked to perform a sprint-float-sprint effort with the zones marked at the 50, 70, and 90 meter marks. The athlete would sprint 50 meters. Since the athlete achieves maximal velocity at the 40 meter mark, the final 10 meters of that zone (approximately 1 sec) are sprinted at maximal velocity. The athlete then continues on for 20 more meters in a relaxed sprint (to the 70 meter mark), then sprints maximally for 20 meters (approximately 2 seconds) resulting in a total effort of 90 meters. Most sprint-float-sprint sessions use 3 to 5 runs, with recoveries of 5 to 6 minutes between them (5).

Variable speed sprinting is typically preferred with athletes who are proficient at sprinting. The training construct is more complex than that used in fly work, resulting in a higher level of challenge to the athlete and may result in higher levels of adaptation as a result. However, developmental athletes or athletes who are not proficient at sprinting might experience excessive injury risk in this type of work. These types of athletes might fare better restricted to fly work.

Key Technical Factors for Maximal Velocity Training

Regardless of the type of sprint-based maximal velocity training used, certain key technical factors must be addressed. An upright posture is critical, and the head and pelvis should show a neutral alignment with respect to the spine. Lordotic postures and anterior pelvic tilt are the most common sprint errors, and the majority of sprint-related injuries are rooted in this problem. The large ranges of motion in the hips established during acceleration should be preserved at maximal velocity. While a high rate of stride frequency is important, posture and ranges of motion should not be sacrificed in an attempt to gain it. The direction of force application is vertical and downward so that the foot contacts the ground only about an inch (a few cm) in front of the body's center of mass on each stride.

SPEED ENDURANCE SKILLS

An athlete who is sprinting at maximal velocity will eventually experience deceleration. As stated earlier, athletes of all levels are capable of exhibiting maximal velocity for about 3 seconds before this inevitable deceleration begins. This deceleration is seldom related to fatigue, but rather results from failures in coordination. When sprinting at high speeds, it is extremely challenging to coordinate high-speed movements for extended periods of time, and ultimately these coordinative failures result before energy systems become challenged at high levels. Speed endurance training is geared to minimize this rate of deceleration. Since the deceleration is more related to coordination losses than fatigue, speed endurance training should be viewed not as a fitness training component, but as high-intensity, highly specific coordination training.

Speed endurance training can be organized in two ways. The first is traditional speed endurance training, using longer sprint distances to challenge the athlete's coordination capabilities. The other is repeat sprint ability training, where shorter sprints (and shorter rest intervals) accomplish similar goals. The demands of the sport the athlete is training for typically determine which method is used.

Speed Endurance Drills and Exercises

In traditional speed endurance training, the goal is to challenge the athlete's coordinative abilities. To do this, distances are chosen and efforts constructed to bring an athlete to maximal velocity and keep him sprinting maximally for periods of time exceeding 3 seconds. Most effective constructs use windows of 3.5 to 5 seconds of maximal intensity sprinting beyond the point in the run at which maximal velocity is achieved.

Fly Work

One way of accomplishing this is with fly work. This fly work is similar but employs longer distances than the fly work used in maximal velocity training. Depending on the level of the athlete and the point at which the athlete achieves maximal velocity, these sprints may range in length from 70 to 120 meters (77-131 yards) in length. Total session volumes range from 400-600 meters (437-656 yards) in most cases. These runs are glycolytically fatiguing, and velocities must be maintained throughout the session, so rest times are long. In most cases rest intervals are 8 to 10 minutes between runs (5).

The distance is chosen so that the athlete sprints at maximal intensity 4 to 5 seconds after reaching maximal velocity. For example, an athlete who achieves maximal velocity at the 40 meter mark might be asked to sprint 80 meters. This would subject the athlete to 40 meters (and approximately 4 sec) of maximal intensity sprinting after reaching top speed. This 4 seconds represents a subtle challenge to the athlete's ability to maintain coordination beyond the 3-second window of maximal velocity capability.

Variable Speed Sprinting

Variable speed sprinting, like the sprint-float-sprint methods discussed previously, can be used to train speed endurance as well. In these cases, zones are identified that provide windows of 3.5 to 4.5 seconds of maximal effort sprinting. Three to five runs are typically used, and recovery times range from 8 to 10 minutes between runs (5).

For example, an athlete who achieves maximal velocity at the 40 meter mark might run a sprint-float-sprint effort over 150 meters, with zones marked at the 80, 110, and 150 meter marks. The athlete sprints maximally to the 80 meter mark. This results in approximately 4 seconds (40 meters) of sprinting beyond the achievement of maximal velocity. The athlete then enters a 30 meter float zone of relaxed sprinting, before entering the final maximal effort zone at the 110 meter mark. The final zone of 40 meters will once again subject the athlete to maximal intensity sprinting over approximately 4 seconds.

Repeat Sprint Ability Training

In repeat sprint ability training, athletes sprint at maximal intensities over shorter distances with short rests. Typically, the repetitions are organized into multiple sets, with longer rest intervals between the sets, in order to preserve intensity throughout the session. Run distances usually are shorter than those used in maximal velocity fly work and should not exceed those distances. Total volumes usually range from 400-700 meters (437-766 yards), with recoveries of 90 seconds to 2 minutes between runs and 5 to 6 minutes between sets (5). For example, if an athlete achieves maximal velocity at the 40 meter mark, that athlete may be asked to sprint 4 × 50 meters at maximal intensity, with short (2 minutes) rest intervals. After a longer rest of 6 minutes, a second set and possibly a third would be done.

Key Technical Factors for Speed Endurance Training

The critical technical factors in speed endurance training are no different than those in maximal velocity training. However, the longer windows of maximal intensity sprinting used will present additional challenges to the athlete. This also presents a challenge to the coach, because higher levels of intervention and error correction are typically needed. In many ways speed endurance training can be an effective environment for an athlete to learn and master sprint skills because of the additional level of challenge presented in this form of training.

CHAPTER 5

Assessment of Speed

Irineu Loturco
John Graham

An important element of designing training programs to enhance speed is the ability to assess (or test) an athlete's speed and performance levels, enabling appropriate training decisions to be made. An assessment administrator, typically the sport coach or strength and conditioning professional (collectively called *tester* in this chapter), with an understanding of exercise physiology can use the results of sport performance assessments to make training decisions that will help athletes to achieve performance goals and maximize potential (14). Physical testing results form the foundation for training programs and provide an objective means of determining the success of a training program. In this chapter we present and describe some of the most commonly used types of speed tests, including the validated curve sprint test for soccer. The speed tests and normative data reported here may assist coaches from various backgrounds and sports in profiling athletes of different levels and ages and monitoring their speed-related performance through training and competition phases.

BENEFITS OF ASSESSMENTS

An assessment is simply a way to measure one's ability in a particular endeavor—in this case, athletic performance. Effective assessment brings a number of advantages, and testers can use speed assessments for a range of reasons, such as evaluating athletic ability, aiding in motivation, and identifying strengths and weaknesses of their athletes (14). The results of these assessments should serve as a basis for developing and adjusting individual strength and conditioning programs.

Effective assessments offer the following important benefits:

- Assessments provide the basis by which achievable goals can be set.
- They serve as a motivational tool because it is probably the most objective and accurate means of documenting and measuring progress and, therefore, adherence to the program. Goal-oriented athletes recognize the importance of positive assessment results and tend to be competitive in their desire to achieve the best rating (14).

▶ They help organize groups. Based on the results, the coach can determine appropriate training partners and can group athletes of similar abilities together.

▶ They predict whether an athlete has the skills or physical potential to play a sport at a competitive level, especially where athletes' test results can be compared against norm scores for a specific sport or playing positions (14).

Because speed plays an important role in many sports, it is essential for testers to be able to assess accurately an athlete's speed, and this requires them to know how to set up valid and reliable speed assessment protocols.

PREREQUISITES

For a testing regimen to be of use, the testing protocol must meet a number of prerequisites. Crucially, assessments must be valid, reliable, and objective in order to produce acceptable measurements for evaluation (14). Unless the issues of validity, reliability, and, where appropriate, objectivity are addressed, testing results will be flawed and, thus, the usefulness of the tests severely compromised.

Validity

Validity refers to the degree to which an assessment measures the characteristic it is intended to measure. Four considerations affect the validity of speed tests (8, 14):

▶ *Construct validity*—whether the speed test actually measures running speed that relates to performance in a specific sport

▶ *Predictive validity*—how the performance on the speed test relates to performance in the sport itself

▶ *Content validity*—how important the speed test selected is to the specific sport

▶ *Concurrent validity*—whether a relationship exists between the speed test and other accepted methods of speed assessment

To better understand the validity of an assessment, consider the use of a 30-yard dash as a speed assessment for baseball or softball athletes. (*Note:* For the purpose of this chapter, distances are commonly provided in yards, but meters can be used instead. The tester should choose the unit of measurement that is associated with the specific sport or the normative or descriptive data to which the test results will be compared. For example, the repeated sprint ability test commonly uses meters.) Specifically, the 30-yard dash has construct validity because it measures a skill commonly used in baseball: running speed between the bases, with 90 feet (30 yards) representing the distance between the bases (8, 14). An athlete with an excellent score in the 30-yard dash theoretically has an advantage in baseball compared to someone with a lower score, because he may be able to make more base hits or steal more bases, thus giving the test predictive validity. A 30-yard dash has content validity because it measures running speed, an important criterion in baseball. Finally, the 30-yard dash measured by an electronic timing device provides concurrent validity by ensuring that the times recorded are accurate and relate to the times that would be recorded with the gold-standard timing systems used at track meets. However, while the 30-yard dash has clear validity for a baseball athlete, its validity for a basketball athlete is not so clear because the typical distances run in basketball are far shorter. For basketball, a 10- or 20-yard dash may offer a greater degree of validity.

Reliability

In athletic performance assessment, reliability refers to the degree of consistency in results during repeat assessments (8, 14). In the example of a 30-yard dash, an athlete performing three 30-yard dashes with an adequate recovery between them ideally should achieve the same score in each trial. In reality, there is always an error score in a test, but a tester should try to minimize the error score by controlling as many of the variables as possible. Scoring deviations or measurement error can include inconsistency in an athlete's effort, examiner error, incorrect protocols being used or a failure to accurately apply protocols, instrument malfunction, and calibration error. While some of these issues are difficult to control (e.g., athlete effort), others are controllable (e.g., test protocols) and need to be considered before setting up a speed assessment. This chapter describes how to construct tests that maximize reliability by addressing the controllable variables, thus producing effective results on which to base evaluation and program design.

Objectivity

Objectivity is the level to which multiple testers agree on the scoring of an assessment; in essence, it is a specific type of reliability. To optimize objectivity and reduce any potential impact of inter-rater reliability (i.e., disagreement between testers), whenever possible, one designated tester should be used. Where repeated tests are required, testing programs should aim to use the same tester for both initial and follow-up examinations, but this is not always possible. A consistent level of objectivity is critical when more than one tester is used, and all testers need to be consistently trained to run all the tests with the same configuration and precision. In these situations, it is essential to use a predetermined scoring system, fixed and clear testing protocols, and identical instruments to maximize objectivity. For example, the tester should know exactly how to set up timing gates, execute the required start protocols, score tests accurately, and so on.

In addition to the issues of objectivity associated with the administration of a test, it is important to address potential issues in score reporting. To avoid inaccurate reporting of assessment results, an unbiased tester should be used whenever possible. It is not uncommon for recorded scores or times to be inaccurately reported for the sake of pleasing a sport coach or parent. Inflating the scores prevents athletes from understanding the normal changes in performance expected over time and can lead to disappointment in the future. In addition, inaccurate scoring negatively affects national statistical norms if these scores are used to generate this data.

SELECTION

Before selecting a test, the speed demands of the sport the athlete participates in should be analyzed. For example, although a 40-yard dash provides an excellent field test for measuring speed for an American football skill position, it does not offer the same validity for a softball athlete, who typically sprints just 20 yards to the next base, including decelerating to a stop.

Not only should the selected tests be valid, reliable, and objective, but they also should provide a positive experience for the athletes and be simple and economical; this will ensure rapid and efficient administration to large groups without the need for expensive or complicated equipment and procedures. Further, an assessment should appeal to the competitive instincts of the athletes so that they will apply maximum effort, and it should provide an experience designed to enhance their physical development.

When selecting assessments, several variables need to be considered:

▶ *Age.* Assessments that are valid for college athletes may not be appropriate for adolescents, who lack experience and perhaps motivation. An example might be to use a 30-yard dash for high school and college baseball athletes but only a 20-yard dash for Little League athletes, who play on smaller fields.

▶ *Experience.* Advanced assessments may prove too difficult for novice athletes, for example, using 20-yard assessments for youth soccer athletes, who compete on smaller fields, instead of the 40-yard assessments used for high school and college soccer athletes.

▶ *Environment.* Certain assessments may not be appropriate when experiencing environmental extremes such as high altitude or excessive heat and humidity. For example, testers should avoid performing assessments outdoors on excessively cold or hot days or days with rain or snow to prevent injury and to improve test validity. Additionally, wind creates a massive variable in performance. Indoor testing can provide more reliable results than outdoor testing because more variables can be controlled.

▶ *Sport-specific characteristics and positions within a sport.* Different sports require adjustments to the test to reflect typical patterns of speed within that sport. For example, because playing basketball or soccer typically requires short accelerations (1, 4, 11), the best speed assessment would be a short test, such as 10 or 20 yards, while baseball speed should be assessed by a longer test: 30 yards to match the distance between bases. Additionally, athletes of different positions within a sport might require different skills and, therefore, different assessments. For example, testers might use a 40-yard dash for a skilled position in football, and a 10-yard dash might better assess the speed of linemen.

▶ *Unbiased assessment.* An assessment should be specific to the activity and the energy system the athlete has trained. For example, basketball athletes never run farther than 30 yards. As a result, testing the 40-yard-dash speed for basketball athletes would not be a wise choice.

▶ *Instrumentation.* Differences in running speed are often marginal, so accurate measurement and evaluation are crucial. Although stopwatches are used, the potential for error is large, especially when the tester is untrained. Research has demonstrated that, even with experienced testers, times recorded by a handheld stopwatch may be 0.20 seconds faster than those measured electronically over the same distance. This is probably caused by the tester's reaction time when pressing the start and stop button at the beginning and completion of the sprint (14). Additionally, handheld stopwatches potentially allow for tester bias, where the tester consciously or subconsciously manipulates the score. If possible, electronic timing should be used. Increasingly low-cost options for electronic timing equipment are available and offer far greater accuracy than a stopwatch.

▶ *Test protocols.* Protocol can significantly affect the results of a test. For example, the score on a 30-yard dash preceded by a 5-yard running start differs greatly from a 30-yard dash performed from a three-point start. Therefore, the protocols used for each test must be identical and accurately recorded for every athlete and every time the test is given. Recording the test protocol allows other testers to adhere to the same protocol each time the testing is conducted. Variation in protocol makes it difficult to compare scores between different programs and to generate norms.

FREQUENCY

Many coaches have their athletes tested three or four times a year; others assess more or less frequently (8). Some sport coaches prefer to have their athletes assessed every couple of weeks, but others may want to test only before the sport season. While three or four times a year is often recommended, this is not a hard-and-fast rule; instead, a testing program should be led by the aims of the training program. Testing also can take place naturally through the training period and does not have to consist of a deliberately set-aside protocol.

Testers should consider two factors when determining testing frequency. First, if formal testing takes place too frequently, valuable training time is lost and athletes do not receive the same level of performance enhancement from assessments as they do from training (8). Second, when athletes are assessed only before preseason camp, they may be less motivated to perform off-season strength training and conditioning. Also, when testing only before the preseason, program changes that could have been made during the off-season are never made, thus neglecting athletes' weaknesses that need attention.

The authors recommend assessing athletes at least three times a year: at the end of the season, at the end of the off-season (i.e., beginning of the preseason), and at the end of the preseason. Testing at these points provides an opportunity to take advantage of the active-rest phase between periods, as well as a chance to understand how athletes respond to training and detraining. This enables an accurate assessment from the training period just completed so that adjustments can be made for the next period and for that same training period in the following year's program. Additionally, for sports that have an extended season, adding an in-season test to assess speed function can reveal adjustments that may be needed.

In addition, performing assessments at least three times annually motivates athletes to continue training during the season, off-season, and preseason and makes each assessment event particularly important. Ideally, assessments are conducted often enough to measure accurately an athlete's progress and the effectiveness of the strength and conditioning program. Assessments should also sustain the athlete's motivation and adherence to the program.

ORGANIZATION AND PREPARATION

Once the assessments have been chosen, an organized format ensures the proper preparation of facilities, testers, and athletes. Areas to address include the following:

- ▶ Pretesting protocols
- ▶ Facility and equipment preparation
- ▶ Test administration and documentation
- ▶ Sequencing
- ▶ Athlete preparation
- ▶ Score recording

Pretesting Protocols

To ensure participation in, and to develop enthusiasm for, the assessment process, testers should announce the assessment date at least three weeks before the assessment and post information about the test in a highly visible area that athletes use frequently. The schedule should include details of the assessment; list athletes to be assessed; the name of the tester; and the location, date, and time of the assessment. To maximize the effectiveness of the testing session, especially when athletes are being tested for the first time, testers can hold an informational meeting a few days before the test to demonstrate all the tests, answer questions, and explain guidelines and procedures.

All athletes should sign an informed consent form or have a parent or guardian sign it if they are high school level or younger. The form will identify medical conditions that may lead to injury or hinder performance. Informed consent forms also give young athletes and their parents a description of the procedure. A copy of all test procedures and guidelines and the purpose of the assessments should be attached to the consent form. See figure 5.1 for an athlete preparation questionnaire; ideally, a copy would be provided to each athlete ahead of the testing session and reviewed by the tester before testing begins if an athlete answered "no" to any question.

Facility and Equipment Preparation

The facility where the assessments are conducted can affect the quality of an athlete's performance, so it should be suitable for the purpose. Assessments should be administered on appropriate surfaces that always provide secure footing. Ideally, the surface should be the same or like the surface used in the sport. For example, field turf is ideal for football, and a wooden floor is preferred for basketball. A challenge for the tester is to ensure that the environment does

Figure 5.1 Athlete Preparation Questionnaire

Athlete: _____ Date: _____

Sport: _____

- I read (if applicable) and understand the testing procedure(s). **Yes | No**
- I completed the informed consent form. **Yes | No**
- I attended the informational meeting (if applicable). **Yes | No**
- I abstained from exercise the day of the test (if applicable or needed based on directions from my coach). **Yes | No**
- I abstained from eating or drinking (other than water) for three hours before testing. **Yes | No**
- I took my physician-required medications (if applicable). **Yes | No**
- I am appropriately rested for testing. **Yes | No**
- I am wearing proper clothing for testing. **Yes | No**
- I am feeling healthy, not sick. **Yes | No**
- I properly and thoroughly warmed up before testing. **Yes | No**

Any "no" answers need to be evaluated by the tester or someone on the sports medicine staff before testing begins.

From National Strength and Conditioning Association, *Developing Speed,* 2nd ed. (Champaign, IL: Human Kinetics, 2025).

not affect performance. Elements such as wind, temperature, humidity, and so on should be controlled. An indoor facility is preferred.

Every tester is ethically responsible for providing a safe assessment environment. The assessment area should be spacious; speed assessments need a considerable distance for deceleration after the finish line. They should also be free of obstacles and hazards. To prevent accidents, the tester must make sure that athletes understand that assessments are no time for horseplay. Additionally, the atmosphere during the assessments should be controlled and private; spectators and other distractions should not be allowed at the facility because these can affect athletes' scores.

Testers know which equipment to use and where it is located, and should make sure that the equipment is on site and appropriately prepared before the assessment is scheduled to begin. The tester also needs to create the testing recording sheets, obtain pencils and clipboards, and be sure that first-aid equipment and emergency procedures are in place.

Test Administration and Test Documentation

Testers should be properly trained in the application of the assessment and have a thorough understanding of all procedures and protocols. If possible, they should administer the same assessments during each assessment period to ensure reliability and objectivity. If the same tester is not available, the replacement tester should have previously conducted assessments with the original tester. An experienced tester should supervise a novice tester to be sure all assessments are carried out and scored identically. Assessment consistency becomes even more critical in a pre- and post-assessment analysis.

To administer a valid assessment with a high degree of reliability and objectivity, all of the elements of the assessment, including test supervision, warm-up, preparation, motivation, safety, number of assessment trials, and cooldown need to be considered. Properly planning and monitoring these elements produces a high degree of reliability in the testing and also maximizes the objectivity between testers, thus lessening the chance of erroneous results.

To facilitate proper test administration, the tester should use a test administration checklist (see figure 5.2) for each test (14). The tester should always have access to a full description of the test protocols for reference. Additionally, all paperwork associated with the administration and recording of the test should be prepared before the testing session.

Speed assessments call for multiple trials, usually two but occasionally three (based on the specific protocol used), and the best score is recorded. The athlete should recover completely before performing subsequent assessments. Assessments that use high-intensity, short-duration activities, which emphasize the phosphagen system, typically require 3 to 5 minutes of recovery after each attempt to ensure the quality of the subsequent effort (7). Therefore, assessments

Figure 5.2 Test Administration Checklist

Athlete: _____ Date: _____

Sport: _____

Ahead of the testing date:
- ❏ The testing protocol(s) has/have been selected.
- ❏ The testing protocol(s) has/have been explained to the athletes and all testers.
- ❏ The location and time of the test(s) have been determined.

Day of the testing:
- ❏ First-aid equipment and emergency procedures are in place.
- ❏ The tester(s) is/are assigned and present for each test.
- ❏ The testing equipment is in working order and on site.
- ❏ The testing worksheet(s), pencils, and clipboards are distributed.
- ❏ The testers understand the testing procedures.
- ❏ The athletes warmed up before testing.
- ❏ The environmental conditions are acceptable and safe.
- ❏ The testing stations or spaces provide sufficient room and are clean and ready.

After testing:
- ❏ The athletes cooled down after testing.
- ❏ The testing data have been analyzed and provided to the appropriate person(s).

From National Strength and Conditioning Association, *Developing Speed,* 2nd ed. (Champaign, IL: Human Kinetics, 2025).

such as vertical jumps and the 30-yard dash can employ a multiple-assessment battery. Every assessment session should conclude with a cooldown including light activities (e.g., stretching, light aerobic, and range of motion exercises). This is particularly important when the final assessment is one that stresses the anaerobic system or is a longer-duration aerobic endurance activity, such as the 300-yard (274 m) shuttle run. An adequate cooldown facilitates recovery.

Sequencing

If a test to assess speed is included in a battery of multiple other tests, appropriate sequencing is important. Testers should assess skills that require a high level of coordination and reaction before conducting tests that may cause fatigue and decrease performance (14). They also should conduct tests of power and strength first because they require just 3 to 5 minutes of recovery time (14). When performed on the same day, speed tests must be conducted early in a testing session and must not take place after assessments that will cause fatigue. Proper sequencing maintains a high level of validity.

Athlete Preparation

Without exception, testers should give athletes a thorough description of each test (this may need to be repeated to ensure full understanding) and one practice trial if possible (14). A warm-up that includes a movement preparation and dynamic activities that build to maximal intensity will prevent injury and maximize performance. Ideally, the warm-up is standardized for each testing session to help ensure reliability between sessions. A cooldown combining light exercise followed by light activities concludes every assessment to reduce the likelihood of potential adverse effects (e.g., muscle soreness and joint pain).

Recording Scores

Testers should develop a scoring worksheet for the specific battery of tests to be given. Each tester needs a worksheet with an alphabetical list of athletes to be assessed at each station, along with space to record each trial and a best score. To ensure unbiased and accurate scoring, the tester or a designated assistant is the only person recording scores at each assessment station. Athletes should not record or verbally provide assessment results.

PROTOCOLS AND THEIR NORMATIVE OR DESCRIPTIVE DATA

Speed is an important attribute for successful sport performance. Consequently, speed-focused assessments are included in most sport performance testing batteries. What may be surprising is that normative data for athletic populations is often difficult to find. A simple explanation may lie in a club, school, or professional program's unwillingness to share results or provide valid, reliable, and objective data. Therefore, testers often develop their own assessment protocols that more closely mimic the requirements of their sport (e.g., 30-yard dash for baseball, 40-yard dash for football, 20-yard dash for women's softball). Unfortunately, there are multiple factors that may limit the development of appropriate statistical data, including protocol issues such as starting position (on the start line, 1 yard back from the start line), starting stance, (sideways, two-point or three-point stance), and timing method (handheld stopwatch or electronic timing device) as well as the variation caused by age, sex and level of play.

To maximize the application of normative or descriptive data to a certain sport or specific group within a sport, the data must be specifically relevant to the tested population and the associated testing protocols must be precisely followed. If those steps are not taken or not possible, an athlete's scores on an assessment (e.g., either before and after training or within the group) can still be compared to each other if the testing protocol used is identical for each testing session.

TYPES OF SPEED ASSESSMENTS

Speed is measured as distance per unit of time and is typically described as the time taken to cover a fixed distance. Assessments of speed are almost always conducted at distances less than 200 yards because longer distance reflects an athlete's anaerobic endurance or aerobic capacity (based on the test distance) more than speed, and normally considerably shorter distances are used (14).

Speed tests normally can be categorized into two types depending on their starting mechanisms.

▶ *Static-start tests.* These are by far the most common tests and commence with an athlete in a stationary starting position. The 40-yard dash is probably the most recognizable speed assessment and commences from a static start. However, other speed assessments are gaining acceptance, probably because of their relevance to their specific sport (e.g., 30- and 60-yard dash for baseball; 20- or 30-yard dash for basketball; 20-yard dash for softball, field hockey, and soccer). To provide the greatest test validity, a tester should determine what distances are typically run in the sport and select those distances for assessment. Measuring split times provides additional information because this allows for an analysis of performance at different parts of a sprint. Timing gates set up at intermediate distances within the sprint can give the tester information about an athlete's strengths and weaknesses within each section of the overall distance. For example, if two athletes have identical 40-yard dash times, split times taken at 10, 20, and 30 yards can help differentiate what training each athlete needs. One may have great 10- and 20-yard splits but average 30- and 40-yard splits, revealing excellent accelerative ability but average ability at higher speeds. The other may have average 10- and 20-yard splits but great 30- and 40-yard splits, revealing average accelerative ability but excellent ability at higher speeds. The additional splits give a tester a more complete picture of each athlete.

▶ *Flying-start tests.* Static-start tests assess an athlete's ability to accelerate from stationary positions. As mentioned in previous chapters, it can take a considerable distance for an athlete to reach maximum speed. Furthermore, in team sports, athletes usually initiate sprints when already moving from moderate or moderate to high speeds (10, 11, 13, 15, 18), which also justifies the use of flying starts during speed measurements. Flying tests assess higher or maximum speeds by allowing a period of acceleration before the timed portion of the test starts. The start line of the flying sprint zone is preceded by an acceleration zone, which should be defined according to the nature of the ability to be assessed (i.e., longer distances for assessing maximum speed, shorter distances for assessing acceleration ability). Timing starts when the athlete breaks the start line of the flying sprint zone and ends when the athlete breaks the finish line. The distances should reflect the precise nature of the given sport.

Assessment	Page number
10-yard to 40-yard dash from a flying start	83
10-yard to 40-yard dash from a static start	82
Curve sprint test for soccer	85
Repeated sprint ability test	86

10-YARD TO 40-YARD DASH FROM A STATIC START

Purpose

To assess the ability to accelerate and achieve higher speeds at distances of 10 to 40 yards from a stationary starting position. (The vast majority of athletes achieve their maximum speed between 20 and 30 yards.)

Application

Forty yards is a commonly tested distance, but shorter distances (10-30 yards) may be selected to reflect typical accelerations and sprints for a specific sport (e.g., soccer or rugby). Tables 5.1 to 5.13 (pages 88-93) provide normative or descriptive data for speed tests for a variety of sports and ages.

Equipment

Electronic timing device or a stopwatch. (If a stopwatch is used, cones need to be placed at the finish line.)

Procedure

1. After completing a general warm-up, the athlete takes two practice runs at submaximal speed over the selected distance (10-40 yards) for a specific warm-up.
2. The athlete stands behind the starting line with one hand on the line on the start switch (modify this position as needed based on the timing device that is used). If a stopwatch is used, the tester should start the watch on the first movement of the athlete's hand and stop the watch as the athlete's torso breaks the finish line.
3. On the go command, the athlete accelerates over the test distance.
4. The athlete's torso breaks the light beam at the finish line to stop the clock (or breaks the finish line if a stopwatch is used). The athlete decelerates for 5 to 15 yards (or longer, if needed).
5. The best score of two trials is recorded to the nearest 0.01 second.

Variation

Place additional beams or cones at 5 yards, 10 yards, 20 yards, and 30 yards, when applicable, to evaluate the athlete at these distances.

10-YARD TO 40-YARD DASH FROM A FLYING START

Purpose

To assess maximum acceleration and speed capacity at distances of 10 to 40 yards.

Application

Forty yards is commonly tested, but shorter distances may be selected (i.e., 10-30 yards) to reflect the distances typically sprinted at maximum speed or the accelerative ability required to reach higher speeds in other sports (e.g., soccer or rugby). Figure 5.3 shows time classifications for boys (a) and girls (b) for the flying 30-meter sprint.

Equipment

Electronic timing device or a stopwatch. (If a stopwatch is used, cones need to be placed at the beginning of the flying sprint zone and at the finish line.)

Procedure

1. After completing a general warm-up, the athlete takes two practice runs at submaximal speed over the selected distance (10-40 yards) for a specific warm-up.
2. The athlete stands 20 to 30 yards behind the beginning of the flying sprint zone. Adjust the acceleration zone according to the athlete's ability (i.e., faster athletes need a greater acceleration distance).
3. On the go command, the athlete accelerates as fast as possible to reach the light beam or cones at the beginning of the flying sprint zone at the highest possible speed, thereby starting the timing.
4. The timing ends when the athlete's torso breaks the light beam at the finish line (or breaks the finish line if a stopwatch is used). The athlete decelerates for 5 to 15 yards (or longer, if needed).
5. The best score of two trials is recorded to the nearest 0.01 second.

Variation

Adjust the beams or cones to create different flying sprint zone distances.

(continued)

10-Yard to 40-Yard Dash From a Flying Start *(continued)*

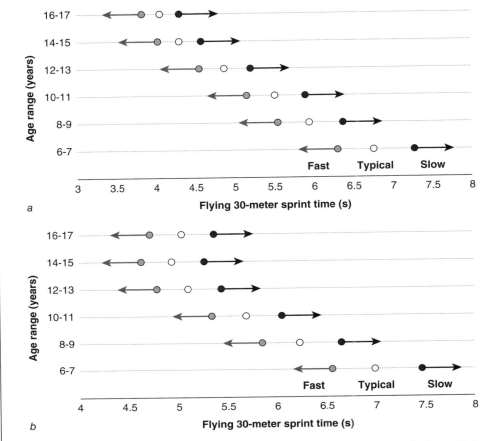

Figure 5.3 Flying 30-meter sprint time classifications for *(a)* boys and *(b)* girls: fast—70th percentile; typical—50th percentile; slow—30th percentile.

Reprinted by permission from D. Fukuda, *Assessment for Sport and Athletic Performance* (Champaign, IL: Human Kinetics, 2019), 122. Data from J. Castro-Pinero, J.L. Gonzalez-Montesinos, X.D. Keating, et al., "Values for Running Sprint Field Tests in Children Ages 6-17 Years: Influence of Weight Status," Research Quarterly for Exercise and Sport 81, no. 2 (2010):143-151.

CURVE SPRINT TEST FOR SOCCER

Purpose

To assess curve sprint ability.

Application

The trajectory of the curve sprint test is the semicircle of the goalkeeper area of an official soccer field, with the following standardized characteristics: a 10-yard (9.15 m) radius (from the penalty spot), a 16-yard (14.6 m) distance from the initial to the final point in a straight line, an angle of 105.84 degrees of amplitude from the point of the penalty spot, and a 19-yard (17 m) total distance (obtained from a trigonometrical analysis). Figure 5.4 shows the setup of the test (12).

Equipment

Two pairs of timing gates are positioned at a 1 yard (or 1 meter) height at the beginning and at the end of the curved path.

Procedure (6)

1. Athletes should complete a general warm-up and two submaximal trials for each side over the curved path.

2. Athletes are then required to perform two maximal trials for each side, starting from a staggered stance position behind the starting line. A 5-minute rest interval between successive trials is recommended.

3. Two variables are recorded from the test: the fastest "good" time (i.e., the fastest time: curve sprint on the good side) and the slowest "weak" time (i.e., the slowest time: curve sprint on the weak side) are recorded.

Figure 5.4   Schematic presentation of the curve sprint test.
Reprinted by permission from I. Loturco, L. Pereira, A. Filter, et al., "Sprinting in Soccer: Relationship with Linear Sprints and Vertical Jump Performance," *Biology of Sport* 37, no. 3 (2020): 277-283, https://doi.org/10.5114/biolsport.2020.96271. Distributed under the terms of the Creative Commons Attribution 4.0 International License (http://creativecommons.org/licenses/by/4.0/).

REPEATED SPRINT ABILITY TEST

Purpose

To assess repeated sprint ability (RSA) in team sport athletes.

Application

The repeated sprint ability test consists of performing six 20-meter (22 yards) maximal straight sprints interspersed by 30 seconds of recovery between sprints. There are other versions of this test that use five 30-meter (33 yards) sprints (2, 5). Figure 5.5 shows the setup of the test.

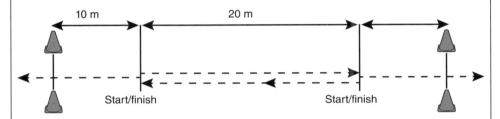

Figure 5.5 Setup for the repeated sprint ability test.

Equipment

Two parallel lines or sets of markers 20 meters (22 yards) apart, and two cones 10 meters (11 yards) past each line as a deceleration zone to allow the athlete to slow down after each sprint.

Procedure (7)

1. Athletes should complete a general warm-up and two or three submaximal sprints before the actual test.
2. The test can be performed on different surfaces (e.g., grass, wood, or sand) depending on the specificity and characteristic of each sport.
3. Athletes start from a staggered stance behind the starting line, sprinting as fast as possible until crossing the second pair of timing gates.
4. The recovery consists of 25 seconds of self-paced jogging with the athletes positioning themselves on the starting line approximately 5 seconds before the next sprint.
5. Three variables can be determined from the test: the best sprint time (i.e., the fastest 20 m sprint from the 6 attempts), the average sprint time (i.e., average of the 6 sprint bouts), and the total sprint time (the sum of all 6 attempts).

Figure 5.6 shows the best and average 20-meter times for recreationally active men and competitive male soccer athletes and figure 5.7 shows their total sprint times for all 6 bouts.

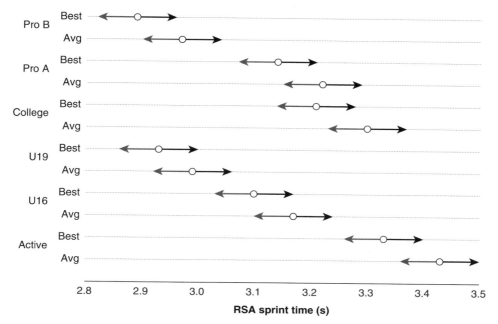

Figure 5.6 Best and average 20-meter times during the repeated sprint ability tests for recreationally active men and competitive male soccer players (electronic timing system).

Reprinted by permission from D. Fukuda, *Assessment for Sport and Athletic Performance* (Champaign, IL: Human Kinetics, 2019), 126. Data from D.P. Wong, G.S. Chan, and A.W. Smith, AW, "Repeated-Sprint and Change-of-Direction Abilities in Physically Active Individuals and Soccer Players: Training and Testing Implications," *Journal of Strength and Conditioning Research* 26, no. 9 (2012): 2324-2330; D.P. Wong, G.H. Hjelde, C.F. Cheng, et al., "Use of the RSA/RCOD Index to Identify Training Priority in Soccer Players," *Journal of Strength and Conditioning Research* 29 (20150): 2787-2793.

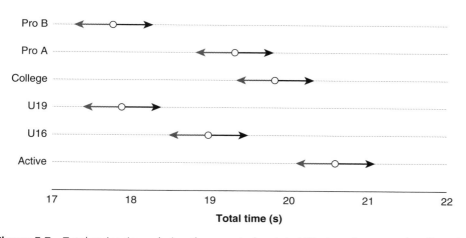

Figure 5.7 Total sprint times during the repeated sprint ability tests for recreationally active men and competitive male soccer players (electronic timing system).

Normative or Descriptive Data for Speed Tests

Table 5.1 High School Baseball

% rank	30-yard dash (sec)	% rank	60-yard dash (sec)
100	3.70	100	6.70
90	3.78	90	6.80
80	3.85	80	6.90
70	3.89	70	7.00
60	3.90	60	7.10
50	3.91	50	7.20
40	3.99	40	7.30
30	4.00	30	7.40
20	4.09	20	7.50
10	4.20	10	7.60

Adapted by permission from J. Hoffman, *Norms for Fitness, Performance, and Health* (Champaign, IL: Human Kinetics, 2006), 110.

Table 5.2 Girls' High School Field Hockey

% rank	40-yard dash (sec)	% rank	100-yard dash (sec)
100	5.55	100	12.77
90	5.70	90	13.73
80	5.88	80	14.11
70	5.92	70	14.32
60	5.97	60	14.55
50	6.04	50	14.71
40	6.15	40	14.95
30	6.24	30	15.43
20	6.36	20	15.85
10	6.52	10	16.25

able 5.3 Various Levels of Football

	40-YARD DASH, MANUALLY TIMED (SEC)						
	Level: high school						
	Position						
% rank	DB	RB	DL and OL	LB	QB	WR	TE
100	4.45	4.50	4.85	4.64	4.64	4.45	4.64
90	4.50	4.51	5.00	4.70	4.70	4.50	4.70
80	4.57	4.61	5.12	4.80	4.80	4.57	4.80
70	4.71	4.74	5.22	4.87	4.87	4.71	4.87
60	4.77	4.81	5.33	4.92	4.92	4.77	4.92
50	4.81	4.86	5.37	4.98	4.98	4.81	4.98
40	4.86	4.90	5.40	5.01	5.01	4.86	5.01
30	4.91	4.95	5.42	5.11	5.11	4.91	5.11
20	4.96	5.00	5.46	5.15	5.15	4.96	5.15
10	5.02	5.05	5.55	5.22	5.22	5.02	5.22

	40-YARD DASH (SEC)					
	Manual	Electronic	Manual	Electronic	Manual	Electronic
	Level					
% rank	14-15 years old	14-15 years old	16-18 years old	16-18 years old	NCAA D1	NCAA D1
100	4.75	4.96	4.60	4.87	4.49	4.68
90	4.86	5.08	4.70	4.98	4.58	4.75
80	5.00	5.17	4.80	5.10	4.67	4.84
70	5.10	5.28	4.89	5.21	4.73	4.92
60	5.20	5.31	4.96	5.30	4.80	5.01
50	5.28	5.43	5.08	5.40	4.87	5.10
40	5.38	5.52	5.17	5.46	4.93	5.18
30	5.50	5.63	5.30	5.63	5.02	5.32
20	5.84	5.84	5.45	5.73	5.18	5.48
10	6.16	6.22	5.73	5.84	5.33	5.70

	40-YARD DASH, MANUALLY TIMED (SEC)						
	Level: college						
	Position						
% rank	DB	RB	DL	OL	LB	QB	WR	TE
100	4.34	4.44	4.72	5.07	4.57	4.60	4.42	4.66
90	4.41	4.50	4.80	5.15	4.62	4.70	4.46	4.78
80	4.48	4.55	4.87	5.21	4.66	4.75	4.50	4.80
70	4.56	4.60	4.90	5.25	4.72	4.79	4.55	4.83

(continued)

Table 5.3 Various Levels of Football *(continued)*

	40-YARD DASH, MANUALLY TIMED (SEC)							
	Level: college							
	Position							
% rank	DB	RB	DL	OL	LB	QB	WR	TE
60	4.63	4.63	4.93	5.30	4.76	4.81	4.60	4.90
50	4.70	4.67	4.96	5.33	4.78	4.86	4.67	4.96
40	4.75	4.74	5.03	5.40	4.81	4.91	4.72	4.99
30	4.79	4.80	5.09	5.47	4.86	4.99	4.77	5.02
20	4.83	4.85	5.15	5.56	4.92	5.06	4.80	5.07
10	4.86	4.88	5.21	5.61	4.97	5.13	4.84	5.11
	40-YARD DASH, MANUALLY TIMED (SEC)							
	Level: NFL							
	Position							
% rank	DB	RB	DL	OL	LB	QB	WR	TE
100	4.30	4.40	4.67	5.02	4.51	4.55	4.34	4.61
90	4.34	4.44	4.72	5.07	4.57	4.60	4.42	4.66
80	4.41	4.50	4.80	5.15	4.62	4.70	4.46	4.78
70	4.48	4.55	4.87	5.21	4.66	4.75	4.50	4.80
60	4.56	4.60	4.90	5.25	4.72	4.79	4.55	4.83
50	4.63	4.63	4.93	5.30	4.76	4.81	4.60	4.90
40	4.70	4.67	4.96	5.33	4.78	4.86	4.67	4.96
30	4.75	4.74	5.03	5.40	4.81	4.91	4.72	4.99
20	4.79	4.80	5.09	5.47	4.86	4.99	4.77	5.02
10	4.83	4.85	5.15	5.56	4.92	5.06	4.80	5.07

QB = quarterback, RB = running back, TE = tight end, WR = wide receiver, OL = offensive lineman, DL = defensive lineman, OLB = outside linebacker, ILB = inside linebacker, DB = defensive back.

Data from Hoffman (2006) and other sources.

Table 5.4 Boys' High School Soccer

% rank	40-yard dash (sec)	% rank	100-yard dash (sec)
100	4.72	100	10.76
90	4.90	90	11.62
80	5.01	80	11.79
70	5.11	70	11.97
60	5.16	60	12.05
50	5.23	50	12.38
40	5.40	40	12.59
30	5.49	30	12.87
20	5.67	20	13.38
10	5.88	10	14.00

Table 5.5 Girls' High School Multisport (Soccer, Softball, and Basketball)

% rank	40-yard dash (sec)
100	5.55
90	5.70
80	5.88
70	5.92
60	5.97
50	6.04
40	6.15
30	6.24
20	6.36
10	6.52

Table 5.6 Boys' 10-Yard Dash (in seconds)

% rank	9 yrs	10 yrs	11 yrs	12 yrs	13 yrs	14 yrs	15 yrs	16 yrs	17 yrs	18 yrs
99	2.12	2.07	2.02	1.97	1.92	1.87	1.75	1.67	1.63	1.58
90	2.19	2.13	2.08	2.03	1.98	1.93	1.81	1.73	1.68	1.62
80	2.27	2.22	2.16	2.11	2.06	2.01	1.89	1.81	1.76	1.70
70	2.36	2.30	2.24	2.19	2.14	2.09	1.97	1.89	1.84	1.78
60	2.44	2.38	2.33	2.27	2.22	2.17	2.05	1.97	1.92	1.86
50	2.58	2.52	2.46	2.40	2.34	2.28	2.15	2.09	2.01	1.95
40	2.70	2.64	2.57	2.51	2.45	2.38	2.24	2.20	2.09	2.03
30	2.79	2.72	2.65	2.59	2.53	2.46	2.32	2.28	2.17	2.11
20	2.88	2.81	2.74	2.67	2.61	2.54	2.40	2.36	2.25	2.19
10	2.96	2.89	2.82	2.75	2.69	2.62	2.48	2.44	2.33	2.27

Table 5.7 Girls' 10-Yard Dash (in seconds)

% rank	9 yrs	10 yrs	11 yrs	12 yrs	13 yrs	14 yrs	15 yrs	16 yrs	17 yrs	18 yrs
99	2.20	2.14	2.09	2.04	1.97	1.92	1.88	1.82	1.79	1.75
90	2.26	2.21	2.15	2.10	2.03	1.98	1.94	1.88	1.84	1.79
80	2.35	2.29	2.23	2.18	2.11	2.06	2.02	1.96	1.92	1.87
70.	2.43	2.37	2.32	2.26	2.19	2.14	2.10	2.04	2.00	1.95
60	2.52	2.46	2.40	2.34	2.27	2.22	2.18	2.12	2.08	2.03
50	2.66	2.60	2.53	2.47	2.39	2.33	2.28	2.21	2.17	2.12
40	2.78	2.71	2.64	2.58	2.50	2.43	2.37	2.29	2.25	2.20
30	2.86	2.79	2.73	2.66	2.58	2.51	2.45	2.37	2.33	2.28
20	2.95	2.88	2.81	2.74	2.66	2.59	2.53	2.45	2.41	2.36
10	3.04	2.96	2.89	2.82	2.74	2.67	2.61	2.53	2.49	2.44

Table 5.8 Boys' 20-Yard Dash (in seconds)

% rank	9 yrs	10 yrs	11 yrs	12 yrs	13 yrs	14 yrs	15 yrs	16 yrs	17 yrs	18 yrs
99	3.11	3.03	2.96	2.89	2.82	2.75	2.68	2.62	2.55	2.49
90	3.18	3.11	3.03	2.96	2.89	2.81	2.75	2.68	2.61	2.55
80	3.28	3.20	3.13	3.05	2.98	2.90	2.83	2.76	2.70	2.63
70	3.38	3.30	3.22	3.14	3.07	2.99	2.92	2.85	2.78	2.71
60	3.48	3.40	3.32	3.24	3.16	3.08	3.00	2.93	2.86	2.79
50	3.58	3.50	3.41	3.33	3.25	3.17	3.09	3.02	2.94	2.87
40	3.68	3.59	3.51	3.42	3.34	3.26	3.18	3.10	3.02	2.95
30	3.78	3.69	3.60	3.51	3.43	3.34	3.26	3.18	3.11	3.03
20	3.88	3.79	3.70	3.61	3.52	3.43	3.35	3.27	3.19	3.11
10	3.98	3.89	3.79	3.70	3.61	3.52	3.44	3.35	3.27	3.19

Table 5.9 Girls' 20-Yard Dash (in seconds)

% rank	9 yrs	10 yrs	11 yrs	12 yrs	13 yrs	14 yrs	15 yrs	16 yrs	17 yrs	18 yrs
99	3.50	3.41	3.33	3.25	3.17	3.09	3.02	2.94	2.87	2.80
90	3.57	3.48	3.40	3.32	3.24	3.16	3.08	3.00	2.93	2.86
80	3.67	3.58	3.49	3.41	3.33	3.25	3.17	3.09	3.01	2.94
70	3.77	3.68	3.59	3.50	3.42	3.33	3.25	3.17	3.10	3.02
60	3.87	3.78	3.68	3.60	3.51	3.42	3.34	3.26	3.18	3.10
50	3.97	3.87	3.78	3.69	3.60	3.51	3.42	3.34	3.26	3.18
40	4.07	3.97	3.88	3.78	3.69	3.60	3.51	3.43	3.34	3.26
30	4.17	4.07	3.97	3.87	3.78	3.69	3.60	3.51	3.42	3.34
20	4.27	4.17	4.07	3.97	3.87	3.78	3.68	3.59	3.51	3.42
10	4.37	4.26	4.16	4.06	3.96	3.86	3.77	3.68	3.59	3.50

Table 5.10 Boys' 30-Yard Dash (in seconds)

% rank	9 yrs	10 yrs	11 yrs	12 yrs	13 yrs	14 yrs	15 yrs	16 yrs	17 yrs	18 yrs
99	4.53	4.42	4.31	4.20	4.09	3.99	3.89	3.79	3.70	3.61
90	4.59	4.48	4.37	4.26	4.16	4.05	3.95	3.86	3.76	3.67
80	4.67	4.56	4.45	4.34	4.24	4.13	4.03	3.94	3.84	3.75
70	4.75	4.64	4.53	4.42	4.32	4.21	4.11	4.02	3.92	3.83
60	4.83	4.72	4.61	4.50	4.40	4.29	4.19	4.10	4.00	3.91
50	4.91	4.80	4.69	4.58	4.48	4.37	4.27	4.18	4.08	3.99
40	4.99	4.88	4.77	4.66	4.56	4.45	4.35	4.26	4.16	4.07
30	5.07	4.96	4.85	4.74	4.64	4.53	4.43	4.34	4.24	4.15
20	5.15	5.04	4.93	4.82	4.72	4.61	4.51	4.42	4.32	4.23
10	5.23	5.12	5.01	4.90	4.80	4.69	4.59	4.50	4.40	4.31

Table 5.11 Girls' 30-Yard Dash (in seconds)

% rank	9 yrs	10 yrs	11 yrs	12 yrs	13 yrs	14 yrs	15 yrs	16 yrs	17 yrs	18 yrs
99	5.10	4.97	4.84	4.72	4.61	4.49	4.38	4.27	4.16	4.06
90	5.16	5.03	4.91	4.79	4.67	4.55	4.44	4.33	4.22	4.12
80	5.24	5.11	4.99	4.87	4.75	4.63	4.52	4.41	4.30	4.20
70	5.32	5.19	5.07	4.95	4.83	4.71	4.60	4.49	4.38	4.28
60	5.40	5.27	5.15	5.03	4.91	4.79	4.68	4.57	4.46	4.36
50	5.48	5.35	5.23	5.11	4.99	4.87	4.76	4.65	4.54	4.44
40	5.56	5.43	5.31	5.19	5.07	4.95	4.84	4.73	4.62	4.52
30	5.64	5.51	5.39	5.27	5.15	5.03	4.92	4.81	4.70	4.60
20	5.72	5.59	5.47	5.35	5.23	5.11	5.00	4.89	4.78	4.68
10	5.80	5.67	5.55	5.43	5.31	5.19	5.08	4.97	4.86	4.76

Table 5.12 Boys' 40-Yard Dash (in seconds)

% rank	9 yrs	10 yrs	11 yrs	12 yrs	13 yrs	14 yrs	15 yrs	16 yrs	17 yrs	18 yrs
99	5.69	5.55	5.41	5.28	5.12	5.02	4.91	4.75	4.68	4.62
90	5.75	5.61	5.47	5.34	5.18	5.08	4.97	4.81	4.74	4.68
80	5.84	5.69	5.56	5.42	5.26	5.16	5.05	4.89	4.82	4.76
70	5.92	5.78	5.64	5.50	5.34	5.24	5.13	4.97	4.90	4.84
60	6.01	5.86	5.72	5.58	5.42	5.32	5.22	5.05	4.98	4.92
50	6.12	5.97	5.82	5.68	5.53	5.44	5.34	5.17	5.09	5.02
40	6.21	6.06	5.91	5.77	5.63	5.55	5.46	5.28	5.19	5.11
30	6.30	6.15	6.00	5.85	5.71	5.63	5.54	5.36	5.27	5.19
20	6.39	6.23	6.08	5.93	5.79	5.71	5.62	5.44	5.35	5.27
10	6.47	6.31	6.16	6.01	5.87	5.79	5.70	5.52	5.43	5.35

Table 5.13 Girls' 40-Yard Dash (in seconds)

% rank	9 yrs	10 yrs	11 yrs	12 yrs	13 yrs	14 yrs	15 yrs	16 yrs	17 yrs	18 yrs
99	6.25	6.09	5.95	5.80	5.69	5.59	5.51	5.43	5.36	5.30
90	6.31	6.16	6.01	5.86	5.75	5.65	5.57	5.49	5.42	5.36
80	6.40	6.24	6.09	5.94	5.83	5.73	5.65	5.57	5.50	5.44
70	6.48	6.32	6.17	6.02	5.91	5.81	5.73	5.65	5.58	5.52
60	6.57	6.41	6.25	6.10	5.99	5.89	5.82	5.73	5.66	5.60
50	6.68	6.51	6.35	6.20	6.10	6.01	5.94	5.85	5.77	5.70
40	6.77	6.61	6.45	6.29	6.20	6.12	6.06	5.96	5.87	5.79
30	6.86	6.69	6.53	6.37	6.28	6.20	6.14	6.04	5.95	5.87
20	6.95	6.78	6.61	6.45	6.36	6.28	6.22	6.12	6.03	5.95
10	7.03	6.86	6.69	6.53	6.44	6.36	6.30	6.20	6.11	6.03

Linear Speed Versus Sport-Specific Speed

Ken Clark
Ian Jeffreys

In both track and field (athletics) and team sports, linear speed is a critical determinant of performance. In the short sprints in track and field, the overall outcomes of race time and race place are determined by the athlete's ability to accelerate rapidly, achieve a fast maximum velocity, and minimize deceleration toward the end of the race (3, 17, 37). In team sports many game-changing plays are preceded by linear sprints (14), and clearly the ability to accelerate to a high speed proffers a potential advantage in many sports. However, it would be wrong to suggest that the fastest runner will necessarily be the most effective on-the-field performer. This is because sport-specific speed and track speed, while having some similarities, also have fundamental differences that directly affect how speed is applied in context and consequently how speed should be developed.

Therefore, for practitioners aiming to maximize transfer of training, it is important to understand the similarities and differences of linear speed in the context of both track and field and team sport competition. One distinct challenge is a paucity of information relating to sport-specific speed, and as a result, a degree of conjecture is necessary when determining how speed as it is applied in sport differs from track speed. However, track speed, given that it is the area with the greater body of literature, provides an effective framework around which to develop an understanding of sport-specific speed. This chapter will first review the biomechanical goals and requirements for the short sprints in track and field and then describe the differences and constraints that apply to team sport athletes on the turf, court, or pitch. To serve as a foundation for explanation, the following sections will discuss each phase of a linear sprint in the context of the 100-meter event in track and field.

THE START AND ACCELERATION

As outlined in previous chapters, the phases of a short sprint in track and field (such as the 100 m) are typically divided into the start, initial and transitional acceleration, attainment of maximum velocity, and deceleration (3, 12). The start includes reaction time, block clearance, and the subsequent two or three steps (1, 25). The initial acceleration phase is often demarcated as the first roughly 10 meters, or approximately the first seven or eight steps in a sprint (32). Sprinters typically exit the starting blocks with a velocity of approximately 3 to 4 meters per second and attain velocities of 7 to 9 meters per second by the 10-meter mark (1, 15, 17). Therefore, both male and female sprinters achieve about 30% of maximum velocity after block clearance and about 75% of maximum velocity or greater by the 10-meter mark. From approximately 10 meters to 40 meters, sprinters complete a transitional acceleration phase, increasing velocity up to approximately 95% of maximum velocity (17, 37).

During the initial acceleration phase, ground contact times are relatively longer and flight times are relatively shorter. Most competitive sprinters reach maximal step rates within the first four to eight steps, indicating that increases in speed after the first few steps are largely due to increases in stride length (32, 35). The start and initial acceleration are characterized by a forward-learning body posture that becomes progressively more upright as the sprint increases (32, 38). The body posture continues to become progressively upright as the torso and shin angles become more vertical, corresponding to contact times that continue to decrease and flight times and stride lengths that progressively increase.

With regards to the kinetic (force)–based factors during the start and acceleration, the runner must apply sufficient vertical force to support and lift the body's weight while optimizing the horizontal forces so that the action–reaction forces will accelerate the runner's center of mass (CoM) forward (5). As determined by Newton's laws, the runners who apply the largest net propulsive horizontal forces and impulses (force × time) will achieve the greatest forward accelerations (24, 28, 29, 30, 36). As the runner continues to increase velocity during the transitional acceleration phase, the ability to apply net horizontal propulsive impulses and to maintain a forward-oriented ground reaction force vector may be key (10, 11, 30, 37). When the runner reaches maximum velocity, the net horizontal forces and impulses (including air resistance) equate to zero, highlighting the importance of the vertical ground reaction forces during this phase (41).

With regards to the kinematic (motion)–based factors during the start and initial acceleration, better acceleration performance is related to more forward-leaning body and trunk angles, the stance foot placed more posteriorly to the CoM at initial touchdown and throughout ground contact, and optimal flight times (24, 25, 40). As it relates to lower extremity kinematics, large thigh ranges of motion and forward shin angles may also be linked to enhanced acceleration performance (23, 40).

THE MAXIMUM VELOCITY PHASE

Competitive sprinters can reach top speeds of 11 meters per second for males and 9 meters per second for females (2), and top speed is directly related to overall 100-meter performance (37). However, while top speed is of paramount importance, a competitive sprinter also needs to minimize deceleration after top speed is attained (35), and it is not ideal for the sprinter to reach top speed too early in the sprint. Therefore, better sprinters typically accelerate for longer distances and achieve faster top speeds deeper into the sprint (37).

The mechanical demands of sprint running change as the runner accelerates and approaches top speed. As speed increases throughout the course of a linear sprint, the contact times decrease while flight times and stride lengths increase as maximum velocity is approached. Because the runner always must apply sufficient vertical impulse to support body weight, the stance-averaged vertical force increases as the runner accelerates toward maximum velocity 32, 34). In fact, peak vertical forces may exceed four to five times the runner's body weight as maximum velocity is achieved (4, 32, 34, 41, 42).

Therefore, with regards to the kinetic factors that determine maximum velocity, faster top speeds require greater vertical force application, with a greater rate of vertical force application specifically occurring in the first portion of ground contact in faster runners (4, 41, 42). Faster top speeds are also linked to greater vertical stiffness, indicating the ability to apply and withstand greater

Competitive sprinters like Gabby Thomas minimize deceleration after reaching top speed.

vertical forces with decreased overall CoM downward displacement during the first portion of the ground contact phase (13, 33). Finally, recent research has indicated that the horizontal propulsive impulses during the latter portion of ground contact may also contribute to top-speed performance (39).

With regards to kinematics, faster sprinters often demonstrate a relatively upright trunk, thigh recovery that occurs more in front of the body (often referred to as *front-side mechanics*), and ground contacts that are initiated on the ball of the foot, with foot–CoM touchdown distances of 0.25 to 0.40 m (2, 25, 31). Faster maximal velocities are typically associated with greater thigh angular velocities and angular accelerations (7, 8, 26, 27) and faster foot velocities at touchdown (6, 9, 16, 31).

SPEED MAINTENANCE AND THE DECELERATION PHASE

During the latter portion of a linear sprint in track and field, the goal is to minimize the amount of deceleration that occurs after achieving top speed. The deceleration phase usually occurs over the last approximately 30 meters of the sprint, depending on the performance capability of the sprinter (17, 37). Typically, competitive male sprinters complete 70 to 100 meters in approximately 2.9 seconds, whereas they complete 40 to 70 meters in 2.7 seconds, indicating a 1% to 4% deceleration over the last 30 meters (35). Similarly, female sprinters complete 70 to 100 meters in approximately 3.2 seconds, whereas they complete 40 to 70 meters in 3.0 seconds, indicating a 5% deceleration over the last 20 meters.

Although relatively less is known about the deceleration phase from a biomechanical standpoint, recent research indicates that deceleration occurs due to decreased step rates during fatigue, as evident by increased ground contact and flight times (35). Interestingly, step lengths were not significantly different during the deceleration phase, likely due to the increased flight times. Sprinting during the deceleration phase demonstrated decreased net horizontal propulsive forces and impulses but slightly greater effective vertical impulses (35). Therefore, increased times to recover the leg (i.e., slower swing times) during the deceleration phase may indicate that it is more challenging to maintain limb reposition speeds under conditions of slight fatigue, potentially due to disturbed inter- and intralimb timing of the thigh muscles (22).

While it is important for athletes to minimize the deceleration phase during the short sprints in track and field, it can be observed anecdotally that deceleration in the latter phases of a sprint will occur only infrequently in a team sport competition. This highlights the importance of several key differences between linear speed in a track and field sprint and linear speed in a team sport competition. Some of these key differences and constraints for team sport athletes are highlighted in the next section.

SPORT-SPECIFIC SPEED APPLICATION

Traditionally, the track model has been the dominant framework around which many speed development programs have been built. However, over the past few years it has been acknowledged that speed application in sport differs from its application in track, and much of this difference can be related to the underpinning goal of each activity. In track, whoever crosses the finish line first (i.e., in the fastest time) wins. The race itself is of a set distance triggered by a predetermined starting sequence and auditory stimulus after which standard strategy can be deployed. As a result, track sprinting lends itself to measurement, which in turn has allowed models to have been developed that are mechanically driven and consequently consistent. As a result the linear models found in this book outlining the distinct phases of the race can be applied across all track settings, allowing for training to be specifically targeted at key constraints within the model. Sport, however, is very different, and the application of speed is ultimately contextually driven. As a result, to understand the application of speed the aims and objectives of the game and the underpinning constructs that dictate its application have to be analyzed.

One Step Forward

There has been a growth in the analysis of movement patterns in sport. Metrics of speed application in different sports reveal major differences in the manner in which speed is applied, in the distances traveled, in the directions of running, in the starting mechanisms, and so on. However, despite this realization, it could be argued that developing truly sport-specific speed is still a work in progress. One challenge is that much analysis is based simply on an analysis of the patterns observed in a game. Now, these undoubtedly have helped make speed training somewhat more contextually relevant, but this analysis often misses a critical component: an appreciation of the underpinning goal of the speed application, or the "why" behind the movement. If we are to ever to truly develop contextually effective speed applications for sport, it is imperative that we first develop a fundamental understanding of what an athlete is trying to achieve in that sport, and to achieve this a very different approach to understanding speed must be taken (21). We have to appreciate that speed is not a goal in itself but instead is a tool by which an athlete is able to better achieve the tasks and goals of the game (18-21). As a result, simply improving a speed score will only ever be a part (albeit an important one) of a bigger picture, a picture that is itself dependent on multiple factors relating to the game.

To achieve this requires a shift from a sole focus on applying track speed models to sport, to the development of a deeper understanding of how—and, crucially, why—speed is applied in a game. This in turn requires engaging more effectively with the coaches and athletes who can provide insight into the sport and to integrate this insight into speed training. It also requires developing a more comprehensive understanding of the movement patterns involved in the sport. This necessitates a move away from a hyperfocus on the highlight reel–type movements of sport to an all-inclusive analysis of all movements to ensure that the gamut of applications is addressed.

Reverse Engineering an Understanding of Sport-Specific Speed

Achieving this wider perspective requires a change in focus and the use of different frameworks. Perhaps the most valuable tool in achieving this more comprehensive understanding is the gamespeed reverse engineering process, whereby the sport itself is the main focus and by breaking it apart piece by piece a greater understanding is developed of how movement and speed specifically relate to performance (18-21). Ultimately, this process can facilitate deeper understanding of the "why" of movement while also ensuring that this "why" is always a key consideration in subsequent training decisions (21).

Developing a deep understanding of many team and court sports is far from easy. Effective performance requires the integration of multiple components, with this integration having both an individual component along with a contextual one. What this means is that individuals will often develop their own unique solutions to given tasks and situations, solutions that ultimately depend on their own levels of gamespeed fitness (20). However, individual analysis is only one aspect; there also needs to be a consideration of how these relate to the capacities of the opponent and also to the environmental setup athletes may face at any given time. In this way the approach taken to solve a sport-related challenge can never be considered in isolation but instead must be considered in relation to their contextual relevance and the likelihood of success.

Clearly, accounting fully for every variable is practically impossible. Instead, what the reverse engineering process tries to do is to progressively break down the challenges of sport into identifiable components, which then shed light on any general principles that affect decisions an individual will make at any one time. This in turn allows key tasks athletes will face within the sport to be identified, and subsequently specific and general capacities that relate to speed and movement can be ascertained, which can then become the focus of training. Importantly, being able to relate these capacities to the tasks and principles of the game enables contextual specificity to be retained as various methods of training are deployed. Indeed, it is this focus on the applicability of speed to achieve sport-related goals that makes gamespeed a more relevant concept than the traditional focus on speed and agility, because by definition it shifts the focus from generic capacities onto capacities directly related to the game.

Reverse Engineering in Practice: A Soccer Example

Given that the reverse engineering process involves breaking a sport down piece by piece into smaller, more identifiable parts that facilitate a deeper understanding of the game as a whole, the process ultimately will be unique to the sport being studied. Additionally, the game's phases, principles and subprinciples, and key tasks to be achieved are specific to the game. Consequently, no one process is universally applicable. However, this is not to say that some aspects of certain approaches may not be transferable providing they are adapted for the sport in question.

Soccer provides a suitable example of how the reverse engineering process can provide an understanding of the movements used within the sport, but also crucially an understanding of the underpinning goals of these movements, or the "why." The four processes are shown in figure 6.1, and what is important is that all of the steps are followed. This is not about looking at the game, identifying how speed is used, and then extrapolating this to a training intervention based on a modification of track training—a process that often results in a bias toward highlight reel movements (21). Instead, the reverse engineering process considers the entire gamut of situations an athlete faces, offensive and defensive, off the ball and on the ball.

Soccer itself can be broken down into two overarching phases, transition phases (figures 6.1*a* and 6.1*b*) and organization phases (figures 6.1*c* and 6.1*d*), both of which can be subdivided into offensive (figures 6.1*a* and 6.1*c*) and defensive (figures 6.1*b* and 6.1*d*) categories. During transition phases there is a turnover in possession—that is, one team loses it and the other gains it. These situations offer opportunities for the team that gains possession while present-ing a risk for the team losing possession. The principles and subprinciples for each team therefore revolve around either maximizing the opportunity for the team gaining possession by moving the ball into positions to exploit the lack of defensive organization, or minimizing the risk for the team losing possession by attempting to win the ball back or reducing the space available for the offense. Clearly, the exact application will depend on many factors such as the position on the pitch where the turnover occurs, the spatial distribution of athletes at that time, and the tactical approach of each team. For example, some teams use a high press to try to win the ball back as soon as they can, while others prefer to drop back into organization. However, key tasks can be identified: The offensive team, for example, will try to exploit the lack of defensive organization by moving the ball into space as soon as they can, occupying multiple channels and trying to get behind the defense with the aim of creating a goal-scoring opportunity. Defensively, the goal will be to minimize the risk by preventing the ball getting forward, channeling play into a low-risk zone, regaining a defensive shape, and minimizing the likelihood of a shot on goal. Armed with this information, specific movement capacities can be identified that facilitate the achievement of these tasks—for example, the ability to accelerate rapidly, to create and exploit

Offensive transition

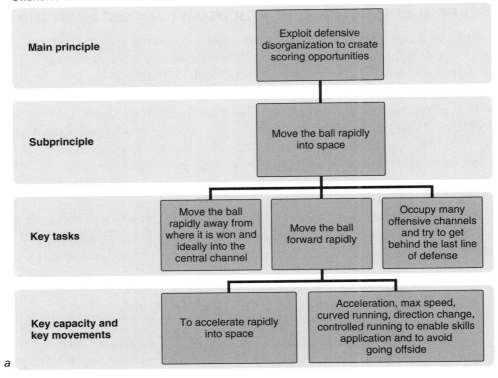

a

Defensive transition

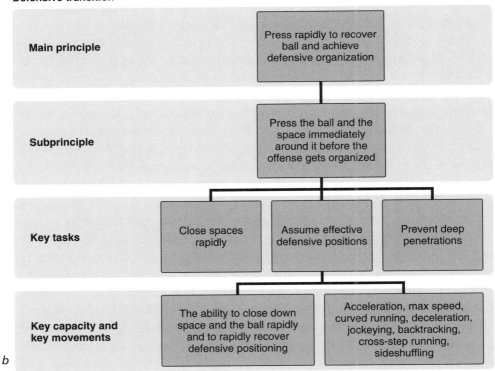

b

Figure 6.1 *(a)* Offensive transition phase or category; *(b)* defensive transition phase or category; *(c)* offensive organization phase or category; *(d)* defensive organization phase or category.

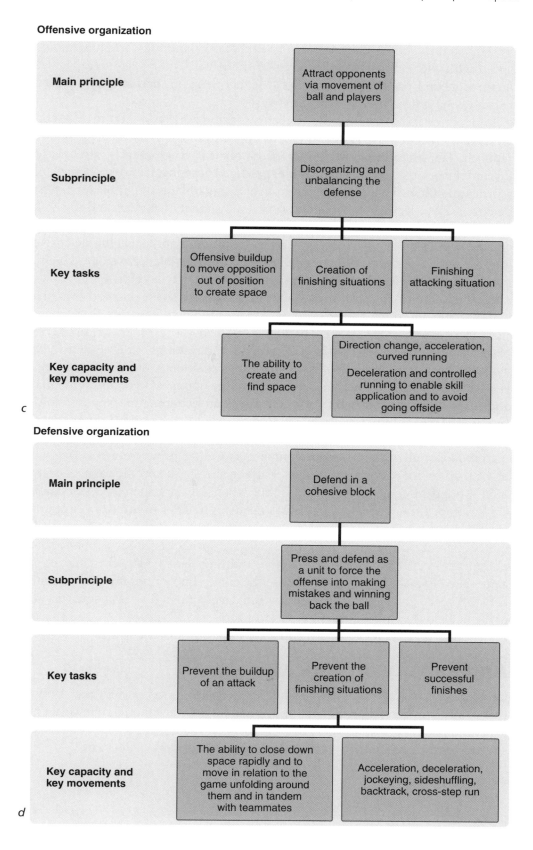

Offensive organization

| Main principle | Attract opponents via movement of ball and players |

| Subprinciple | Disorganizing and unbalancing the defense |

| Key tasks | Offensive buildup to move opposition out of position to create space | Creation of finishing situations | Finishing attacking situation |

| Key capacity and key movements | The ability to create and find space | Direction change, acceleration, curved running / Deceleration and controlled running to enable skill application and to avoid going offside |

c

Defensive organization

| Main principle | Defend in a cohesive block |

| Subprinciple | Press and defend as a unit to force the offense into making mistakes and winning back the ball |

| Key tasks | Prevent the buildup of an attack | Prevent the creation of finishing situations | Prevent successful finishes |

| Key capacity and key movements | The ability to close down space rapidly and to move in relation to the game unfolding around them and in tandem with teammates | Acceleration, deceleration, jockeying, sideshuffling, backtrack, cross-step run |

d

space, to adjust speed and movement to exploit opportunities, and to combine speed with the technical requirements of the game. These specific capacities in turn depend on general capacities (e.g., acceleration, deceleration, curved running, maximum speed capacity).

In organization situations, the challenges facing athletes are quite different. Here, defenses are set and the offensive opportunities are necessarily greatly reduced. The overarching principles of the offense, consequently, are how to disrupt the defense, pulling them out of position through effective movement of athletes and the ball with the ultimate aim of disorganizing and unbalancing the defense. Key tasks involve rapid and varied movement of athletes and the ball, with the goal of creating separation in instances where individual space is to be created, but also creating space for others by pinning and dragging defensive athletes out of position, thus negatively affecting the defensive shape. Again, specific capacities can be identified, such as the ability to accelerate into space, often after undertaking a deceptive movement such as a shape or speed shift, the ability to pin and drag, and so on. It is important to note here that throughout these movements athletes need to be able to carry out the technical requirements of the game such as receiving the ball, passing, and shooting. Consequently, the ability to decelerate and adjust body shape and position to achieve these tasks is crucial. Defensively, the goal is, once again, the opposite: to retain individual and team positions through controlling space and channeling play into low-risk areas, thus minimizing the likelihood of goal-scoring opportunities. Here, capacities such as the ability maintain a position of control from which to read, manipulate, and react to the environment as well as to accelerate to the ball or with an opponent become crucial. Once again, these specific capacities are built around more general capacities, but when capacity such as acceleration are developed the ultimate goal always needs to be kept in mind. An important consideration in organization settings is that many of the movements look quite different from what is generally viewed as speed, instead resembling that more traditionally associated with agility training. This is why the concept of gamespeed is extremely useful, because the game simply does not differentiate between speed and agility. What gamespeed development does is ensure that all of the key movements required for effective gameplay are developed, and this is framed around the tasks that athletes have to perform in the game.

Applicability of Track Models

Given the diversity of sports and the different scenarios faced within these sports, there will always be differences in the applicability of track models. However, in general the following key differences can be identified, all of which affect how speed is developed in sport-specific scenarios.

- The ability to accelerate is typically more important than maximum speed in most sports.

- This acceleration often requires an athlete to reach as high a speed as possible in as short a distance as possible, and as a result, the long acceleration pattern typical of track sprinters is not one that transfers well to sports. Given that many of these distances are very short and often cannot be determined in advance, athletes who are able to initiate movement effectively, thus gaining separation on the first step, are at a distinct advantage. Indeed, in many instances the distances covered do not allow this advantage to be overridden.

- Acceleration is initiated from a more upright position in many sports and often from a position where the athlete is already moving. As a result, a clear differentiation between initial and transition acceleration is impossible. Additionally, the ability to accelerate from a range of positions requires skills often associated with agility. This stresses that in the majority of sports speed and agility can never be separated.

- Movement is triggered by a range of stimuli, many of which are visual. As a result, the ability to see the relevant stimulus is crucial. As a result, the track model of acceleration, where the focus is on the ground for a number of early steps, is ineffective.

- Sport speed is used to carry out a given task, whether offensive or defensive. This requires the ability to adjust speed to that which is optimal to carry out the skill. Similarly, the ability to change speed is an important offensive weapon, and this also requires that defensive athletes are similarly able to adjust their speed accordingly. As a result, gamespeed does not fit the classic track model and is typically nonlinear in nature. This requires the ability to both increase and decrease speed in response to the game. Thus, the ability to accelerate from a range of prior movements and at a range of speeds together with the ability to decelerate and to control movement throughout are important components of gamespeed.

- Sport performance often requires frequent adjustment of movement, and this adjustment can only be initiated when the feet are on the floor. As a result, in many sports a model based on cadence rather than stride length is deployed. In this way the classic maximum speed model may not be suitable for the majority of sport scenarios. This is also the case when skills such as dribbling, catching, and passing need to be deployed and a lower body carry is needed in order to carry out these skills.

- In many sports athletes rarely run in a straight line for any length of time and movement paths are more curved in nature.

CONCLUSION

While much remains to be understood about the precise nature of sport-specific speed, this chapter has outlined some key considerations. Ultimately, there will always be a degree of contextual specificity to the way speed is applied within different sports. What is clear is that track speed and gamespeed have some similarities and also significant differences. As a result, using a track speed model will not always transfer seamlessly to speed in a sport, and different or supplementary approaches need to be deployed to ensure speed is developed in a manner that optimizes transfer to performance.

CHAPTER 7

Program Design for Linear Speed

Adam Noel

Developing a linear speed program that elicits exceptional results requires a methodical and well-organized training plan that assures the development of the mechanical, physiological, and neurological adaptations discussed in previous chapters. While this may seem daunting, this methodical plan should include similar periodization strategies to those used to improve, for example, an athlete's 1RM bench press or vertical jump. Programming strategies such as manipulating and progressing intensity, volume, and frequency will help create the desired adaptations. Furthermore, like any quality training program, a phasic progression with multiple training blocks with specific objectives to improve either acceleration or maximal velocity is vital in improving speed performance. Finally, a comprehensive program should consider the specific demands of the athlete's sport and his or her strengths and weaknesses. By implementing an effective program for linear speed training, athletes can improve their performance and reach their full potential on the field or court.

SPEED ANALYSIS

The first step to developing a linear speed program is analyzing each athlete's sport and positional requirements. All sports will vary in their linear speed demands based on factors such as the playing surface dimensions and the athlete's technical and tactical obligations. For example, basketball athletes and soccer athletes should train their linear speed differently because of the physical demands of their respective sports. While both sports require linear speed, its use on the court or field is unique. Basketball athletes require short, explosive bursts of linear speed to create separation from defenders, quickly change direction, and get to the basket or defend against fast breaks. Therefore, the training program should focus on developing short-distance and quick accelerations.

On the other hand, soccer athletes require more varied applications of speed including longer sustained bouts of linear speed to run up and down the field, make runs behind the defense, and keep up with the play. Their training program, therefore, should include a focus on developing the ability to maintain speed for more extended periods and developing quick bursts of acceleration to create separation from defenders.

In addition, basketball athletes typically play on a court with a smaller playing area, while soccer athletes play on a larger field. Due to the unique size of the playing dimensions, the sports' movement patterns and physical demands vary and therefore require different training programs to optimize performance.

While basketball and soccer athletes require linear speed, the specific demands of their respective sports differ, and the distances trained for linear speed should reflect those differences. More details on how these differences are manifested in training is covered in the sport-specific sections in the last chapter of the book.

Finally, while linear speed distances vary depending on the sport, it is also essential to understand the differences in positional speed requirements. No sport may have more considerable differences in positional demands than American football. For example, wide receivers and cornerbacks may focus on developing top-end speed over longer distances to excel in deep routes and pass coverage. Running backs and linebackers may prioritize acceleration and short-distance speed to be effective in tight spaces and quick changes of direction. Conversely, linemen may focus on building explosive power and strength to drive the opposing athlete forward in short bursts.

Simon Bruty/Anychance/Getty

Sports vary in their linear speed demands. Soccer players like Lionel Messi need to maintain speed for extended periods and use quick bursts of acceleration to create separation from defenders.

All positions in football require a level of linear speed; however, to optimize the athlete's performance, the practitioner must identify the exact distances and speeds the athlete needs to be highly skilled at his or her position. Further information on this will be provided in the specific football chapter later in the book.

TIME–MOTION ANALYSIS

Considerations about how to ascertain the specific nature of sport-specific speed are covered in later chapters, but one way a coach can better understand the differences between the sport and the positional demand of the athlete is by using data collected by a *time–motion analysis*. Time–motion analysis is a method used in sport science to objectively quantify the physical demands of the sport by measuring the movement patterns and physical activity of athletes during training or competition. The analysis involves recording and analyzing the time spent performing different activities or movements, such as sprinting, jumping, and throwing, and assessing the intensity and duration of each activity; the results of a range of analyses can be accessed in various research journals and online (11).

By analyzing the time–motion data, performance coaches can develop a training program focusing on the specific skills and movements needed to excel in the athlete's sport. The information gathered from the analysis can guide the practitioner in designing specific drills and exercises that simulate the movements identified in the time–motion analysis. Additionally, the data can monitor the athlete's speed and progress over time, allowing adjustments to the training program as needed to ensure continued improvement (11).

PHASIC PROGRESSION

Once a specific benchmark has been identified for each position, the coach can begin planning a training program to enhance linear speed over those desired distances and applications. When designing a program to increase the athlete's overall linear speed outputs, it is best to break down the components of sprinting into blocks or phases of training. The three phases commonly broken down in a linear sprint include the acceleration phase, transition phase, and maximal velocity phase. Each program block should emphasize a specific physical quality that will enhance an aspect of the sprinting phase.

While it is best to start programming with the end in mind, the actual training of the athlete should begin with the development and maturation of acceleration abilities before implementing longer distances at higher speeds. This seamless build-up of acceleration to maximal velocity is modeled after the theoretical speed progression called the *short-to-long method* (6). The short-to-long method aims to develop the athlete's acceleration and propulsive forces before transitioning to longer sprints, focusing on top-end speeds through more upright running positions.

In the short-to-long method, the athlete typically starts with short distances of around 5-20 meters (or yards), focusing on proper acceleration mechanics, explosive power, and reaction time. As the athlete progresses and becomes more comfortable with these distances, the training distance will gradually increase, eventually working up to top-end speed distances of 40-60 meters (or yards) or longer, depending on the athlete's goal and positional requirements. This approach also has an added advantage in that in the majority of sports sprinting distances are short, and thus this training potentially has the greatest immediate impact on performance.

Acceleration Phase

As mentioned, the acceleration phase is the first training block in the linear speed progression. As outlined previously, the acceleration phase in a sprint is the initial portion when athletes attempt to overcome their body weight from a stationary or slow-moving position by increasing speed and velocity as fast as possible. This ability to accelerate rapidly depends highly on an athlete's capacity to create significant force in the proper direction as fast as possible (8).

The ability to accelerate and create force in the proper direction involves a combination of resisted sprints and explosive movements that put the athlete in advantageous positions to project the body horizontally. The recommended drill prescription for obtaining these angles is through hill sprints and sled pulls and starts from a low and crouched, push-up, or half-kneeling position (figure 7.1). These exercises are a great option to help the athlete feel the posture and positions needed for horizontal projection and low heel recovery, equating to efficient propulsion forces in the early stages of the sprint (10).

Figure 7.1 Acceleration training using a sled pull.

Transition Phase (Mid- to Late Acceleration)

Once the athlete has trained for several weeks on reaction time and the first 10-20 meters (or yards), the linear speed program shifts to longer acceleration distances in preparation for faster speeds. As previously outlined, the transition phase is the sprint portion that occurs after the acceleration phase and before the maximal velocity phase. It typically occurs between the 10-30-meter (or yard) mark in the sprint. It involves the athlete transitioning from the forward lean and powerful strides of the acceleration phase to a more upright posture and faster strides for maximal velocity.

During the transition phase of the linear sprint program, the athlete should be introduced to maximal velocity mechanics and longer flat-ground sprints to help with the seamless transition from acceleration to top-end speed. The goal of the transition phase is to help teach the athlete how to shift effortlessly from a horizontal projection angle to a more upright running position with faster ground contact. The sprint prescriptions for the athlete should include longer acceleration distances of 20 to 40 meters (or yards), along with the execution of technical top-end speed exercises such as dribbles, straight-leg shuffles, and bounds. These maximal velocity movements can help the athlete develop the proper torso, hip, and thigh positions needed for efficient high-speed running, and by blending the longer acceleration runs with these technical movements, the athlete should be able to demonstrate proper transitional mechanics and therefore be fully prepared for the final stage of the program.

Maximal Velocity Development

As outlined in previous chapters, the maximal velocity phase in linear sprinting occurs in the latter portion of the sprint, when athletes have reached their highest speed and attempt to maintain it for as long as possible. While most athletes may never reach their actual top-end speed in a game, exposing them to the stimulus of maximal velocity running is vital due to the training effect and neuromuscular enhancements gained through such intense training. Athletes also learn to be fluid and relaxed while demonstrating the proper upper and lower limb synchronization needed to run as fast as possible. In many sports, such as football, soccer, and track and field, an athlete's ability to achieve and maintain high speeds over a range of distances is critical to success.

The development of maximal velocity sprinting should be through longer runs when the athlete has the distance necessary to build up to their fastest speed. Once the top speed has been built up, the goal should be to maintain that speed for as long as possible. Some of the conventional prescriptions used to develop and maintain maximal velocity include fly-ins, wickets (figure 7.2), and easy-fast-easy, and fast-easy-fast sprints.

Figure 7.2 Maximal velocity training using wickets (short hurdles).

Finally, it is essential to note that the athlete should not neglect acceleration training through the maximal velocity phase. While the goal is to improve the athlete's operational output to sprint fast, the athlete must work on retaining the skills and improvements made in the acceleration phase. Although the volume will be lower, short sprint distances of 10 to 20 meters (or yards) should be included within this phase to maintain the qualities acquired within the early steps of the program.

SPEED TRAINING COMPONENTS

Once the training blocks have been designed, the following steps consist of drawing out the number of days the athlete will perform a speed or recovery workout, outlining and periodizing the intensity, frequency, rest, and volume needed to elicit a specific training response. Furthermore, the fundamental concept of progressive overload should be strictly adhered to, allowing the athlete to adapt to the training stressors on the body gradually and reducing the chances of injury or overtraining.

Intensity

Sprint *intensity* can be defined in multiple ways. One way to define sprint intensity is the percentage of the maximum effort an athlete can produce, such as a percentage of their maximum speed or strength (2). Like weight training, the percentage used for high-intensity efforts is anything above 85% of the athlete's fastest time or speed. For example, suppose an athlete's personal best in 40 meters is 4.5 seconds, and during a training session that athlete is running multiple 40-meter sprints at 5 seconds. In that case, that athlete runs at 90% of maximum output for that given distance, which would be considered a high-intensity stimulus.

The second way sprint intensity can be defined is through the mechanical cost created by the exercise prescription. Not all sprint distances are created equal, and the physical cost of sprinting 10 meters at a 100% effort, for example, is far less demanding than sprinting 40 meters at a 95% effort. While muscle and connective tissue stress is present during the acceleration phase, the forces experienced in short-distance sprinting do not rival the physical cost needed to sprint at maximal velocity (2). Therefore, sprints performed close to maximal velocity or top-end speed should be carefully monitored and progressed due to the severity of stress on the body.

Frequency

Training *frequency* refers to the number of times per week the athlete engages in a particular training session. When it comes to the development of sprinting, weekly training sessions are commonly broken down into either high or low intensity. The model is based on alternating high- and low-intensity training sessions throughout the training week to allow sufficient recovery and overload from each high-intensity session (3).

High-intensity training sessions focus on developing speed, power, and explosiveness through sprinting drills, plyometrics, and weightlifting exercises. These workouts are highly demanding on the athlete's body and nervous system due to the speed and output required to complete the exercises. Low-intensity sessions, on the other hand, focus on recovery and building aerobic endurance through tempo runs, pool workouts, and resistance training workouts with lighter loads. The goal of the low-intensity session is to promote recovery while improving work capacity and endurance (3).

The frequency of high- and low-intensity training sessions will depend on the athlete's current fitness level and specific phase in the program. Typically, the athlete will perform two to three high-intensity and two to three low-intensity sessions per week, with 48 to 72 hours between high-intensity workouts.

Rest

Rest is one of the essential ingredients to creating an optimal training program. While rest between high-intensity training sessions was previously covered, the rest between sprints is just as crucial to understand. Sprinting at high speeds requires the contribution of both metabolic and neural factors (1).

The primary metabolic energy system used for high-speed running is the anaerobic alactic energy system, also known as the ATP-CP energy system. This system relies on the immediate availability of adenosine triphosphate (ATP) and creatine phosphate (CP) stored within the muscles. When an athlete performs a high-intensity exercise such as sprinting or jumping, the body rapidly breaks down ATP and CP to release energy to fuel muscle contractions. Because most sprints should be performed at 90% to 100% and last anywhere from 2 to 10 seconds, the recommended work-to-rest ratio to replenish creatine phosphate is typically 1:12 to 1:20 (9).

While the replenishment of CP stores is essential for the recovery time between max-effort sprints, the coach must also consider the stressors placed on the nervous system. During a max-effort sprint, the nervous system plays a central role in generating high levels of muscular force quickly and efficiently. When the athlete is not given enough rest between sprint efforts, the rate at which the muscles contract may be dampened, potentially affecting key factors to sprint performance such as stride frequency and stride rate (4). Although the time it takes the nervous system to recover between sprints and repetitions remains unclear, a general rule of thumb is to take 60 seconds for every 10 meters (or yards) performed at 100 percent of maximum effort. This ratio gives the athlete's CP levels and nervous system ample time to replenish for the subsequent sprint effort, allowing for similar sprint outputs from repetition to repetition.

Volume

Running *volume* is generally expressed as the total amount of work completed during a training session, typically measured in terms of the distance covered and the number of repetitions performed. The volume of sprints an athlete performs daily, weekly, and monthly should be monitored and progressed to ensure appropriate build-up to avoid over- or undertraining.

In the short-to-long method, the athlete begins the linear-speed program at short acceleration distances with more repetitions per set. During this phase, the distances covered are roughly 5 to 20 meters (or yards). While these sprints should be performed at 95% to 100% of maximal intent or effort, the neural fatigue from these accelerations is less taxing than those performed at maximal velocity. Due to the shorter distances and lower neural fatigue, the athlete can perform many sprint repetitions per set within an acceleration workout.

Once the athlete has built up the muscular and neurological system to handle longer distances, the number of repetitions decreases; however, the overall volume of distance accumulated during this phase will be elevated.

The volume of sprint distance per workout should gradually build from phase to phase. Huge spikes in weekly or monthly running volume should be avoided at all costs, because this acute spike could harm the athlete if he or she has not performed the proper build-up prior to the increase.

There is no perfect formula for volume or how many sprint repetitions an athlete should perform for a particular workout, so it is best to work backwards from the goal and progressively overload distance and intensity from phase to phase.

Warm-Up

Sprinting at high speeds places significant demands on the muscles and nervous system, and a proper warm-up can help to ensure that these systems are ready for the task at hand. By increasing blood flow to the muscles, improving range of motion, enhancing nervous system activation, and improving mental focus, a well-designed warm-up can help athletes perform at their best during high-speed sprinting (7). In addition, a warm-up can help to reduce the risk of injury by preparing the body for the activity and improving the ability of the muscles and joints to handle the stress of high-speed sprinting.

A well-constructed warm-up prior to sprinting is generally broken up into three phases. The first phase of the warm-up, the *raise phase*, begins with light exercises to increase blood flow, increase core and muscle temperature, and elevate the athlete's heart rate. Using this raise phase of the warm-up to practice low-intensity technical movements is a highly time-efficient method of adding extensive skill practice but without a significant increase in training time. Once the heart rate is elevated and the athlete's core temperature increases, the athlete performs various muscle activation and mobilization exercises via the application of dynamic stretches (in the *activation and mobilization phase*). This phase aims to stabilize and mobilize the joints and muscles needed to achieve optimal sprint angles and positions. *Activation exercises* can include movements performed in the supine or quadruped position, such as glute bridges, planks, or quadruped scorpions. *Dynamic stretches* are a type of stretching that involves actively moving a muscle or joint through a range of motion. Dynamic stretches may include movements such as leg swings, lunge variations, knee hugs, or various active hamstring stretches designed to enhance the athlete's overall movement capacities and reduce the likelihood of a muscle strain (7).

The third and final phase of the warm-up is the *potentiation phase*. The primary objective of the potentiation phase is to perform skill-specific movements that closely mimic the speeds and intensities of the upcoming activity. Running and power-speed drills are heavily employed within this phase to prepare the nervous system and muscle tissue for intense work and serve as an extra opportunity for the athlete to improve sprint posture and coordination (5). The athletes' running and power-speed drills should closely mimic the patterns and positions related to the sprinting phase. For example, in the acceleration phase, running drills such as A-marches, A-skips, and A-runs are often prescribed to help the athlete reinforce more significant knee and hip flexion and extension capacities

(5). On the other hand, during the maximal velocity phase, the running drills performed should closely mimic a cyclical leg action with a more pronounced heel recovery. Dribbling drills where the athlete must progressively cycle over various heights of the opposite limb can serve as an ideal learning tool for top-end speed mechanics.

The intensity and speed of the running drills should be increased gradually as the athlete moves closer to the actual sprint prescription. Following the running drills and before the high-intensity sprints, the athlete should perform three to four warm-up sprints starting around 70% to 75% and gradually increasing in intensity or distance. Once the athlete has performed the last warm-up sprint, the athlete should begin to complete the high-intensity sprints prescribed for that workout.

PUTTING IT ALL TOGETHER

Developing a linear speed program requires careful planning and close attention to detail. The coach should have a high understanding of the athlete's sport and positional requirements as well as current fitness levels. Once the athlete has been assessed and a goal distance has been determined, a phasic progression that emphasizes the specific qualities of the sprint should be drawn out and progressed. Within each phase, the intensities, volumes, durations, rests, and frequencies should align with the current adaptation the athlete is trying to achieve. The training variables should be constantly monitored and progressed so the athlete continues to develop and see improvements in speed and running mechanics from phase to phase. Finally, once the phases and training variables are set, the practitioner can begin prescribing the specific drills to be performed during the warm-up and actual speed prescription.

The most important aspect of creating a linear speed program is to keep the end goal in mind, work backwards from the goal distance when assembling the program variables, and constantly monitor and assess the athlete's speed and technical deviations. By following these essential aspects, the athlete can set a new personal best while staying healthy along the way.

See tables 7.1 and 7.2 for sample week-long acceleration and maximal velocity training programs for a collegiate wide receiver. (*Note*: For simplicity, distances are provided in meters, but yards can be used instead.)

In this sample training week, the primary goal is the development of maximal velocity speed. The athlete will complete three high-intensity training sessions and two low-intensity sessions, followed by two days completely off. During the high-intensity training session, the athlete will complete longer-distance sprints to enhance top-end speed, short sprints to retain acceleration abilities, multiple-response plyometrics and explosive medicine ball throws to aid in overall power output, and finish with a total body exercise. Tuesday and Thursday will be dedicated to low-intensity training, where the focus is on building aerobic

Table 7.1 Sample Acceleration Training for a Collegiate Wide Receiver

Day	Session type	Activities	Weight room (resistance training) emphasis
Monday	Low intensity	Tempo runs: 2 × 6 × 60 m @ 75% effort Extensive med ball throws Abdominal exercise circuit	Upper body exercises
Tuesday	High intensity	Hill sprints: 1 × 8 × 10 m (30 sec rest) 1 × 6 × 20 m (60 sec rest) Incline broad jumps: 3 × 5 Med ball overhead throw: 3 × 5 Med ball underhand throw: 3 × 5	Lower body exercises
Wednesday	Recovery	Foam roll, light stretching, mobility circuit	Off
Thursday	Low intensity	Tempo runs: 2 × 8 × 80 m @ 75% effort Extensive med ball throws Abdominal exercise circuit	Upper body exercises
Friday	High intensity	Heavy sled-resisted sprints: 1 × 5 × 10 m (60 sec rest) 1 × 5 × 20 m (2 min rest) Hurdle jump + stick: 3 × 5 Med ball diving chest pass throw: 3 × 5 Med ball rotational throw: 3 × 4 each	Lower body exercises
Saturday	Recovery	Foam roll, light stretching, mobility circuit	Off
Sunday	Off	Off	Off

endurance and proper running technique at submaximal intensities using tempo runs, extensive medicine ball throws, and abdominal exercise circuits. The athlete will finish the low-intensity day with light auxiliary (assistance) exercises in the weight room to train any areas neglected during the total body workout. Finally, because the athlete trained five days in a row, two off-days are prescribed to help with the regeneration process and mental preparation for the next week of training.

In this sample training week, Tuesday and Friday are the high-intensity days when the emphasis is placed on acceleration development and lower body resistance training. Hill sprints and heavy sled–resisted sprints are the primary acceleration prescriptions to help the athlete understand proper force

Table 7.2 Sample Maximal Velocity Training for a Collegiate Wide Receiver

Day	Session type	Activities	Weight room (resistance training) emphasis
Monday	High intensity	Wickets (8 hurdles): 6 × 20 m build + 20 m wickets (2 min rest) Two-point falling start: 6 × 20 m (2 min rest) Continuous bounds (3 jumps): 3 × 4 Med ball push-press throw: 3 × 5	Total body exercises Primary lower body exercises Primary upper body exercises
Tuesday	Low intensity	Tempo runs: 2 × 8 × 100 m @ 75% effort Extensive med ball throws Abdominal exercise circuit	Light auxiliary (assistance) exercises
Wednesday	High intensity	Two-point start: 1 × 6 × 20 m (2 min rest) Fly-ins: 1 × 5 × 20 m build + 20 m fly	Total body exercises Primary lower body exercises Primary upper body exercises
Thursday	Low intensity	Tempo runs: 2 × 8 × 100 m @ 75% effort Extensive med ball throws Abdominal exercise circuit	Light auxiliary (assistance) exercises
Friday	High intensity	Three-Point Start: 1 × 4 × 30 m (4 min rest) Sprint-float-sprint: 1 × 4 × 20 m sprint; 20 m float; 20 m sprint (5 min rest) Continuous hurdle jump (5 hurdles): 3 × 4 Med ball overhead backwards throw: 3 × 4	Total body exercises Primary lower body exercises Primary upper body exercises
Saturday	Off	Off	Off
Sunday	Off	Off	Off

application and body position. Effort during the sprints should be near 100%, with full recovery between repetitions. Monday and Thursday are dedicated to low-intensity training and upper body resistance training. The focus during the low-intensity session is on building aerobic endurance and proper running technique at submaximal intensities using tempo runs, extensive medicine ball throws, and abdominal circuits. Finally, Wednesday and Saturday are active recovery days to let the muscles, connective tissue, and central nervous system fully recover for the next high-intensity training session.

CHAPTER 8

Developing Sport-Specific Speed

Ian Jeffreys

In many traditional speed development programs speed is seen as a general capacity, with the idea that just by improving linear speed as measured by a generic test, such as the 40-yard dash, sport performance will improve. However, this view has challenges and the application of speed requires a far greater bandwidth than is provided by a solely linear track-based focus. This chapter expands on these ideas and identifies factors that should be considered when designing sport-specific speed development sessions and programs.

TOWARD SPORT-SPECIFIC SPEED APPLICATION

Chapter 6 demonstrated how the specific requirements for speed in sport depend on the tasks to be achieved and ultimately on the environmental setup being faced at any one time. Ultimately, athletes use movement to solve the challenges presented at any given time, and coaches need to provide athletes with the capacities to use speed to solve the challenges they face.

These considerations should clearly influence how speed training should be applied within a given sport, and as a result no speed training program can ever be optimally effective unless it addresses the challenges of a specific sport. The reverse engineering process helps elucidate the underpinning "why" of sport movement, which dictates the expression of speed (3, 4).

It is important to keep in mind that the ultimate aim of sport-specific speed training is to develop speed in a manner that translates to optimal performance in the sport being played; this is known as *gamespeed* (3). This requires both general and specific approaches to speed development. While the basic abilities of accelerating and achieving high maximal running speeds will always form a basis of an effective speed training program, it is when this is supplemented by activities that focus on the tasks to be addressed in the sport that optimal transfer to performance occurs.

The remainder of the book addresses speed in the context of specific sports, allowing coaches and athletes to develop speed in a way that benefits performance of the sport. The following chapters provide sport-specific programs for many major sports, but if a particular sport is not covered, this chapter provides a general system of analysis that can be used to develop sport-specific speed development programs that can be applied to any sport.

ANALYZING THE SPEED REQUIREMENTS OF A SPORT

As outlined in the chapter 6, developing effective gamespeed requires an understanding of how speed is applied to achieve sport-specific tasks. Clearly, there will always be differences between sports, and this can be made even more challenging by the differences between playing positions within the same sport, the differences dictated by the tactical approach of individuals and teams, and the spatial setup experienced at any one time. Luckily, the reverse engineering process allows for a deeper understanding of these variables and facilitating an approach that best engenders transfer between training and performance. This should always be the first stage in developing a sport-specific speed development program. Only when the "why" of speed application is established can speed training truly reflect context, thereby ensuring that key contextual considerations are always kept in mind whenever a training method is used (3, 4).

While getting to the "why" of movement must always be the first stage in any sport-specific training program, once the tasks are identified focus can shift to the specific and general capacities required to best perform these tasks. Here asking a few key questions can help further refine the approach to training. Working through the following questions will reveal a clearer picture of the speed requirements of a specific sport, which in turn are addressed through a well-planned development program.

- ▶ What distances are typically run?
- ▶ In what direction does movement typically occur?
- ▶ What are the typical starting methods?
- ▶ What are the typical movement combinations?
- ▶ What considerations trigger and control movement?
- ▶ What is the temporal distribution of speed efforts?
- ▶ How does speed relate to sport-specific skills and requirements?

These questions provide a framework on which to build a speed development program consisting of exercises and drills that maximize the transfer of basic speed qualities into sport-specific gamespeed.

TYPICAL MOVEMENT DISTANCES

Previous chapters have outlined the difference between maximum speed and acceleration and how these relate to the running distances involved. In sport, distances are often dictated by external factors, such as the court size in basketball and tennis, the rules regarding run and pass offense for offensive linemen in American football, and the distances between bases in baseball and softball. In these instances, it is relatively easy to identify typical distances of sprints, which can be used to guide the relative importance of maximum speed capacity. For other field sports such as soccer, it is not as straightforward because a host of distances must be covered, many being position specific. However, even here, analysis that focuses on one athlete and his or her movement will reveal general patterns of movement distances at different phases of the game. Analyzing the movement of most sports reveals a far greater reliance on acceleration than on maximum speed, so this should be reflected in the allocation of training time and effort spent on this aspect of performance.

Running backs in gridiron football, like Christian McCaffrey, accelerate and attain maximal speed over long distances to evade opponents and score touchdowns.

Importantly, this analysis should include movement both on and off the ball. In many sports the vast majority of movement occurs off the ball, and this may involve different movement patterns than what are observed on the ball. In rugby, for instance, when on the ball, a scrum half's runs are predominantly short; however, watching off the ball reveals longer runs when in a supporting, or defensive covering, position. These patterns should be reflected in the allocation of sprint distances, and they also affect the role of maximum speed development. These longer distances and rolling starts may reveal that the athlete approaches and achieves maximum speed much more frequently than if on-the-ball movements had been analyzed in isolation.

While the distance of runs can be useful, it is crucial that the "why" of movement is always kept in mind, because this will affect the application of acceleration and maximum speed. Unlike track, in which the distance to be covered is fixed, in most sport situations the exact distance of acceleration cannot be known in advance. For example, for a defensive back chasing down a running back, the distance of sprint will depend on the athletes' relative running speeds. Where the defensive back is significantly faster he may be able to catch the running back in a short distance. However, if their speeds are more similar, it may take significantly longer to achieve the goal. Thus in many sports the distances may vary between application, and it is important to look not only at averages but also at worst-case scenarios in determining their speed needs. Additionally, even when longer distances are required, the running patterns are often unlike the long acceleration patterns used in track. Instead, athletes are far more likely to need to reach a high speed as quickly as possible in order to make the play as early as they can. The defensive back in the previous example will look to make the tackle as quickly as possible and not aim to accelerate over a longer distance to make the tackle further downfield.

TYPICAL MOVEMENT DIRECTIONS

As well as being one dimensional in terms of distance, track sprinting is also one dimensional in terms of its direction, simply requiring movement from the start to a finish 100 meters away in a straight line. Most sports are not like this and require sprints in a multitude of directions. Similarly, once in motion, the running pattern is far more likely to be curved in nature, adjusting to the evolving game rather than being purely linear. What is critical is the ability to start in different directions and to be able to change directions as required once in motion. These starting movements are termed *initiation movements* (1, 3), and coaches can identify the typical directions in which an athlete will be required to sprint. Starting movement, for example, occurs in one of three predominant directions: to the front, to the side, and to the rear, with other directions being subtle variations of one of these types. Once an athlete has initiated movement in one of these directions, a more typical acceleration pattern, albeit often curved, takes place. Therefore, the ability to accelerate is fundamental to the vast majority of sports, with the major differences being the distance of acceleration and the actions following acceleration.

Importantly, and unlike the track sprinter, field and team sport athletes are unlikely to continue to accelerate in one direction. Instead, it is highly likely that they will be required to change direction at some point. In terms of direction change, this is generally lateral in nature, with two patterns dominating depending on how sharp the direction change is: changing direction sharply or changing direction in a gentler curved pattern. The "why" of these direction changes always has to be kept in mind from offensive and defensive perspectives. Here maintaining speed is but one consideration, and direction changes often have a specific task-based goal such as beating an opponent. In this way, sharp changes of direction often require a large lateral component, and achieving this requires a period of deceleration to allow an athlete to assume a position from where a sharp cutting pattern can be achieved. Indeed, many top performers are adept at optimizing their deceleration to enable them to make sharp cuts. This also demonstrates the folly of assessing change of direction capacity solely from a time-based perspective as much current analysis does.

However, sharp cuts are not the only, or indeed the most common, type of direction change. Many times an athlete's movement is not entirely straight but makes subtle direction changes in response to the actions of the game. Here, direction changes are not sharp, but instead athletes run curved patterns, with the aim of maintaining running speed during this process but also facilitating adjustment where necessary to allow the tasks of the game to be achieved. Analysis of the typical directions of movement in sport reveals that these curvilinear movements occur frequently in sport, often being far more common than purely linear runs. Speed and control in these curvilinear patterns can be developed by carefully selecting exercises that reflect this movement.

TYPICAL STARTING PATTERNS

Another key element of movement to ascertain is the initial starting position and especially whether starts are predominantly static (e.g., a batter at first base in baseball) or rolling (e.g., a tennis athlete coming forward into the net after a serve). Again, team and field sports differ greatly from track sprinting, where the sprinters start uniformly in blocks.

In reality, few team and field sports use a universal start pattern. Even when starts are static, these vary in their setup positions (standing square, standing staggered, or three point) and the initial direction of movement (forward, lateral, to the rear, or a combination of these). Given these variations, athletes should master all of the typical starting scenarios they will face in a game. This can be achieved by varying the runs conducted in a training session.

While most traditional sprint training programs predominantly practice static starts, this may not allow full transfer to a game situation because in many sports speed is not typically initiated from a static start. Far more common are starts where an athlete is already in motion, termed *rolling starts*. Here athletes already in motion need to accelerate in response to the requirements of the game unfolding around them. In sports where these movements are common, speed training needs to include these actions to develop an athlete's capacity to accelerate from a rolling start.

Rolling starts vary in terms of their direction, their distance, and the preceding movement pattern. For example, soccer athletes accelerate while they are already in motion. However, while this movement is generally linear, it also includes a multitude of directions, and the athletes could be shuffling or backpedaling before they accelerate. Subsequent acceleration, therefore, could be initiated from a range of preceding movement patterns. These initial patterns can vary in type and distance. To further complicate matters, the subsequent motion may require acceleration in a linear direction but could just as easily include acceleration laterally or to the rear. Clearly, these variables add a sport-specific aspect to speed that needs to be practiced. Coaches and athletes should look at the typical patterns they need to produce in a game and integrate these into their speed training program.

Additionally, the purpose of the rolling start needs to be evaluated. In many instances, rolling starts are transition-based movements, which are movements that prepare the athlete for the main action. The athletes move while waiting to react to key aspects of the game. In this way they must be in a position that allows them to react quickly and effectively in response to a perceptual trigger from the game, such as the movement of the ball, an opponent, or a teammate. Because the quality of the subsequent movement often depends on the quality of the transition movement, this movement should be practiced and mastered. Similarly, the associated movement combinations need to be practiced so the athlete can effectively carry out the movements required by the game.

Sport-specific speed training requires an analysis of the typical starting patterns. To facilitate this analysis, the following areas need to be assessed:

▶ *Static starts.* The essential components of static starts include the following:

- *Stance.* In general, a staggered stance in which one foot is placed ahead of the other is preferred because it places the athlete in a more effective acceleration position. This is the preferred stance if the athlete has a choice. However, in some instances, the sport dictates a square stance in which the feet are even with each other. If this is the case, the athlete should practice from this stance.

- *Subsequent movement direction.* Although subsequent movement is often linear, this is not always the case. For example, a baseball athlete at first base assumes a square stance to be able to see the pitcher and then accelerates laterally toward second base before turning to sprint.

▶ *Key variables of rolling starts.* Five key variables need to be ascertained.

- *Distance.* The distance of the rolling start affects the speed the athlete will achieve. If the rolling start is relatively long, the athlete will be able to attain a higher speed. In many sports a range of distances are used, so rolling starts of different lengths should be practiced.

- *Direction.* The direction of the rolling start must be determined.

- *Typical movement patterns.* Once the typical patterns used in a rolling start (e.g., shuffling laterally) are identified, the athlete can practice the specific movement combinations to be able to accelerate rapidly from rolling starts.

- *Direction of subsequent motion.* Rolling starts may be predominantly linear, but they may also be multidirectional. Tennis, for example, requires rapid accelerations laterally from a split step or shuffle.

- *Rolling start as a transition.* Rolling starts may be used while an athlete is waiting to react to a stimulus. In this case, the focus of the rolling start should be on control and the quality of the movement after the stimulus, rather than speed.

TYPICAL MOVEMENT COMBINATIONS

The discussion of rolling starts leads naturally into a discussion of movement combinations. Seldom in sport does a burst of speed happen in isolation. Instead, it happens during the flow of a game and is always preceded by either an initiation or transition movement (1, 2, 4). A task as simple as stealing second base can be broken into separate components: set up in a square stance, make a hip turn, accelerate, decelerate, and slide. In this instance, the movement combinations can be pieced together and practiced so that the whole movement becomes a well-honed skill. This is analogous to movements being joined together in a dance routine, with the quality depending on the individual moves and on how they flow into one another.

Even the most complex skills can be broken down so that typical movement combinations are identified, practiced, and developed. Here again, speed and agility intertwine and cannot be separated, because sport performance requires an ever-changing balance between these abilities. This is why it is generally best to look at sport speed training as movement training or gamespeed (3, 4). For example, a basketball athlete trying to drive to the net may initiate a cut move to try to change direction and create space (agility) and follow this up with a rapid acceleration to the basket (speed).

Ronald Acuña Jr. combines many movements to steal second base.

CONSIDERATIONS THAT TRIGGER MOVEMENT

Sport speed is nearly always triggered by an external stimulus emanating from the sport. It is not uncommon to see athletes with better 40-yard (37 m) dash times being beaten to the ball by supposedly slower athletes who are able to move rapidly in the context of the game and in reaction to the game itself. Track sprinters often talk about moving on the *B* of the bang, with the gun providing an external, aural stimulus to trigger movement. This is a simple stimulus and reflects the relatively closed nature of track sprinting. In many sports, speed is triggered by a range of stimuli, both aural and visual. Basketball athletes, for example, read, anticipate, and react to the movement of the opposition, the movement of their teammates, and, obviously, to the movement of the ball. The nature and location of these stimuli provide the context for highly sport-specific speed training, where movement is triggered by a range of stimuli rather than simply starting on the "Go" or the whistle. As with all speed training, these abilities can be improved through training both underpinning speed and gamespeed. Incorporating a range of activities that prepare athletes for their sport challenges is important. However, care must be taken to ensure that these capacities are built on sound technical models (see chapter 3) and should not be introduced at the expense of effective techniques.

Faf de Klerk sprints down the field, using the stimuli of the opponents and his team-mates to trigger his movements.

TEMPORAL DISTRIBUTION OF SPEED EFFORTS

Although these consideration may not relate to speed development directly (and thus not covered in this book), they do play an important role in determining the ultimate effectiveness of speed application. Unlike track and field, where speed is applied as a singular event (e.g., as a single sprint in the 100-meter dash or as a series of distributed efforts such as in the long or triple jump), most sports require the ability to repeat speed application. In these instances, while maximal speed capacity is important, it can be rendered obsolete if the athlete is unable to repeat the speed application. In American football, wide receivers, for example, perform a series of sprints repeated on every down and thus require the ability to sustain speed across all of these applications. As a result, an effective speed development program must consider the temporal nature of speed application and ensure that this is built into the overall considerations when designing speed training interventions. Again, all the above considerations play a role—the sprint distances, the directions, the starting patterns, and so on—but to this needs to be added repeatability considerations such as the number of sprints performed, the work-to-rest ratios, and the type of recovery (active rest versus complete rest). This can guide appropriate development of repeated sprint ability and ensure that not only does the athlete have a high-speed capacity, but that he or she is also able to sustain this throughout competition.

SPORT-SPECIFIC CONSIDERATIONS

All technique development must enable the athlete to carry out the sport-specific requirements, which is why the track sprinting model of maximum speed is often not effective in sports scenarios. Simply asking the questions, "Why?" and "What comes next?" can be enlightening. Track sprinting models typically involve static starts, running a fixed distance, and then having a long deceleration period. These will always have a place in a general speed development program, but this approach also misses critical components of gamespeed. In sport athletes are accelerating to perform a task. As we have previously seen the patterns of acceleration required to get to high speeds quickly will be different from those used in track, but also, performing the task will require an adjustment into a position from where the task can be performed successfully. This will often require an adjustment to a more transition movement position, and training needs to ensure that the athlete is capable of these adjustments. Interestingly, this often involves a decelerative component, yet assessments of speed and agility performance continue to be based on time as the sole indicator of performance capacity. Similarly, maximum speed is rarely attained in sport and far more common is the ability to move through the speed gears, increasing speed, decreasing speed, curving runs, running at a high but controlled speed, and so on.

Establishing the "why" and keeping it in mind throughout training are crucial to developing gamespeed (3, 4). To this end, it is important to integrate sport-specific requirements into training where appropriate. Acceleration, for example, for a tennis athlete can involve the use of a racket, and any position attained must enable the athlete to play the required shot. In this way, elements such as balls can be integrated into the speed training session, providing a sport-specific practice.

Armed with the results of this analysis, coaches and athletes should be able to break down the specific speed requirement of a sport and identify key elements that need to be developed. The analysis should have identified fundamental patterns from which to construct programs that develop the athlete's ability through to sport-specific application. Chapter 9 provides advice from expert coaches on how to develop speed to enhance performance in specific sports. However, even if a sport is not covered, the information presented here should allow a coach or athlete to develop a sport-specific training program that can maximize the transfer of training directly into enhanced sport performance.

CHAPTER 9

Sport-Specific Speed Training

The chapters up to this point have taken us on a journey from the mechanically derived world of linear speed to the more complex realm of sport-specific speed application. The remainder of this book is dedicated to the application of speed in specific contexts. Here, leading experts describe how a variety of speed training applications can be applied to specific sports.

What is important here is not the exercises themselves but rather how to apply them to address a specific speed requirement of the sport. It is not the exercise itself that is sport specific—indeed some exercises are used in a number of the chapters; instead it is how the exercise is used to address a sport-specific objective. Much of the recommendations focus on the initial development of fundamental abilities such as acceleration, deceleration, and running at maximum speed, skills that are common to a multitude of sports. The programs use a range of basic exercises but crucially as basic competency is developed these are also combined with exercises that apply these in sport-specific situations. For coaches or athletes working in sports not covered in this section, the information in chapters 6 and 8 should enable the speed requirements of any sport to be analyzed, and then application exercises can be devised to ensure that the ability to apply speed in context is enhanced.

Note: for drills, distances are commonly provided in yards with a metric conversion in parentheses when needed, unless there is a reason to use meters. In general, though, meters can often be interchanged with yards unless a precise distance is needed, such as for a standardized assessment protocol.

▶ BASEBALL AND SOFTBALL

Adam Ross
Frank Spaniol*

"Speed never slumps" is an adage often used in baseball and softball. While it may seem an oversimplification, it is no secret that speed, both offensively and defensively, has a significant impact on baseball and softball performance. Whether it is the need to have greater range as a defensive fielder or the ability to change the game as a baserunner, speed has the undeniable ability to affect the outcome of the game. With the pursuit of game-changing speed comes the need to pursue training for specific physiological adaptations such as explosive power and reactive agility, which are central to this exhibition of speed in both baseball and softball.

SPEED IN BASEBALL AND SOFTBALL

Generally speaking, an athlete who can move faster than an opponent creates an advantage in performance. For this reason, speed is identified as a "tool," such an important one that it is one of the five tools (hitting, hitting for power, running speed, fielding, and throwing) that professional and collegiate scouts look for when assessing talent. Interestingly, of these five tools, speed is the only tool that can be used on both offense and defense, which increases the magnitude of impact if trained appropriately. When you look around the baseball and softball field, it is not hard to see where speed can affect the outcome of specific individual plays and, ultimately, the game in general. Offensively, athletes with great speed will move from base to base faster, advancing on balls

*Adam Ross was contracted to author this section; Frank Spaniol's name was added to acknowledge his significant contribution partially retained from the previous edition.

in the dirt, stealing bases to move into scoring position, and pressuring the defense on each batted ball. Defensively, speed affects the probability of batted balls ending up as hits by creating a greater coverage of the open field, which ends up saving more runs.

SPEED ASSESSMENT IN BASEBALL AND SOFTBALL

For many years, the 60-yard (55 m) dash has been used to test baseball speed and is considered the gold standard by many coaches and scouts. The average professional baseball athlete runs the 60-yard dash in approximately 6.92 seconds. Outfielders are typically the fastest athletes, with an average time of 6.89 seconds, while infielders run an average of 6.97 seconds. Catchers are typically the slowest position athletes, with an average time of 7.19 seconds (6, 13, 14). The fastest position athletes typically are centerfielders, shortstops, and second basemen.

In addition to the 60-yard dash, some professional baseball teams measure 30-yard (27 m) split times. Again, outfielders are the fastest position athletes, averaging 3.69 seconds in the first 30 yards and 3.20 seconds in the last 30 yards. Likewise, infielders average 3.73 seconds in the first 30 yards and 3.24 seconds in the last 30 yards, while catchers are the slowest with an average of 3.83 seconds in the first 30 yards and 3.36 seconds in the last 30 yards (6).

While traditionally the 60-yard dash has been considered the gold standard evaluation for assessing speed in baseball, softball has more consistently used a 40-yard (37 m) dash assessment (13). Due to the nature of gameplay, the 30-yard dash, home-to-first, and home-to-second tests could be the more appropriate assessments for determining gamespeed in both baseball and softball athletes (7, 13, 15). Due to the similarities between the game requirements and the lack of research on softball specifically, it must then only be hypothesized that these three factors might also predict softball performance in a similar way.

IMPLICATIONS OF SPEED IN BASEBALL AND SOFTBALL

While simple sprint speed can be useful in baseball and softball, sport-specific speed is often a better indicator of success. One of the most common assessments of baseball- and softball-specific speed is the home-to-first base time, measured from the time batters make contact with the ball to the time they reach first base (4). In Major League Baseball, the average right-handed batter reaches first base in 4.35 seconds, while the average left-handed batter reaches first base in 4.31 seconds (5). While the difference of 0.04 seconds may not appear significant, it actually equates to a left-handed batter reaching first base approximately 10 inches (25 cm) before a right-handed batter. Clearly, this can affect whether an athlete gets on base or is thrown out. Anecdotal research suggests that elite-level softball athletes at the college and national team level have average home-to-first base times of approximately 3.0 seconds for right-handed batters and between 2.7 and 2.8 seconds for left-handed batters (1). With bases being 90 feet (27 m) apart in baseball and 60 feet (18 m) apart in softball, this equates to relatively similar outcomes in feet-per-second and ultimately miles-per-hour speed expression, with right-handed baseball athletes running an average of 20.69 feet per second (6.31 m/sec) or 14.1 miles per hour (22.7 km/h) and right-handed softball athletes an average 20 feet per second (6.10 m/sec) or 14.1 miles per hour (22.7 km/h). From the left-hand side, baseball athletes gain a small advantage over right-handed batters, covering an average of 20.88 feet per second (6.36 m/sec) or 14.24 miles per hour (22.92 km/h), while left-handed softball batters gain a large advantage over their right-handed counterparts, reaching first base much faster at 21.43 feet per second (6.53 m/sec) or 14.61 miles per hour (23.51 km/h) due to batting techniques that place the batter in an advanced starting position at contact.

As in the 60-yard dash, outfielders are the fastest home-to-first runners, with an average time of 4.24 seconds (center fielder: 4.16 sec; left fielder: 4.30 sec; right fielder: 4.29 sec). Infielders are second fastest with an average of 4.36 seconds, with middle infielders averaging 4.27 seconds (shortstop: 4.26 sec; second baseman 4.27 sec) and corner infielders averaging 4.44 seconds (first baseman: 4.50 sec; third baseman: 4.39 sec). The average catcher runs from home to first in 4.48 seconds (5). With these times in mind, how might programming be better designed to target sport specific speed?

To answer these questions, consider the implications in baseball of a routine ground ball and subsequent close play at first base. The average centerfielder arrives at first base 2.1 feet (0.64 m) ahead of a shortstop, 4.91 feet (1.50 m) ahead of a third baseman, and 6.82 feet (2.08 m) ahead of a catcher. The average shortstop arrives at first base 0.73 feet (0.22 m) ahead of a right fielder, 0.80 feet (0.24 m) ahead of a left fielder, 2.88 feet (0.88 m) ahead of a third baseman, and 4.56 feet (1.39 m) ahead of a catcher. The average second baseman arrives at first base 0.52 feet (0.16 m) ahead of a right fielder, 0.59 feet (0.18 m) ahead of a left fielder, 2.68 feet (0.82 m) ahead of a third baseman, and 4.34 feet (1.32 m) ahead of a catcher (5). Obviously, in a sport often referred to as "a game of inches," such differences are significant to the success of athletes reaching base safely and having a greater impact on their team's success.

Additionally, speed can have an important effect defensively. Given the dimensions of baseball and softball fields, along with the varied positioning of athletes, empirical evidence suggests that in a single play, these athletes may be required to cover more than 39 to 43 feet (12-13 m). When evaluating the requirements of specific positions, observational evidence also suggests that infielders commonly cover between 10 and 20 feet (3-6 m) in a single play, whereas outfielders commonly cover a range of 20 to 43 feet (6-13 m) (10). In the outfield, faster athletes can cover more ground in a given time. This allows faster athletes to make more plays, resulting in fewer hits for the opposition. In the infield, faster athletes may also be able to make more plays than slower athletes, improving a team's defensive scores. All this illustrates that speed can make an individual athlete better, and enhanced speed can improve a team's performance.

Based on these results, it is apparent that speed plays a vital role in successful baseball and softball performance. Ironically, because of the short distances involved in the game, athletes rarely, if ever, achieve maximum speed (7). In actuality, it is acceleration that plays a much greater role in baseball than maximum speed because of the explosive starts and stops needed for success in the sport (8). Since overall success in baseball and softball is not solely based on athletes' ability to produce maximum linear speeds, their ability to identify and respond to task relevant cues in a timely manner is also of great importance (10).

FORCE AND SPEED

As outlined in chapters 1 and 2, Newton's second law of motion (law of acceleration) states that the acceleration of an object depends directly on the net force acting on the object and inversely on the mass of the object. Therefore, it is the ability of athletes to impart peak muscular force and maximal rate of force development, all in relation to their body mass, that contributes to greater relative acceleration (7). As the force acting on an object increases, the acceleration of the object increases. As the mass of an object increases, the acceleration of the object decreases. Therefore, when body mass goes up, acceleration goes down, unless force increases proportionally. Subsequently, an athlete's body composition plays an important role in acceleration, so when an athlete gains weight, every effort should be made to increase lean body mass (muscle), which has the potential to produce greater force.

In addition to improving force (strength), athletes should also pay careful attention to appropriate body composition. The percent body fat for the average professional baseball pitcher is about 12.3%, catchers are 11.5%, infielders are 9.4%, and outfielders are 8.4% (2) with rookie athletes being notably leaner (9). Percent body fat for most college and high school athletes is slightly higher (12, 14). To achieve maximum speed, baseball athletes should strive to maintain the optimal balance between lean body mass, fat mass, and force (strength).

Baseball and softball are highly dependent on not only the ability to produce force but also the athlete's ability to respond to visual and auditory cues both offensively and defensively. Defensively, athletes are tasked with retrieving batted balls quickly and efficiently, with the ultimate goal of taking away potential hits and scoring chances from the opposition. Offensively, an athlete's job is only partly done upon reaching base. At this point, successful baserunners must be able to react to and track batted or thrown balls and have an awareness of game situations and defensive alignments while also identifying signals from coaches and teammates. Due to these presuppositions, baserunners who have good reactive agility will be better able to read and respond to ever-changing game situations in an efficient manner. Therefore, reactive agility drills are equated with the development of sport-specific speed for baseball and softball (10).

BASEBALL- AND SOFTBALL-SPECIFIC DRILLS

While understanding the science behind speed in baseball and softball is important, it is the practical application of that knowledge that is most critical for the athlete and coach. From the analysis just provided, it is clear that baseball and softball performance requires effective acceleration, which in turn requires an athlete to react to some type of external stimulus, usually a batted or thrown ball. When selecting speed and agility drills for baseball and softball athletes, acceleration drills simulating both offensive and defensive scenarios should be considered, using both open and semi-open drills. Open drills are those that require a reaction to a specific stimulus with a reaction that is not predetermined (11). Semi-open drills have elements that are preplanned; however, they require some additional perceptual and decision-making skill in successful completion of the task, such as responding to a batted, rolled, or dropped ball (10).

From a defensive standpoint, athletes must train in an open environment, ready to react in any direction. The first drill trains this. Ball drops are excellent drills because they are easy to administer, are competitive, and train the stimulus–reaction–acceleration response that is so crucial to successful baseball performance. From an offensive standpoint, baserunning in baseball and softball requires powerful acceleration that transitions from a static baserunning position, which could be from a lateral (baseball) or forward-facing (softball) start position to a sprinting position. The drills in this section are excellent for working on the transition to full acceleration (3).

Baseball and softball drills	Page number
10-yard start	136
30-yard sprint	137
Ball drop	135
Curve run (first base to third base)	138
Curve run (home to second base)	139
Fly-ball sprint	141
Ground-ball sprint	140

Ball Drop

Aim

To develop the stimulus–reaction–acceleration response that is crucial for good defensive play.

Action

The drill uses tennis balls and a surface that is firm enough for balls to bounce at least twice. The athlete starts in a fielding position, which may be a square or staggered athletic stance, facing a partner or coach who is approximately 5 yards away. As the partner or coach drops the ball from shoulder height, the athlete explodes forward to catch the ball before it bounces twice. (The athlete should not dive unless the surface makes it safe to do so.)

Coaching Points

- The athlete initiates and maintains an acceleration posture on the ball drop.
- Arm drive is powerful, and the hand ranges from shoulder level in the front to a point behind at or just past the hip. *Acceleration posture* is also known as the *drive phase*, which is a body position that is used to optimize mechanical advantage to enhance force and power as the athlete seeks to propel the body forward. For this position, the athlete will seek to have a torso lean with the chest and shoulders slightly ahead of the hips as the athlete powerfully pushes against the ground with each step. The knee drives forward and up explosively while the other leg drives powerfully into the ground.

Variations

Difficulty can be increased by having the athlete move farther away from the partner or coach or by lowering the release point of the drop. Most athletes find it challenging to take a half or full step away from the partner or coach after each successful catch. The athlete can repeat the drill using a crossover step to the left, then a right crossover step. The drill can also be performed with the athlete's back to the partner or coach. The athlete turns, finds the ball, and catches it before it bounces twice. A variation that enhances the reaction–response component uses three partners or coaches positioned equal distances from the athlete (left, front, and right). They drop balls at random, requiring the athlete to react and accelerate in multiple directions, thus enhancing the reaction component.

10-Yard Start

Aim
To develop accelerative ability from a base-running stance.

Action
The drill uses a starting line and a set of cones 10 yards away to mark the finish line. After an appropriate warm-up, baseball athletes start in a base-running stance (photo *a*) and softball athletes start from a two-point staggered-stance start position (photo *b*). At a self-start or visual or auditory cue that requires the athlete to react (e.g., pitcher), the athlete transitions from the initial stance to straight-ahead sprinting (photo *c*) and accelerates through the 10-yard line. This can be performed as a drill in itself, or it can be timed if required. If timed, the coach should time the sprint from the athlete's initial body movement until the runner crosses the 10-yard line. Athletes take two or three practice starts and then perform three to five runs for time. The athlete walks back and recovers for an additional 10 to 15 seconds after each run.

Lateral base-running start position. **Staggered stance forward-facing start position.** **Sprint through finish.**

Coaching Points
- An effective acceleration posture is initiated and maintained.
- Arm drive is powerful, and the hand ranges from shoulder level in the front to a point behind at or just past the hip.
- The knee drives forward and up explosively while the other leg drives powerfully into the ground.

30-Yard Sprint

Aim

To develop initial and transition accelerative ability.

Action

The drill uses two cones set up 30 yards apart. For baseball athletes, the runner starts at one cone, taking a baserunner lead (photo *a*), initiating movement (photo *b*), crossing over (photo *c*), and sprinting forward (photo *d*) through the 30-yard mark. To make this 30-yard sprint drill specific to softball, athletes should start in a two-point staggered stance (photo *b* of the 10-yard start), simulating this different starting position for the baserunner. Again, this can be performed simply as a drill or timed if required. If timed, the watch is started on the first movement and stops when the runner crosses the second marker. The athlete performs two or three practice starts and then performs three to five runs for time. The athlete walks back and recovers for an additional 10 to 15 seconds. This is the approximate rest that they will receive on an aborted steal or a hit and run.

Lateral base-running start position.

Initiating movement.

Crossing over to forward sprint position.

Forward sprinting.

Coaching Points

- Watch for the same acceleration posture, arm drive, and knee drive as for the 10-yard start.
- The athlete slowly shifts to a more upright running position.
- Perform an effective hip turn followed by an effective acceleration. To properly execute a hip turn, the focus will be on a swift and controlled rotation of both hips and shoulders. The inside foot may either pivot or drop step as the trail leg drives to create rotation of hips and shoulders into acceleration posture. The arms will play a crucial role in both maintenance of balance and generation of rotational force as this movement is executed.

Curve Run (First Base to Third Base)

Aim
To develop the athlete's ability to sprint from first to third base. This is an important ability because offensive runs include this curved portion, and considerable time can be lost through ineffective curve-running mechanics.

Action
This drill uses three cones set up 10 yards apart on the warning track around the curve in the outfield from the right-field power alley to the left-field power alley. Cone 1 (start) is on the right-field side of center field, cone 2 is in center field, and cone 3 is on the left-field side of center field. The objective is to simulate going from first to third base. To execute this drill with baseball athletes, runners will take a base-runner (lateral) lead and then a secondary lead (shuffle) (figure a). From the secondary lead, the athlete crosses over using hip turn mechanics, runs the outfield curve, and sprints through the third cone for time. Softball athletes will execute this drill from a two-point staggered-stance start position without a secondary lead (figure b). The watch starts on the first movement and stops when the runner crosses the third cone. Athletes take two or three practice runs and then perform three to five runs for time.

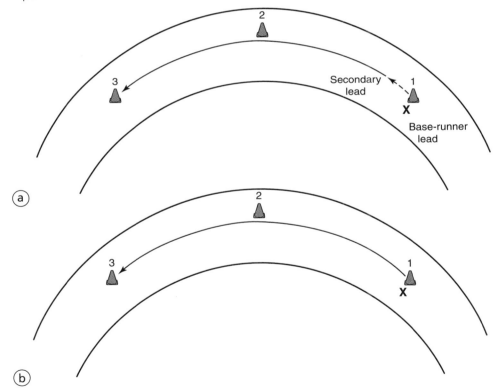

Coaching Points
- The athlete transitions from initial acceleration to high-speed running mechanics, becoming more upright in their running action in the process.
- The athlete maintains speed through the curve.
- The athlete leans into the curve while maintaining an effective posture.

Curve Run (Home to Second Base)

Aim
To develop the ability to sprint from home to second base.

Action
The drill uses three cones set up 10 yards apart on the warning track around the curve in the outfield from the right-field power alley to the left-field power alley. Cone 1 (start) is on the right-field side of center field, cone 2 is in center field, and cone 3 is on the left-field side of center field. The objective is to simulate going from home to second base. The action is similar to the previous drill, but this time the athlete starts from a hitter's stance instead of a base-runner stance. The run can be timed from the runner's first movement until the body crosses the third cone. Athletes take two or three practice runs and then perform three to five runs for time. Athletes walk back and recover for an additional 10 to 15 seconds.

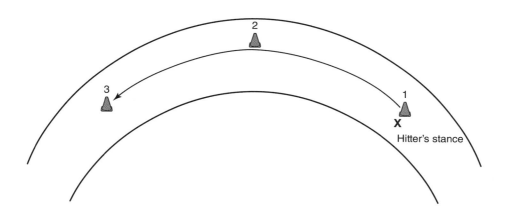

Coaching Points
- The athlete transitions from initial acceleration to high-speed running mechanics, moving from a low driving position to a more upright position.
- The athlete maintains speed through the curve.
- The athlete leans into the curve while maintaining an effective posture.

Ground-Ball Sprint

Aim
To develop the stimulus–reaction–acceleration response that is crucial for good infield defensive play.

Action
As the partner or coach hits a ground ball, the athlete accelerates forcefully to field it. The athlete starts in a fielding position facing home plate. The coach sets up in a batting position and hits ground balls toward the athlete. The difficulty can be increased by moving the athlete nearer to the partner or coach. The coach or partner hits the ball in various directions and various distances away from the athlete. This requires the athlete to react and accelerate in multiple directions, thus enhancing the reaction component.

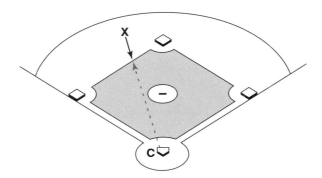

Coaching Points
- From the initial fielding position, the athlete initiates and maintains an acceleration posture.
- Arm drive is powerful, and the hand ranges from shoulder level in the front to a point behind, at, or just past the hip.
- The knee drives forward and up explosively while the other leg drives powerfully into the ground.

Fly-Ball Sprint

Aim

To develop the stimulus–reaction–acceleration response that is crucial for good outfield defensive play.

Action

As a partner or coach hits a fly ball, the athlete accelerates forcefully to catch it. The athlete starts in a fielding position, facing home plate. The coach sets up in a batting position and hits fly balls in the direction of the athlete. The athlete sprints to catch the ball. The difficulty can be increased by having the athlete cover a greater area. The coach or partner hits the ball in various directions and various distances away from the athlete. This requires the athlete to react and accelerate in multiple directions, thus enhancing the reaction component.

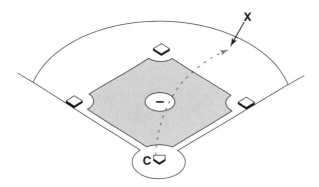

Coaching Points

- From the initial fielding position, the athlete initiates and maintains an acceleration posture.
- Arm drive is powerful, and the hand ranges from shoulder level in the front to a point behind, at, or just past the hip.
- The knee drives forward and up explosively while the other leg drives powerfully into the ground.

▶ *BASKETBALL*

Chris Chase

In the sport of basketball, it is expected that each athlete contributes in some capacity on both offense and defense. Not only that, but athletes are often expected to solve offensive and defensive problems against several other positions on the court that are different from their own. Quick and shifty 6-foot (1.8 m) guards, for example, will match up against athletes who have a similar athletic profile, but they will also be challenged by lumbering 7-footers (2.1 m) with 7-foot wingspans.

SPEED IN BASKETBALL

To find solutions to these challenges, athletes use a variety of movements to accelerate, decelerate, and change direction. These movements include running forward and backward, running around curves, defensive sliding side to side, and crossover running, among others. Since basketball is played on a relatively small court (94 ft × 50 ft [29 m × 15 m]) with 10 athletes, a particular movement is usually performed for a short period of time or distance before a change of direction occurs. Due to the short amounts of time spent performing one movement, it is rare that athletes reach top speed in any movement before having to decelerate.

Fatigue also plays a role in how effectively athletes can showcase their speed. Team-generated unpublished Kinexon data on athletes collected by this author indicate that, on average, the distance a starter covers during an NBA game is between 1.9 and 2.2 miles (3.1-3.5 km), while role athletes cover 1.1 to 1.6 miles (1.8-2.6 km). It has also been shown that approximately 75% of that playing time is spent at greater than 85% of max heart rate (2). Continuous game action can go on for upwards of 1 to 2 minutes before a foul or time-out stops play. A trip to the free throw line may provide 20 to 40 seconds of rest, while a full timeout is 75 seconds in the NBA and 60 seconds in the WNBA. During these periods of rest, it is beneficial for energy systems to recover quickly. Recovering quickly allows the athlete to continue to play at the highest percentage of maximum capacity in the three primary elements of basketball specific speed: acceleration, deceleration, and change of direction. The following sections will use drills as the basis for describing how to prescribe, progress, and evaluate work in this area of training.

IMPLICATIONS OF SPEED IN BASKETBALL

The ability to produce high outputs in these three elements of basketball speed is a general physical quality that is advantageous. However, to take full advantage of the value of speed in basketball, athletes must be able to react quickly, no matter what movement they are using. More than other sports, basketball necessitates that all positions react on both offense and defense while frequently transitioning from one movement to another. Athletes not only react to other athletes, but also react to the movement of the ball. Athletes on defense may have to sprint forward after a pass is thrown and then change direction while transitioning into a defensive slide. They then may have to transition from that slide to a crossover run if they are losing a step to the athletes on offense.

Acceleration, deceleration, and change of direction should not be confused with high-speed running. There are elements of the game that significantly reduce the time an athlete spends running at a high percentage of their max speed. Velocity is equal to distance multiplied by time, and because the court is small, it does not provide a long distance to frequently reach max speeds. Even if the court were bigger, there are 10 athletes on the court, and each athlete is directly challenged by another for much of the game. Whether an athlete is being challenged to make a move around a defender or is defending against an athlete on offense, it is rare to get the opportunity to sprint in a straight line for 2 to 3 seconds without interruption. The basketball itself is another constraint to consider, because the increased complexity of dribbling while running inherently slows down an athlete.

Understanding the demands of the sport is critical for a strength and conditioning coach when performing a needs analysis. As previously stated, basketball is not characterized by significant amounts of time spent at high percentages of max speed. From this author's experience as a coach in the NBA, high-speed running with maximum velocity mechanics serves as a secondary element of speed training for basketball. Acceleration, deceleration, and change of direction are the primary elements.

BASKETBALL-SPECIFIC DRILLS

The foundational elements of a basketball-specific speed development program are acceleration, deceleration, and change of direction. An effective basketball-specific program should balance these three elements in a progressive structure. This program can be progressively overloaded by manipulating speed, change-of-direction angle, number of changes of direction, movement variety, reactivity, and impulse.

Consider speed, which is calculated by dividing distance by time. If the distance is far and the time short, then speed is high. A program can progress

Stephen Curry trains acceleration, deceleration, and change-of-direction speed to beat opponents.

from low to high speeds by increasing the distance traveled and shortening the time it takes to cover that distance.

Manipulating change of direction angles is another way to progress a basketball-specific speed program. A progression from a lower angle cutting to 180-degree changes of direction is recommended. For reference, the change-of-direction angle describes how much athletes turn away from the direction in which they originally running. Using an analog clock as a visual, an athlete runs in a straight line if the hour hand is on the 6 and the minute hand is on the 12, showing six o'clock. When the hour and minute hands are positioned to show a time close to 6:07, that forms a change of direction angle close to 45 degrees. A 135-degree change of direction is shown with the hour hand on 6 and the minute hand on 22 or 23.

Running is not the only movement that should be used when training to get into and out of changes of direction. A basketball-specific speed program can include running, defensive sliding, and crossover running. Athletes also walk forward and retreat backward during the game, which can be used in training as soft starts to transition into another movement. Less movement changes within drills are recommended early in programming. The program can increase variety as it progresses, necessitating the athlete to transition from sprinting to sliding to a crossover run, for example.

Since we know that several changes of direction can occur in one possession, it is important to progress drills by increasing the number of changes of direction within that drill. Multiple changes of direction can add stress by increasing the time it takes to complete the drill while also requiring multiple accelerations, decelerations, and reaccelerations.

Reactivity and competitiveness are also considerations when programming for basketball-specific speed. Initially, drills can be nonreactive and noncompetitive to minimize distractions. The program then progresses to drills that are reactive but not competitive. This means that an athlete may react to a visual or auditory stimulus to start the drill and change direction during the drill. Finally, reactive and competitive drills are used. For example, two athletes may be tasked with reacting to a stimulus, or each other, to start a drill. After that reaction, they may have to race each other to finish the drill (1).

Progression of drills and exercises is an important consideration in developing effective speed training programs. An understanding of how to progress impulse, especially during deceleration and change-of-direction drills, is the final piece to the speed programing puzzle. Impulse is the product of the force applied and the time it is applied for. The majority of coaches do not have access to triaxial force plates but can follow some general guidelines to help progressively overload elements of impulse without acute spikes in loading. Progressing from long ground contact times to shorter ground contact times is one way impulse can be manipulated. For example, a longer ground contact time during a change of direction allows the body more time to produce force eccentrically to control the deceleration. That long ground contact time also allows for a higher velocity to be achieved during the concentric phase to propel the athlete forward in a new direction. With impulse equaling average net force multiplied by time, one can see how a higher number for time can lead to higher impulse. Therefore, high impulse can come from a longer ground contact time multiplied by a moderate average net force, or a shorter ground contact time multiplied by a high average net force. As the elements of speed training are progressed, it is important to understand how they affect the components of the impulse equation.

For example, an athlete's program may call for an increase in velocity going into a 180-degree change of direction. To achieve that velocity, a longer run-up distance is prescribed. The athlete is then expected to change direction with a short ground contact time. That short ground contact time likely leads to a high peak force from the athlete trying to stop and reaccelerate quickly. If an athlete is not having success, it may be because he or she is not ready for that high peak force in such a short time. Cueing the athlete to allow for a longer ground contact time may reduce the peak force experienced and spread the force out over a longer duration. If this cue does not work, we have already described other ways to manipulate impulse to make the change of direction more trainable. To adjust entry velocity, the coach can shorten the distance the athlete must run into the change of direction. This reduces the time available to build up to higher speeds. If a change in total distance is not desired, a coach can mark a distance at a point in the drill that indicates when the athlete should start decelerating. Providing a longer distance to decelerate prior to the change of direction can allow for a greater number of braking steps. This can lead to a slower entry speed into the change of direction.

The following drills are meant to provide practical examples to train and progress the three elements of basketball-specific speed.

Basketball drills	Page number
5-0-5 drill	150
Acceleration drills	146
Change-of-direction drills	148
Curved acceleration drills	150
Deceleration drills	147
Drills to transition from movement into jumps and bounds	151
Linear reacceleration drills	149

Acceleration Drills

Aim
Acceleration drills are characterized by progressively longer accelerations. The aim is to decrease the time it takes to cover distances between 5 and 25 yards. It is recommended that a long distance is provided after the finish line to slow down and minimize deceleration forces.

Action
A coach can initially program hard starts, which require the athlete to initiate the acceleration from a stationary position. Progressing to soft or rolling starts can add complexity by having the athlete perform a low-intensity movement prior to the start. Since the focus is acceleration, that low-intensity movement should not require a change of direction.

The coach can program linear and lateral hard and soft starts. A linear start positions athletes in the direction they will be going, while a lateral start positions athletes perpendicular to the direction they will be going. For example, a lateral hard start looks like a baseball athlete stealing a base. The athlete positions his body facing the batter's box and then turns 90 degrees to direct the acceleration toward the base. To make that 90-degree turn toward second base, for example, the athlete uses a directional step. The directional step is performed by initiating the movement with a left foot push and opening the right leg, directing the knee drive toward second base. An example of a linear soft start has the athlete bouncing around in place like boxers staying light on their feet. In one motion, the athlete then drops into an acceleration position and drives forward into the acceleration itself. An acceleration position can be described as initiating the movement from a staggered stance, similar to how an American football wide receiver would initiate route running.

Distance can also be manipulated. Starting at a distance of 5-10 yards does not allow for high speeds to be achieved and is considered to be the low end of intensity. The ground contact times of the first several steps are longer, producing high impulse due to time and lower peak forces.

Finally, accelerations can progress to being reactive. It is recommended that an athlete has success with nonreactive, noncompetitive linear and lateral starts before making the starts reactive and noncompetitive and finally, reactive and competitive. Auditory and visual stimuli can be used to make a hard or soft start reactive. For example, a reactive linear soft start would have the athlete lightly bouncing up and down in place, similar to boxers' bouncing to stay light on their feet ready to strike, before reacting to the command "Go" by dropping into a staggered stance and accelerating. Coaches can also use visual cues by having the athletes react to them waving their arms. This same drill can become reactive and competitive by adding more athletes responding to the same stimulus.

Coaching Points

Acceleration drills should not require much cueing. Although technique is important, if an athlete is doing acceleration drills, it is assumed that adequate technique has been achieved. Acceleration drills require high amounts of effort and output in a task that is very dynamic. During such a task, it does not benefit athletes to force them to think about how they are moving. If a coach sees a technique flaw, it may be beneficial to break out into a technique drill or remember to include that technique drill at the start of the next session. Feedback on performance can be a positive supplement to acceleration training. Recording and reporting finishing times directly to athletes is highly recommended during training.

Deceleration Drills

Aim

Deceleration drills are the second element of basketball-specific speed training. The aim of these drills is to train athletes to stop effectively in a variety of ways.

Action

As in acceleration drills, a progression can be followed by manipulating several variables. The first of those variables is acceleration and deceleration distance, which allows the coach to manipulate the entry speed and braking distance into the deceleration. Deceleration distance progresses from long to short. A long deceleration distance gives more opportunity to decelerate due to a greater number of braking steps.

The programming entry point into deceleration drills would be a linear hard start into a short acceleration of 5-7 yards, followed by a long deceleration distance of 2-4 yards, and then coming to a stop at around 10 yards. The athlete can stop and come to balance in a symmetrical stance or an asymmetrical stance, also referred to as a *staggered stance*. A symmetrical stance looks like a classic defensive stance position, with both feet parallel to each other and moderately wider than hip width. An asymmetrical stance is similar but is meant to load the lead leg more than the back leg on the final braking step. Both of these stopping positions may be programmed at the same time. Whichever deceleration strategy is used, the athlete should be cued to decelerate quickly, using as few steps as possible. Even if the deceleration distance is long, it is not recommended that the athlete chops the feet excessively to slow down. When a defensive athlete is closing out to an offensive athlete, the classic deceleration strategy in basketball usually sounds pretty squeaky. The athlete seems to use the traction of the bottom of the shoes and takes several more steps than what is needed to stop. If the coach is seeing this, the athlete can simply be cued to use fewer steps. The coach also can cue the athlete to improve by dropping into a more squatted position as those braking steps occur. This squatted position can more effectively leverage the muscles used for deceleration, especially the quadriceps.

An athlete should have success decelerating from high entry speeds and short deceleration distances before making these drills reactive. Deceleration drills can become reactive by having the athlete decelerate on command. For example, an athlete may be required to perform a nonreactive, noncompetitive lateral soft start. After that start, the athlete is cued to listen for the command "Stop," and then decelerate and come to balance as quickly as possible.

Coaching Points

Putting on the brakes can be an intense movement challenge and can easily look unstable. This instability is not helpful, especially when that athlete is going to be called on to change direction and reaccelerate after decelerating. It is important to cue the athlete to maintain an athletic posture when completing a deceleration. The athlete should come to a balanced stop with center of mass over midfoot. Since the sport has visual requirements, it is beneficial to cue athletes to keep their eyes up and be aware of what is going on around them.

Change-of-Direction Drills

Aim

The third element of basketball-specific speed training is change of direction. The components of change of direction are acceleration, deceleration, and reacceleration. Drills that challenge change of direction are meant to mimic the sport more closely. Basketball is characterized by frequent changes of direction that require high forces to decelerate and reaccelerate in a different direction. Change-of-direction drills serve as the last specific physical preparation prior to the drills that will be done in practice or a game. Therefore, the forces during change-of-direction drills need to be at a high relative percentage to the forces experienced in a practice or a game.

Action

All variables outlined earlier can be manipulated when programming these drills. Velocity has already been discussed at length, so this section will focus on drills that progress change-of-direction angle, number of changes of direction, movement variety, impulse, and reactivity.

Change-of-direction angles can start at around 45 degrees for basketball athletes. Starting at a change-of-direction degree that is less than that is acceptable, but those angles are not commonly expressed in basketball. Lower-angle changes of direction may better serve a football wide receiver running a skinny post pattern, or a wing in soccer redirecting himself slightly when sprinting along the sideline. Higher-angle changes of direction are frequent in basketball, so the programming should progress quickly to those higher angles.

It is recommended that a program start with one change of direction and progress to several changes of direction. As the drill becomes longer due to these changes of direction, fatigue must be considered. Since this section is focused on basketball-specific speed, it is recommended that fatigue is minimal to maximize output. As the number of changes of direction increase, it may be beneficial to consider longer rest periods.

Movement variety and reactivity are high priorities in an athlete's change-of-direction programming. Running, defensive sliding, and crossover running can be the primary movements showcased. Transitioning from one movement to another after a change of direction can make the drill easier or harder. For instance, an athlete may be tasked with running for 10 yards, decelerating into an asymmetrical stance, then changing direction at a 135-degree angle into a defensive slide. Even though two different movements are being used and one leg is being stressed over the other, it is easier to transition into the slide since the body continues to face the same way. If this athlete was required to run into and out of the change of direction, he or she must turn the body around to achieve the angle.

Coaching Points

Programming to make changes of direction reactive follows the same progression as acceleration and deceleration drills. After success is had with nonreactive, noncompetitive drills, an athlete can progress to reactive, noncompetitive drills. For example, an athlete may have to perform a change of direction at a predetermined angle without knowing which direction until the coach points to the right or left.

Linear Reacceleration Drills

Aim

Linear reacceleration drills are meant to challenge an athlete's ability to reaccelerate in a straight line after a deceleration.

Action

Although reacceleration happens during changes of direction, linear reacceleration drills keep the athlete moving forward in a straight line. These drills can be used to progress and add variety to acceleration and deceleration programming. The programming entry point into these drills would be nonreactive, noncompetitive. The athlete would accelerate and then decelerate into a balanced defensive stance position and then transition into a relaxed boxer's bounce. The athlete would then be required to perform a plyo step, which is characterized by splitting into a staggered stance and pushing predominantly through the front leg. This facilitates reacceleration in the same direction.

Coaching Points

Reacceleration drills highlight a point of emphasis that should be placed on how quickly athletes can drop into an acceleration position and propel themselves into forward movement. Getting into an acceleration position usually requires the athlete to split into an asymmetrical stance by dropping into some degree of flexion. Hip, knee, and ankle flexion are meant to eccentrically load muscles that will then contract as the athlete pushes forward into the acceleration. It is important for coaches to emphasize this positioning during reacceleration training. Before making these drills reactive, the athlete should be able to execute nonreactive, noncompetitive transitions into acceleration positioning.

Variations

Linear reacceleration drills work well as reactive drills and noncompetitive or reactive and competitive drills. A reactive, noncompetitive version of this drill would require the athlete to decelerate and reaccelerate from a visual stimulus. For example, the coach could hold up a hand to show a stop signal, requiring the athlete to decelerate and get into the boxer's bounce. The athlete bounces until the coach gives another hand gesture to signal reacceleration.

Making this drill reactive and competitive can look similar to shadow drills, which require an athlete to follow the leader's movement. For example, two athletes may be tethered together by a short elastic cord. They would start level with each other, with one athlete assigned as the leader and the other athlete assigned to be the follower. The leader initiates the accelerations, decelerations, and reaccelerations. The follower must keep up, making sure the elastic cord stays loose. If the cord stretches, the drill is considered unsuccessful for the follower.

Curved Acceleration Drills

Aim

Accelerating around a curve could be considered a variation or a progression of a linear acceleration drill, depending on the population being programmed for. Basketball athletes frequently perform curved running, especially in the half court when attempting to get around screens, for example. The purpose of these drills is to expose athletes to a stressor that they will be subjected to in their sport and maximize their ability to execute this movement strategy.

Action

Curved running drills simply require cones to be set up in a curved shape of the coach's choosing. A similar progression could be followed as has been outlined in previous examples of how to manipulate acceleration drills. Progressing velocity, curve angle, and number of curves within a drill is recommended.

Coaching Points

Athletes may have a tendency to start running tall during curved acceleration drills. It is important to emphasize a more squatted, or flexed position to create more favorable angles from which to produce force. A lower position also creates more stability, which is needed when affecting other athletes on the court.

5-0-5 Drill

Aim

The 5-0-5 drill can be considered a terminal task for a basketball-specific speed program. The aim of the drill is to challenge the athlete with a difficult change of direction at a high entry speed. This drill can be used to evaluate all three elements of basketball-specific speed: acceleration, deceleration, and change of direction.

Action

The drill is characterized by a 180 degree change of direction after sprinting a distance of 5 yards. After that 180-degree change of direction, the athlete must sprint 5 yards through the finish line. The 5-0-5 can serve as a training drill and a test. As a test, the 5-0-5 can be used as a proxy for success in the acceleration, deceleration, and change-of-direction drills already programmed. It includes the three elements of basketball-specific speed, as well as exhibiting high velocity, change-of-direction angle, and impulse. The primary result of the drill is the total time it takes to complete the 5 yard distance before the change of direction and the 5 yard distance after the change of direction.

Depending on the tools available to the coach, it can be beneficial to get information on entry speed. Information on ground contact times and force production of the last three steps, known as the *anti-penultimate step*, *penultimate step*, and *final foot contact*, would also be beneficial.

Coaching Points

The 5-0-5 drill highlights reacceleration as a point of emphasis in basketball-specific speed training. After any change of direction occurs, it is usually beneficial to reaccelerate at a high rate for several steps. A coach can emphasize this during change-of-direction drills like the 5-0-5, cueing athletes to reaccelerate aggressively through a finish line or into the next cut.

Drills to Transition From Movement Into Jumps and Bounds

Aim

Even though the focus of this section is basketball-specific speed, it is well-known that basketball athletes must transition from a movement into a jump or bound. Adding jumps and bounds to the acceleration, deceleration, and change-of-direction drills can be considered a progression for both of these methods of training. Jumps and bounds may be programmed independently of speed training but can be made more specific to the sport by combining them together.

Action

For example, an athlete can perform a linear hard start, accelerate for 8 yards, decelerate for 2 yards, and immediately perform a jump. This drill is an essential progression to general jump training, because it adds the challenge of stopping horizontal momentum and transferring that into vertical force. Success in this drill is demonstrated by jumping and landing in the same spot. This is not only meant to train for higher outputs, but it can teach a defensive athlete to avoid fouling a shooter. If a defender cannot control forward momentum, he or she may jump into and contact the shooter instead of simply contesting the shot.

The euro step also highlights a need for combination training. A euro step is considered a bound, because it is characterized by jumping off one leg and landing on the contralateral limb. Athletes are usually running into the euro step and must use the penultimate step to apply high braking forces to slow the athlete down. The athlete then bounds at an angle to move past the defender and elevates off that leg in an attempt to score. Impulse can be very high for these bounding steps due to the higher entry velocity. If the athlete's general bounding drills never progress to this combination drill, the program would be underpreparing the athlete for the forces that will experienced in the game.

Coaching Points

Accountability is important during these drills. If the athlete does not control momentum and lands in a different place after the jump, for example, that is considered an unsuccessful rep. Showing control throughout the transition from running to a jump or bound is the primary focus. If an athlete cannot control the 45-degree angle bounding after a run-up, it may be beneficial to slow down entry velocity.

▶ *GRIDIRON FOOTBALL*

Loren Landow

Gridiron football, named for its grid-lined field of play, is a North American descendant of football and rugby. Along with other hybrid rugby-football offshoots such as Australian football and Gaelic football, the sport involves advancing a ball past a goal line by carrying, throwing, or kicking. However, gridiron football differs from its distant cousins because it is broken up into individual downs, or plays. Each play begins when the possessing team's center snaps the ball to a teammate and ends when a referee whistles the play dead.

Within gridiron football, there are two primary offshoots: American football and Canadian football. Although these two sports grew from similar roots, they have a few distinct differences such as playing field size, number of downs, and athletes per side. However, the expressions of speed are virtually the same regardless of the different rulebooks. In this section, American football and Canadian football will be referred to collectively as *gridiron football*.

SPEED IN GRIDIRON FOOTBALL

Speed is the most valuable asset for a gridiron football athlete, but it is expressed differently among the sport's different positions. An interior defensive lineman and a wide receiver both sprint at various points in a game, but the context of their sprinting is different. The defensive lineman first engages and sheds blockers, then sprints in pursuit of the ball. Meanwhile, the receiver spends

Patrick Mahomes uses a variety of speed expressions throughout a game.

much more time in open space, sprinting to elude defenders who are in coverage or pursuit. Elite-level football teams recognize speed as a prized resource and incorporate it into nearly every aspect of their program, ranging from training to personnel decisions to in-game tactics.

Expressions of Speed in Gridiron Football

Gridiron football athletes are faced with a near-constant need to decelerate, change direction, and then reaccelerate. The sport's various offensive and defensive position groups display speed differently on the field. To facilitate discussion, it is helpful to break these speed expressions down into distinct skills. The primary skills falling under the umbrella of speed are short-area quickness, acceleration, deceleration, top-end speed, curvilinear sprinting, and maneuverability.

Short-Area Quickness

Sitting squarely at the intersection of speed and agility, *short-area quickness* is a combination of perceptive, cognitive, and athletic attributes. It requires anticipation and reaction. When athletes perceive and interpret a signal (e.g., an incoming tackler), they must instantly decide how to respond and then take physical action. This skill is most important for position groups operating in tight physical spaces; some of the best examples are linebackers and running backs during inside running plays. When people talk about running backs who have great vision, they are often talking about short-area quickness. These great running backs can read running lanes and make quick cuts to accelerate through a hole in the defense.

Acceleration

Perhaps the most important speed-related skill in gridiron football, *acceleration* describes how quickly an athlete can gain velocity. Since each play begins with a dead ball, athletes must be able to accelerate since they cannot get much of a running start. If athletes have superior top speed but accelerate slowly, they will rarely be able to display their maximum velocity abilities because they will be tackled or the ballcarrier will accelerate past them.

The first few steps of an athlete's acceleration are strongly affected by *relative strength*, and exercises like a heavy back squat can help to improve force output during these initial steps. However, more explosive exercises like power cleans and medicine ball throws can provide more benefit for later acceleration steps (9).

Deceleration

Deceleration is acceleration's often neglected twin. In speed training for gridiron football the emphasis is usually about how fast an athlete can reach maximum velocity, but the ability to quickly reduce speed can be just as critical. The integral concept of a juke or cut—vital tools for a ballcarrier to evade defenders or for a receiver to get open—is built entirely on deceleration. The most elusive offensive skill athletes are excellent at faking acceleration one way, then decelerating and reaccelerating in another direction.

Defenders need deceleration just as badly as their offensive opponents, because the sooner athletes can stop, the sooner they can redirect and accelerate in a new direction to cover a route runner or pursue the ballcarrier. Athletes therefore should learn and practice the nuts and bolts of how to slow down. The ability to decelerate repeatedly in gridiron football is extremely important to maximizing performance and minimizing injury risk.

Top-End Speed

On a given play, gridiron football athletes rarely get the chance to accelerate all the way to their highest sprinting velocity—referred to here as *top-end speed* or *maximum velocity*. They are accelerating, decelerating, and making contact with opponents so often that they rarely get the chance to reach full speed. However, the skill of maximum velocity sprinting can still have a major impact on games. Athletes who can reach their maximum velocity quickly are known for making big plays and avoiding potential disasters.

Improving the absolute highest speed athletes can reach is certainly important, but in gridiron football they need to be able to sprint at high speeds for a significant number of repetitions. National Football League (NFL) wide receivers often cover hundreds of yards at high speeds during a game (1), so their bodies must be prepared to handle this level of exertion.

Curvilinear Speed and Maneuverability

Sprinting fast in a straight line is important, but in gridiron football that line usually cannot stay straight for very long. Athletes who have the skill and lower body capacity to make sharp turns while continuing to sprint can set themselves apart from other athletes who would need to make a decelerative cut in the same scenario. This type of speed—sprinting along a curve rather than a straight line—is known as *curvilinear speed*. Athletes who can sprint in a curved line while gaining or maintaining speed—like 200-meter track sprinters turning the corner during a race—have good curvilinear sprinting ability. This quality is displayed often during a game: the offensive guard pulling and turning upfield to become a lead blocker; the defensive end or outside linebacker executing a speed rush around the offensive tackle to sack the quarterback; or the running back breaking contain and getting outside the defense on a toss play.

Maneuverability describes an athlete's ability to strategically move between linear speed and curvilinear speed in an in-game scenario. For example, during a kickoff or punt return touchdown the return specialist's path often follows a long winding route rather than a zigzag pattern with many sharp decelerative cuts. With the entire kick coverage unit bearing down on the returner, quick acceleration while navigating behind blockers and finding an open running lane is critical. Maneuverability is a key attribute that allows an athlete to make fast and effective on-field decisions, enabling movement adjustments in response to the movements of the opponents, the ball, and other teammates, all while maintaining speed and balance.

An athlete's *multidirectional ability* combines these components of speed with lateral and backward movement, along with the bridging movements needed to change direction efficiently. *Agility* specifically describes an athlete's multidirectional ability in response to a stimulus, such as a ballcarrier making a sudden jump cut to evade an incoming tackler. Not all movement skills carry the same level of importance for each position group, so it is helpful to examine the aforementioned speed qualities as relative priorities between positions.

Key Performance Indicators for Speed

The five speed skills described in this section (short-area quickness, acceleration, deceleration, top-end speed, and maneuverability) are all involved in gridiron football but in varying degrees depending on each athlete's on-field position. *Key performance indicators (KPIs)* describe the highest-priority skills for different position groups (table 9.1). For example, acceleration is a KPI for defensive linemen, whereas top-end speed is not.

Table 9.1   Speed KPIs for Gridiron Football

Position	Short-area quickness	Acceleration	Deceleration	Top-end speed	Maneuverability
QB	☆☆☆	☆☆☆☆	☆☆☆	☆☆	☆☆☆☆
RB	☆☆☆☆☆	☆☆☆☆☆	☆☆☆☆☆	☆☆☆	☆☆☆☆
TE	☆☆☆	☆☆☆☆	☆☆☆☆	☆☆☆☆	☆☆☆☆
WR	☆☆☆☆	☆☆☆☆☆	☆☆☆☆	☆☆☆☆☆	☆☆☆☆☆
OL	☆☆☆☆	☆☆☆☆	☆☆☆	☆	☆☆
DL	☆☆☆☆☆	☆☆☆☆☆	☆☆☆☆	☆☆	☆☆☆☆
OLB	☆☆☆☆	☆☆☆☆☆	☆☆☆☆	☆☆☆	☆☆☆☆☆
ILB	☆☆☆☆☆	☆☆☆☆☆	☆☆☆☆	☆☆☆	☆☆☆
DB	☆☆☆☆☆	☆☆☆☆☆	☆☆☆☆☆	☆☆☆☆☆	☆☆☆

QB = quarterback, RB = running back, TE = tight end, WR = wide receiver, OL = offensive lineman, DL = defensive lineman, OLB = outside linebacker, ILB = inside linebacker, DB = defensive back.

IMPLICATIONS OF SPEED IN GRIDIRON FOOTBALL

Gridiron football often is nicknamed a "game of inches" because the sport has an extremely slim margin for error. Especially at the professional level, action on the field unfolds at a blistering pace. A mere split second can make the difference between a big play or a disastrous one. This means speed influences nearly every dimension of the sport. Scouting and selecting athletes, tactics employed during the game, and training methods all ultimately revolve around speed.

Athlete Evaluation

Just to get on the field—especially at gridiron football's collegiate and professional levels—athletes need to be fast. To prove their speed to potential future teams, athletes participate in athletic combine testing events, which include a battery of general performance assessments as well as position-specific drills.

The NFL Combine—the annual invite-only combine for a select few prospective NFL athletes—is the most famous of these events. Analysis of NFL Combine data shows that college and NFL athletes consistently have been getting faster and more powerful over the years, as measured by their performance in combine tests such as the 40-yard (37 m) dash, vertical jump, three-cone drill, and standing broad jump (2, 7).

The 40-yard (37 m) dash and its 10- and 20-yard (9 and 18 m) split times are some of the most intensely scrutinized combine testing numbers, and their relationship to future NFL success is real. Research has found that NFL athletes named to the Pro Bowl or All-Pro teams during their playing careers tend to run a faster 40-yard dash at the NFL Combine than their NFL peers who receive no accolades; the 40-yard dash was the only test to display this relationship across all the main position groups (3).

Strategy

Gridiron football is a constant cat-and-mouse game in which the fastest athletes can transform the game even when they are not touching the ball. Much of a team's weekly game preparation involves studying the opponent's previously taped games to glean strategic information about how the other team operates. One aim of this film study is to identify the other team's fastest athletes and plan for how to account for them. During the game, speed has a massive effect on a team's offensive and defensive schemes.

Once the offense has lined up on the ball, they can use the tactics of shifting or sending a player in motion to reveal the opponent's defensive strategy and locate advantageous one-on-one matchups. Offenses move their athletes around with the intention of getting a fast running back or tight end matched up against a slower linebacker in pass coverage. A savvy quarterback can read the other team's defense before the snap, then exploit these matchups to create big plays. Meanwhile, defenses attempt to neutralize faster offensive athletes by rotating and disguising their pass coverages.

Kicking plays to score points or change possession, also known as *special teams plays*, rely heavily on speed. Teams with faster special teams units have advantage in the battle for field position, especially in covering punts and kickoffs. It is possible for a punter or kickoff specialist to "outkick the coverage" by kicking the ball farther than other teammates can catch up to, giving the opposing returner ample space to catch and return the kick or punt. If the teammates are fast enough, however, they can arrive at the same time as the ball and prevent a return.

Energy System Demands

Sports like rugby, soccer (association football), lacrosse, or basketball all involve a more flowing pace with occasional stoppages in play. Gridiron football, on the other hand, features brief bouts of intense action interspersed with frequent stoppages and longer periods of rest. Rather than experiencing periods of walking, jogging, and sprinting at various intensities throughout a game, gridiron football athletes exert maximal or near-maximal effort for the duration of each play.

A football play usually lasts between 2 and 13 seconds, with an average of 5.5 seconds in college and 5.0 seconds in the NFL (5). After each play, the referee starts a play clock counting down 25 or 40 seconds until the offense must begin another play. This gives athletes a short break between downs. Studies have shown that college athletes rest between plays for about 32.7 seconds on average, while NFL athletes rest an average of 26.9 to 36.4 seconds (5). However, these numbers can vary depending on the offense's playing tempo and how much of the play clock they use. Athletes sometimes get longer periods of rest—up to 10 minutes or longer in some cases—when they are on the sideline waiting to return to the game.

All three energy systems (phosphagen, glycolytic, and oxidative) are involved in gridiron football, but the sport's unique structure makes it overwhelmingly powered by the phosphagen system (4). On sustained play drives that keep athletes on the field for 10 or more plays at a time, the glycolytic system starts to play a more prominent role. The oxidative system is important—especially between plays and drives—for helping to clear metabolites accumulated during repeated bouts of sprinting, thereby replenishing the anaerobic systems (8).

Speed Training Considerations

Athletes need dedicated field-based speed training sessions to improve sprinting skill as well as speed quality and capacity. Coaches should take an approach that stresses improving movement quality, but to meet gridiron football's demands, great emphasis also must be placed on movement capacity.

Movement Skills Training

Mastering smooth and effective movement patterns to maximize on-field speed is like studying a new language. Athletes can rehearse the smaller components of a movement pattern with simple drills, like a language learner studying a verb conjugation chart or a list of vocabulary words. Practicing and honing these movement "chunks" helps athletes improve movement quality and efficiency. A more efficient athlete is a faster athlete.

In the context of speed training for gridiron football, this coaching philosophy advocates rehearsing basic drills along with practicing actual sprinting. Athletes at all levels can benefit from universal speed drills discussed elsewhere in this book, such as the acceleration A-Skip and Wall Drill. These drills emphasize the four Ps of sprinting technique: *posture* (the body's overall alignment in space), *position* (creating ideal shapes during the sprint), *placement* (where the feet strike the ground), and *patterning* (overall rhythm and coordination).

Level of Competition and Training Age

Athletic ability and training background are major considerations when designing speed training programs for football athletes at different levels. A youth or high school athlete with limited training experience can benefit greatly from consistent exposure to basic speed drills. Young athletes need to develop better general coordination patterns to set a foundation for future speed gains. Improving their overall coordination helps them learn to better express elastic energy during their sprints.

High-level athletes generally should be executing a greater share of football-specific speed drills than their younger counterparts. Athletes with a higher training age (including most college and professional athletes) should still return to basic low-impact drills at certain times such as early off-season training or returning from an injury to work on regrooving movement patterns and clearing up any lingering issues.

In-Season versus Off-Season Training

Clever planning of sprint volume, intensity, and frequency throughout the calendar year can boost both speed *quality* (how fast and how well athletes run) and speed *capacity* (the ability to sustain high speeds in a single sprint and across multiple sprints). Athletes need to build high levels of capacity to withstand gridiron football's immense physical toll.

An ideal starting point for most athletes' off-season speed training would include at least 3 days per week that feature on-field movement training (6). These training days can have a standalone hourlong movement session followed by a similar duration weight room session; if less time is available, movement and lifting can be combined into one session, with movement prioritized early in the session.

Ideally, 1 of these 3 suggested movement days per week would be dedicated primarily to sprinting acceleration, multidirectional training, and maximum velocity sprinting. Speed capacity can be trained on the second or third day near the end of the session. The third day would be either a top-end speed sprinting day or a speed capacity day. The multidirectional or agility day serves as a sort of hybrid session when athletes use "bridging" movements to blend acceleration with shuffling, backpedaling, and crossover running.

During the season, athletes get most of their speed conditioning from practices and games. One creative way that coaches can continue to work on sprinting technique is by integrating basic acceleration and maximum velocity drills into athlete warm-ups. Drills that are less taxing on the nervous system should be employed earlier in the warm-up so athletes can rehearse quality movement patterns. At or near the warm-up's end, the athletes can perform some short acceleration starts.

Speed Conditioning

Running a fast 40-yard (37 m) dash time may be an athlete's ticket to the next level, but long-term success rides on conditioning the ability to replicate that speed many times over the course of a game—their *repeat sprint ability*. This is different from *speed capacity*, which is a broader term. Speed capacity covers both an athlete's ability to sustain high speeds in a single sprint and the effectiveness in maintaining that speed across multiple sprints. Repeat sprint ability has a narrower definition, referring specifically to an athlete's competence in sustaining speed over several sprints. Perhaps the toughest challenge in planning speed conditioning for gridiron football is finding the right training dosage to maximize repeat sprint ability.

Especially in the weeks leading up to the season, athletes need enough sprint repetitions to help their bodies become figuratively calloused and more injury resistant. However, if these high-volume repetitions are too low of an intensity, athletes' bodies will be inadequately prepared to withstand gridiron football's repetitive high-intensity efforts. Sprint repetitions need to be both fast enough and copious enough to drive the specific adaptations needed for gridiron football.

Speed bands are a helpful framework coaches can use when thinking about how best to dose speed training for different gridiron football position groups. In this author's experience, most pro-level skill position athletes typically get their capacity-based work at around 12 miles per hour (5 m/sec), and their quality-based work closer to around 16 to 20 miles per hour (7-9 m/sec) for skill position athletes. (Some athletes can run in the range of 21-23 mph [9-10 m/sec]). The band concept simply means that these numbers are a general target, and actual sprint speeds should fall within a reasonable bandwidth of that target.

Elite-level teams use GPS tracking technology during training, practice, and games to monitor the number of sprints and overall distance covered within these different speed bands. Youth and high school athletes without access to this technology can perform their capacity (high-volume) work at roughly 60% speed, and their quality (high-intensity) work at 90% (±10%) speed.

Another useful off-season speed programming strategy is to flip the sprint distance progressions for acceleration and top-end speed days, creating a dovetailing effect. Acceleration training is structured from short to long: earlier off-season phases focus more heavily on acceleration quality using short sprints, then sprint distances ratchet up over the course of the off-season to build more acceleration capacity, ranging from 10 yards on the short end to 30 yards on the long end. Meanwhile, top-end speed training works in reverse from long to short, using longer distances (60 yards) to build a solid base of speed capacity, then gradually transitioning to shorter distances in subsequent weeks (30 yards at the shortest) to refine speed quality.

The dovetailing effect of working from both ends creates a gradual and complementary buildup of both acceleration and top-end speed, ensuring that neither quality nor capacity is developed in isolation. By starting with a focus on short acceleration sprints and gradually extending distances, athletes develop the acceleration quality needed for quick bursts. Conversely, by starting with longer distances for top-end speed training and gradually reducing them, athletes enhance their ability for repeatability. The integration of these two methods creates a synergistic transition between different speed training phases, allowing for the development of both quality and capacity in acceleration and top-end speed in a balanced manner.

FOOTBALL-SPECIFIC DRILLS

The most useful football-specific speed drills re-create movement demands each football athlete will experience based on position. Coaches can ramp up the overall volume of these drills late in off-season training to build athletes' capacities within the types of speed skills they will use most often on the field. These drills also can be useful at the end of a speed training session, allowing athletes to take the speed skills they have been honing during the session and apply them in a more relevant context.

Football drills	Page number
All positions: position-specific acceleration starts	161
Defensive athletes and running backs: brake and gas	162
Defensive line: pursuit drill	163
Offensive line: pin and pull	165
Quarterbacks: scramble drill	164
Running backs: stepover bag acceleration	167
Running backs: wheel route	166
Wide receivers: inside/outside release "go" route	166

All Positions: Position-Specific Acceleration Starts

Aim

This drill replaces the generic stances used for 10- to 20-yard acceleration starts with a stance that more closely resembles each athlete's offensive or defensive position group.

Action

This drill looks different for each position group, and the goal is to select a starting stance relevant to that position. Quarterbacks and running backs use an even-footed two-point stance with their feet hip- to shoulder-width apart, bending slightly at the hips and knees. Running backs can start with a slight forward trunk lean and hands on their thighs if this is how their coaches want them to line up on the field. Wide receivers can use their staggered two-point receiver stance as taught by their position coaches and can practice their footwork to beat press coverage prior to accelerating.

Tight ends, offensive linemen, and interior defensive linemen can use their normal three-point stance. Inside linebackers typically line up in a wide athletic stance. Outside linebackers can take their usual staggered two-point stance, and defensive ends who use a three-point stance can line up like they are in a wide nine-technique alignment preparing to rush the passer. Once an athlete is lined up in a position-specific stance, a normal acceleration start for a predetermined distance can be executed.

Coaching Points

- Regardless of the stance used, athletes still need to be capable of executing their acceleration technique as coached.
- Position groups with wider stances, such as linemen, should still use their football-specific stance and focus on driving their feet first before transitioning into acceleration.
- If an athlete's position-specific stance interferes with the ability to practice the desired skill, the stance should be regressed to a more generic staggered two-point stance or a three-point sprinter's stance.

Variations

Position groups who use different stances in various in-game scenarios can practice them all. For example, quarterbacks can set up their stance like they are under center, using a staggered two-point stance with a low crouch, or they can use an even-footed or staggered two-point stance as if they are taking the snap from a shotgun formation. Similarly, defensive backs can practice starting from both an even two-point stance and a staggered two-point stance.

During the drill, athletes starting from an even two-point stance or athletic stance may take a *rhythm step* to begin their sprint. In this transition movement, they take a step backward before sprinting forward, creating forward body lean. After taking a quick backward step with one foot, they can punch the other foot forward into an acceleration position and start sprinting.

Various sprint distances can be used depending on session goal and time of year. The drill also can be made more reactive. Offensive athletes could start off a pre-snap quarterback cadence, whereas defenders could react off a coach or teammate who pretends to snap the ball at the line of scrimmage.

Another useful variation of the drill for defensive athletes is to line up in the same two-point stances just mentioned, but instead of accelerating straight ahead, they can initiate a *drop step* to turn and sprint in the opposite direction. To execute a drop step to the right, the athlete quickly lifts the right foot and opens the right hip, allowing the right foot to punch out into an acceleration step pointing about 45 degrees back and to the right. At the same time, the athlete starts to extend the left leg forward and to the left, leaning the body back and to the right. The right foot then drives back into the ground beneath the hips, and the left foot takes a crossover step across the body into another acceleration step. After two to three steps, the athlete should be sprinting in the complete opposite direction from the original stance alignment. The athlete does not need to make a 180-degree turn in just one step. Instead, the path takes a slight initial curve, which allows the athlete to get the body fully turned around. This version of the drill is essentially a stationary edition of the brake-and-gas concept highlighted in the next drill.

Defensive Athletes and Running Backs: Brake and Gas

Aim
This drill trains athletes moving in a different plane of motion to quickly decelerate and explosively accelerate forward.

Action
Athletes can start this drill either backpedaling or moving laterally, but the goal to change direction smoothly and efficiently remains the same.

To perform the backpedaling version of the drill, the athlete starts in an even or staggered two-point stance, with feet hip- to shoulder-width apart, low hips, and a forward trunk lean. Either on the athlete's own or at a coach's signal, the athlete begins to backpedal straight back, reaching a foot under the hips and pushing the ground away to the front with each step. The arms swing lightly at the elbows in rhythm with the backpedal.

At a designated spot or number of steps, the athlete performs a braking sequence by shifting the body weight: Instead of pushing out in front of the body to travel backward, the athlete needs to push behind the body to move forward. The base of support (the feet) is moved back behind the hips to brake momentum, initiating the sequence with a braking step. The athlete reaches behind the hips and plants the foot to halt the backward movement.

With the planted brake leg behind them, the athlete aims the body into an acceleration position. As the athlete comes to a stop, the braking leg is extended and the other foot punches forward to hit the gas into an acceleration position while splitting the arms opposite from the legs. The front-side thigh is now roughly perpendicular to the trunk, the knee is flexed at roughly 90 degrees, and the foot dorsiflexes to prepare for an elastic ground strike.

From this point the athlete drives the gas leg back into the ground to propel the body forward and continues sprinting for a predetermined distance or number of steps, driving the arms back forcefully to match the timing of the strides. The goal is to decelerate on one leg while the other leg accelerates.

The other main version of this drill starts with the athletes moving laterally after starting from an athletic stance. They could be shuffling, crossover running, or stepping over agility bags or hurdles prior to braking and accelerating forward. Instead of placing their braking foot directly behind their hips, they will need to brake at more of a 45-degree angle to stop their lateral movement and redirect into forward acceleration. Otherwise, the principles of the brake-and-gas transition remain the same whether the athlete is moving backward or sideways before accelerating.

Coaching Points

- Coaches should look for good athletic bend to start the drill.
- Depending on coordination, relative strength, and the initial speed of travel, the athlete may need to take two decelerative braking steps instead of just one.
- Athletes should aim the final braking step in the opposite direction from where they want to go.

Variations

Defenders can also use a T-step as their braking step for this drill. Instead of planting on the ball of their back foot with toes straight ahead, they turn their foot slightly outward and plant on the full surface of the shoe or cleat. Using either of these strategies works well. The T-step technique tends to be more applicable for defensive backs and linebackers who are coached to use it, but it can be useful for all position groups on defense.

The drill start, as well as the athlete's brake-and-gas sequence, can be on a coach's signal or ball movement. The drill also can become multiplanar; instead of backpedaling straight back and then accelerating straight forward, the athlete can drop straight back and then accelerate forward at an angle (either predetermined or based on a coach's signal), or shuffle to the right then reaccelerate forward and to the left.

The athlete can react to a coach or teammate who mimics throwing a football, indicating when to decelerate and in which direction to reaccelerate. To make the drill even more sport specific, the quarterback can throw the ball, so the athlete must break on the ball and make an interception.

Athletes and practitioners can construct this drill in virtually limitless ways, so the goal of the session needs to be in mind when determining which version to use. Early in the off-season, athletes are best served with a more closed and basic version of the drill in which the transition spot is predetermined. Then as the off-season program progresses, the drill can become increasingly more open and complex.

Defensive Line: Pursuit Drill

Aim

Defensive linemen use exceptional power to engage and shed blockers, but they need to practice how to sprint once they have disengaged from a block and begin to pursue the ball.

Action

The athlete first lines up in a three-point stance as taught by the football coaches. Either on the athlete's own or on a coach's signal, the athlete fires out of the stance into the offensive backfield similar to a defensive line get-off drill. Once the athlete has reached a set point in the backfield—typically around 2 to 3 yards deep—the athlete decelerates and then sprints either upfield or to the sideline in pursuit of an imaginary ballcarrier.

Coaching Points

- Ensure that the athlete stays low when firing out of his stance.
- Coaches should keep an eye on how well the athlete can redirect and transition into acceleration, watching for adequate arm drive as the athlete sprints in pursuit.

Variations

Adding reactivity helps make this drill more specific and complex. To start the drill, a coach or athlete can hold a football down on the line of scrimmage and move it to simulate the snap. The lineman must watch the ball and fire off the line as soon as it moves. The next layer of reactivity would be to have a coach or teammate in the backfield, pointing in one direction as the lineman reaches the backfield to indicate which direction to pursue. Coaches can even add an actual ballcarrier whom the lineman must pursue and tag.

Another way to add more specificity would be to place a blocking dummy or a teammate holding a blocking pad directly across the line of scrimmage from the athlete performing the drill. When athlete fires out of the stance, the athlete strikes the pad with both hands and executes a push-pull technique followed by a rip or swim move to disengage from the blocker and penetrate the backfield.

Quarterbacks: Scramble Drill

Aim

This drill is for quarterbacks to practice using speed to evade pass rushers when they are flushed out of the pocket.

Action

Starting either under center or in a shotgun alignment, the quarterback calls out the cadence to start the drill and then executes a standard three- to seven-step drop with the football, pretends to scan the field, then takes off sprinting as if to avoid getting sacked. The quarterback rolls out into the flat by sprinting parallel to the line of scrimmage, then after reaching a predetermined landmark, the quarterback turns the corner and runs a curvilinear sprint past the line of scrimmage for a predetermined distance.

Coaching Points

- As the quarterback initially rolls out of the pocket while still looking downfield, prepared to throw the ball. The quarterback can then tuck the ball while turning upfield.
- The athlete's initial scramble running parallel to the line of scrimmage should not be extremely fast, but as soon as the quarterback tucks the ball and turns upfield, the sprint should be at maximum intensity.

Variations

This drill can be performed sprinting to the quarterback's left or right. A more reactive version would include a coach or teammate who stands across the line of scrimmage facing the quarterback, then points right or left to tell the quarterback which way to roll out of the pocket. Quarterbacks can also practice this drill with different stances and pass dropbacks, such as bootleg plays that have a designed quarterback rollout.

Offensive Line: Pin and Pull

Aim

Pulling plays are one of the most speed-centric scenarios offensive linemen will face in a game, primarily training the curvilinear sprinting skill described earlier in this section.

Action

On a pulling play, the lineman's assignment is to take a step back and turn to sprint down the line of scrimmage, then turn up the field to block a second-level defender in space. The lineman starts on the line of scrimmage in either a two- or three-point stance, depending on how the team's offensive playbook works.

Either on an internal prompt or with a quarterback cadence, the lineman takes a short step behind and turns the toe out to point down the line of scrimmage in the ball's direction. Simultaneously, the same side arm is pulled back to help the body turn toward the opened step. The lineman immediately transitions into a sprint, running parallel with the line of scrimmage roughly 1 to 2 yards in the offensive backfield. After reaching a designated spot, the lineman turns a corner and sprints down the field for 10 to 20 yards as if to block a second-level defender.

Coaching Points

- Ensure that each lineman's stance, initial pulling step, and backfield depth during the pull are all executed according to how the athlete's position coach teaches those football techniques.
- Coaches should stress to linemen that the purpose of this drill is to improve the skill of curvilinear sprinting in a more relevant situation, and it may not perfectly resemble their on-field playing techniques.

Variations

The initial stance can vary depending on the athlete, because tackles and guards are sometimes asked to pull from a two-point stance. A center can practice snapping the ball to a quarterback in shotgun formation before initiating their pull.

Sometimes it can be helpful to line up another lineman next to the athlete who is performing the drill. If the athlete is pulling to the right, this second lineman lines up on the athlete's right side and performs the pin part of the pin and pull play: executing a down block to the left on an imaginary defender lined up across from the pulling lineman. Placing this second lineman ensures that the lineman performing the drill does not pull too tight to the line of scrimmage.

This drill's other major variations are changing the pulling direction and target hole. These tweaks should reflect what the team's playbook calls for their linemen to execute. For example, on one play a left guard may pull to the right across the formation, aiming for the B-gap between the right guard and right tackle; on another play, a right guard may pull to the left and sprint to the D-gap outside the tight end's shoulder in search of a defender to block. Athletes can practice both these variations but should get more exposure to the type of pull they will make more often in games.

Wide Receivers: Inside/Outside Release "Go" Route

Aim
Hand fighting is an integral part of gridiron football for wide receivers; they need to first be able to get past a defender's press coverage, and then they need to transition into a sprint.

Action
The receiver lines up on the line of scrimmage in the usual coached football stance. A coach or teammate is lined up across the line, holding a blocking pad or wearing arm pads. The drill starts with an offensive cadence, and when the ball is snapped the dummy defender holds out the arms or pads as if to press the receiver. The receiver executes a press release technique as taught by the position coach. Once the receiver has worked past the defender, the receiver immediately runs a "go" route straight down the field.

Coaching Points
- Coaches should keep an eye on how seamlessly receivers can transition into their acceleration technique once they have fought off the defender, as well as how well they can carry speed down the field.
- Taking a false step to initiate the release is allowed.

Variations
The wide receiver's alignment and stance can be changed depending on where the athlete lines up most often in a game, and then work on releasing to both the right and left sides. The receiver can also start the drill as a player in motion, running down the line of scrimmage, then turning upfield once the ball is snapped.

The route can be modified according to the athlete's needs. For example, the receiver could run a different deep route such as a post or corner to add a curvilinear aspect. The point is to use a longer distance that stretches the field and allows the receiver to reach high speeds. Adding a quarterback with a football also can challenge the receiver's ability to make speed adjustments and catch a deep throw.

Running Backs: Wheel Route

Aim
One of the most important routes for a running back is the wheel route: a curved path that runs first toward the sideline and then turns toward the line of scrimmage before shooting straight up the field.

Action
The running bacs starts the drill in a shotgun formation, lined up in an even two-point stance next to a coach or teammate who acts as the quarterback. Following a quarterback cadence or on an internal prompt, the athlete turns and sprints out into the flat area located behind the line of scrimmage outside the tight end or offensive tackle. Once the running back reaches a predetermined spot, the athlete executes a curvilinear acceleration to turn upfield, sprinting at full speed for another 10 to 30 yards.

Coaching Points
- As the athlete rounds the corner of the route, attention should be given to maintain arm drive and lean the body inside to keep speed high.

- Coaches should monitor the athletes' stride length and ensure they are not overreaching in their sprint, and are getting their feet back to the ground quickly.

Variations

Route direction, depth, and width all can be modified according to the team's offensive playbook to make it feel more realistic for the athlete. Distance sprinted downfield can be prescribed according to the time of year, with longer distances used for training sessions that are more focused on speed capacity. For added challenge and skill development, a live quarterback can be added, throwing a pass for the running back to catch along their route.

Running Backs: Stepover Bag Acceleration

Aim

This drill is essentially the offensive counterpart to the defensive brake-and-gas drill aimed to improve change of direction into acceleration.

Action

The coach lines up three to five agility bags in a parallel sequence so they resemble the hash marks on a football field. The athlete takes an even two-point stance just outside the left-most bag, with the feet parallel to the bags. To initiate the drill the athlete essentially performs an A-run moving sideways to the right; the right foot is punched up into an acceleration position, moved over the first bag then driven back down into the space between the first and second bags so the left foot can be punched into an acceleration position next. Then the left foot comes down to meet the right foot, and this sequence is repeated at a running pace to get over all the bags.

Upon clearing the final bag with the right foot, the athlete uses this foot as a brake behind the hips to direct the body into a forward acceleration lean and then the right leg should be pointed in the opposite direction from the intended sprint direction, while pointing the left foot in the intended direction. The left foot becomes the gas to begin sprinting forward.

Coaching Points

- The athlete should maintain a good body posture throughout the drill. When stepping over each bag, the athlete should keep the thigh perpendicular to or slightly higher than the trunk, with the knee flexed at roughly 90 degrees and the foot fully dorsiflexed.
- The athlete should be spending minimal time on the ground between each bag, moving quickly and rhythmically.
- Upon clearing the final bag, the athlete's leading foot should land far enough behind the hips to allow the body to lean forward into an acceleration position.
- The athlete should point the brake foot in the opposite direction of the intended sprint direction, then point the gas leg in the intended direction as it punches into acceleration.

Variations

The athlete can start the drill on an internal prompt, with a coach's cue, or with a quarterback cadence. Mini hurdles can be used in lieu of agility bags. Sprint angle can be modified as well: Instead of stepping over the bags and then sprinting straight ahead, the athlete can plant the brake foot further outside the hips to accelerate back inside at a 45-degree angle.

► ICE HOCKEY

Devan McConnell
Mark Stephenson*

Ice hockey is considered one of the fastest games in the world. Athletes reach speeds of over 20 miles per hour (32 km/h) (1). Because of this, training for high levels of acceleration and maximal speed should be a priority in ice hockey performance development. In a typical phase of play, an athlete may skate all out for 30 to 45 seconds, requiring bursts of speed and acceleration and abrupt changes of direction (4). Within this 30- to 45-second shift, high speed acceleration and maximal speed skating accounts for about 7% of the total time (2). Although this may seem like a small amount of total time at these highest intensities, it is during these brief periods when game-changing plays are often made. Therefore, an improvement in an athlete's speed and acceleration may increase performance (8).

Although the kinematics of the skating stride are different from land-based running—namely, external rotation about the hip and more of a frontal plane of action on the ice rather than a sagittal plane action at high speeds (7)—the movement signature during the first few strides of acceleration on the ice are quite similar to land-based acceleration (1). In fact, resisted sprinting off ice has been shown to predict skating speed more than other commonly used off-ice performance tests (6). Because of this, it is of the utmost importance to focus on acceleration mechanics and the underlying physiology that contributes to speed and acceleration both on and off the ice.

SPEED IN ICE HOCKEY

As in most other sports, enhanced speed can give an ice hockey athlete an advantage in both offensive and defensive situations. One primary commonality between running speed and skating speed is that strength and power training are critical in developing speed and acceleration. The ability to create linear motion from a standstill comes down to the same basic principles, regardless of whether locomotion is occurring on the ice or on land. As outlined in chapter 2, creating high levels of force very quickly in the proper direction is ultimately what propels the athlete forward during acceleration. As similarly outlined in chapters 1 and 2, Newton's third law states that for every action in nature, there is an equal and opposite reaction. This is essential to understand, because it is the force applied to the ice through the skate blade by the athlete that allows motion to occur. Therefore, a major portion of speed training for ice hockey should develop the strength and power characteristics required for effective skating performance. This should focus on developing the explosive-strength capacities of the leg musculature responsible for the skating motion.

Strength and conditioning training for ice hockey should take place both on and off the ice. Incorporating various on-ice speed training methods with off-ice strength, power, and plyometric training will develop speed to enhance

*Devan McConnell was contracted to author this section; Mark Stephenson's name was added to acknowledge his significant contribution partially retained from the previous edition.

overall performance. Off-ice training should focus on developing key physical capabilities such as unilateral lower body force, explosive power, and horizontally directed movement such as resisted and unresisted sprinting. On-ice training should focus on acceleration and speed mechanics as well as maximal speed sprinting at different distances to develop the technique and neuromuscular patterns necessary to translate strength and power to skating speed.

Repeat sprint ability and change of direction or agility are also key components of the athleticism necessary to play ice hockey at a high level. The ability to repeatedly produce high power outputs throughout a competition gives a competitive edge to an athlete over an opponent and is an important fitness component in repeated sprint sports (5).

Depending on the periodization model being used, the majority of off-ice physical development usually occurs during the off-season. However, off-ice strength and conditioning during the in- season period should not be neglected. Though volumes of off-ice training will be lower during the competitive season than they are during the off-season, maintaining and continuing to improve the physical characteristics that underpin speed and power are especially important to continue all year long.

Whether speed development is on ice or off ice, several factors need to be addressed. Speed training involves explosive power and therefore should be performed only when the body is fully recovered (3). Additionally, adequate rest between work bouts allows the athlete to perform at full capacity and with proper technique. It is important to note that the adaptations required to increase maximal speed are highly neurological, and as such, it is necessary to respect the work-to-rest ratios necessary to allow for near-full recovery of the central nervous system when speed development is the goal. Improving speed and improving conditioning are not the same thing. Repeating efforts during speed work without near-full recovery will not result in improvements in acceleration or maximal velocity sprinting. Training tips for developing explosive speed are summarized here:

- ▶ Perform speed training at the beginning of the workout.
- ▶ Use at least a 1:4 work-to-rest ratio between repetitions.
- ▶ Perform all work at 90% of full velocity or higher. Time the sprints.
- ▶ When using resistance, allow no more than a 10% decrease in velocity for high-velocity speed work, and 50% decrement for short acceleration work.
- ▶ Incorporate drills that move both linearly and laterally.

Although running and skating have biomechanical differences at maximal velocity speeds, athletes can apply many of the concepts that traditionally would be used in developing running speed to on-ice sprinting. In many of the sprint drills, athletes and coaches can substitute skating for running. Similarly, drills that train key movement combinations can be used to develop on-ice speed. Additionally, on-ice training can incorporate resisted drills, such as those that use elastic bands or mechanical resistance, to provide an overload to the drive phase of acceleration.

IMPLICATIONS OF SPEED IN ICE HOCKEY

While speed is not the only factor affecting successful ice hockey performance, improved speed can offer a great advantage to any athlete, both offensively and defensively. In ice hockey, rapid skating acceleration and sprint speeds are tactically important in the game for an athlete to achieve correct positioning on the ice, catch and cover opponents, and win the race to the puck. (1)

Athletes with greater speed get to the puck faster, enhancing the opportunity to maintain or win possession and providing more time to make effective game-based decisions. Offensively, greater speed offers an enhanced attacking threat, enabling a wider choice of attacking options. Defensively, greater speed provides a potent defense against a range of attacking threats. A seemingly small increase in one's maximal speed ability allows the game to be played at a lower relative cost overall. For example, if the average speed of a play is around 17 miles per hour (27 km/h), an athlete who has a maximal speed ceiling of 22 miles per hour (35 km/h) will have to work at 77% of maximum ability, while an opposing athlete whose speed ceiling is only 20 miles per hour (32 km/h), will have to compete at 85% to maintain the same pace. This difference between maximal speed ability and the pace of play is commonly referred to as *speed reserve*. Over time, the difference in speed reserve between these two hypothetical athletes can easily take its toll from a fatigue standpoint for the slower athlete.

ICE HOCKEY-SPECIFIC DRILLS

These exercises supplement a basic strength and conditioning program to produce physical adaptations that will increase ice hockey speed. They are divided into two categories: *on-ice training* and *off-ice training*. The on-ice work is speed specific, and the off-ice work develops the key physical characteristics that support and enhance on-ice speed.

Ice hockey drills	Page number
5, 10, 5	172
Acceleration running speed	173
Acceleration speed: on ice from a standing start	171
Back and forward transition	172
Cruise, sprint, cruise	171
Diagonal bound	177
Double-leg broad jump	175
Lateral hurdle hop	176
Sled pull	178
Slide board sprint	174
Uphill running	178

On-Ice Speed Development

Speed and acceleration are key physical characteristics of some of the best hockey athletes in the world. Because of this, speed development for hockey athletes should be a key component of a hockey-specific strength and conditioning program. Dedicated work on and off the ice is necessary to maximize one's ability to rapidly accelerate over short distances as well as skate at high velocities over longer distances. To increase on-ice speed, athletes need to develop the ability to accelerate as rapidly as possible over short distances from static starts and, more commonly, from rolling starts. Rolling starts are performed in a range of directions: forward, laterally, and to the rear, and the preceding movements occur in a range of distances and speeds that reflect the nature of the game.

Acceleration Speed: On Ice From a Standing Start

Aim
To develop the ability to accelerate over a range of distances.

Action
From a standing start, the athlete skates as rapidly as possible for the chosen distance, typically 5 to 15 yards (or meters).

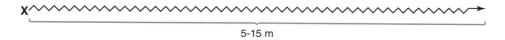

Coaching Points
- Rapidly assume an effective skating acceleration posture.
- Use a driving skating action to accelerate rapidly.

Cruise, Sprint, Cruise

Aim
To develop the ability to accelerate from a rolling start.

Action
The athlete begins by skating 5 yards (or meters) at a moderate pace as if cruising in a game situation and then accelerates to a full sprint for 10 yards (or meters). Finally, the athlete decelerates back to the initial pace.

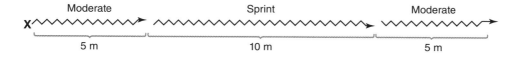

Coaching Points
- Control movements during the buildup.
- Rapidly assume an effective skating acceleration position.
- Use a driving action to accelerate as rapidly as possible.

Variations
The initial movement can take place in a range of directions and speeds to reflect the movement of an athlete on the ice. The idea is to adjust the body position and accelerate from a range of movement patterns. Additionally, the acceleration can be initiated in response to an external stimulus such as a coach's command.

Back and Forward Transition

Aim
To develop the ability to accelerate forward after the athlete has been moving backward.

Action
The athlete skates backward 10 yards (or meters), then rapidly stops and accelerates forward for 10 to 15 yards (or meters). The athlete uses a driving acceleration action.

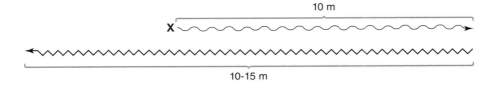

Coaching Points
- Maintain control while skating backward.
- Perform a skating stop.
- Reposition the body into an acceleration posture.
- Skate forward powerfully for the required distance.

5, 10, 5

This drill is an ice hockey–adapted version of the traditional pro-agility shuttle, often used for American football.

Aim
To develop the ability to accelerate, stop, and reaccelerate.

Action
Three cones are set up 5 yards (or meters) apart. The athlete stands next to the center cone, then turns to one side and accelerates 5 yards (or meters) to the end cone. The athlete turns back the other direction and accelerates 10 yards (or meters) to the cone at the opposite

end. The athlete turns the other direction and accelerates 5 yards (or meters) to the center cone. The athlete repeats the drill, completing the accelerations in the opposite directions.

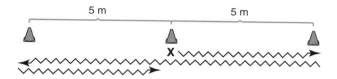

Coaching Points

- Initiate the movement with a powerful driving action.
- Emphasize appropriate posture.
- Stop rapidly, then accelerate rapidly and powerfully.

Off-Ice Conditioning

Off-ice training develops key physical capacities that can translate to more effective on-ice performance. These drills consist of traditional running sprint drills and plyometric-based activities.

Acceleration Running Speed

Aim

To develop the ability to accelerate over a range of short distances.

Action

From a standing start, the athlete accelerates as rapidly as possible for 10 to 20 yards (or meters).

Coaching Points

- Maintain an effective acceleration posture with a whole-body lean being generated (see chapter 3).
- Emphasize the generation of force through a powerful extension of the rear leg.
- Emphasize a powerful leg drive with the knee of the lead leg being driven forward and up.
- Use a powerful arm action to supplement the drive.

Slide Board Sprint

Aim

To develop lateral driving ability together with deceleration mechanics.

Action

The athlete assumes a starting position on the slide board and pushes off explosively in a lateral direction. The athlete decelerates to stop the movement in that direction using the outside leg, which initially flexes and then rapidly extends to immediately drive off in the opposite direction. The duration of the drill depends on its purpose (e.g., energy system development or explosive power work).

Coaching Points

- Emphasize the leg drive of the outside leg, driving the body across the board.
- The arms are held in a bent comfortable position at the side of the body and move rhythmically across the body to support the movement and maintain balance.
- Maintain an athletic posture, with the head in a neutral position; the eyes looking forward; the back flat; and flexion at the ankle, knee, and hip.
- Initiate direction change as rapidly as possible using a cutting action, where the outside leg is flexed and then extended powerfully.

Double-Leg Broad Jump

Aim

To develop explosive strength when moving horizontally.

Action

The athlete assumes a two-footed square stance (photo *a*) and executes a maximum-effort broad jump by pushing off powerfully with both legs (photo *b*). The athlete lands on the balls of the feet with the thighs no lower than parallel to the ground, with a flat back, and with knees aligned with the feet. The athlete jumps as far as possible without compromising the landing mechanics.

Starting stance.

Broad jump.

Coaching Points

- Emphasize full extension in the hips during the push-off.
- Use a powerful arm action as shown, with arms driven initially backward and then powerfully forward.
- Land on the balls of the feet (can be a flat foot if a single jump is performed).
- When landing, keep the thighs parallel to the ground or higher.

Variation

The athlete can progress to performing two to five jumps in a sequence. When performing multiple jumps, the athlete lands on the balls of the feet and tries to spend as little time on the ground as possible to emphasize the stretch-shortening cycle (see chapter 2).

Lateral Hurdle Hop

Aim

To develop explosive strength when moving laterally.

Action

The athlete stands on the right leg to the right of a 3-inch (8 cm) hurdle. The athlete explosively hops to the left, aiming for maximum distance over the hurdle, and lands on the left leg. The athlete holds the landing for a moment before hopping back over the hurdle with the left leg, landing on the right.

Coaching Points

- The hop is initiated with a powerful triple extension of the hip, knee, and ankle of the outside leg.
- Emphasize a powerful arm action.
- The landing is on the ball of the foot, shifting rapidly to the full foot when the athlete holds the position. (When performing repetitions, the landing stays on the balls of the feet.)

Variations

Athletes can hop off and land on the same leg. Once athletes master stability on the landing foot during single hops, they can perform a series of hops in which they change direction immediately on landing, returning to the start position. When performing a series of hops, emphasis is always on the quality of the movement, so athletes should perform no more than 10 repetitions (5 per leg) in a sequence.

Diagonal Bound

Aim

To develop elastic strength when moving laterally.

Action

A line 10 to 20 yards (or meters) long is marked on the ground. The athlete stands adjacent to one end of the line, facing the other end. The athlete bounds forward diagonally over the line, initiating the movement with the inside foot and landing on the outside foot. Immediately on landing, the athlete bounds forward diagonally off the outside foot back over the line, landing on the other foot. The athlete repeats for a specific number of bounds or a specific distance.

Coaching Points

- Initiate the bound by a powerful triple extension.
- Emphasize a powerful arm action, with both arms initially driven back and then immediately forward.
- Maintain stability by landing on the ball of the foot.

Uphill Running

Aim

To develop explosive strength in triple extension.

Action

The drill takes place on a 20-yard (or meter) gentle slope of 3 to 6 degrees. The coach or athlete should inspect the surface to make sure there are no hazards such as holes, roots, or large rocks. The athlete accelerates powerfully up the slope for 20 yards and recovers fully by walking slowly back to the start before starting the next repetition.

Coaching Points

- Use the acceleration technique outlined in chapter 3.
- Triple extend powerfully with each step as if pushing the ground away.
- Emphasize a powerful arm action, driving the arms forward to chin level and then powerfully back behind the body.

Sled Pull

Aim

To develop effective driving mechanics and enhance capabilities.

Action

The athlete dons a shoulder harness or waist belt attached to a sled. Approximately 10% of the athlete's body weight is added to the sled. Alternatively, athletes can use a weight that slows them down no more than 50% of their unresisted sprint time over the prescribed distance, if acceleration development is the primary goal. The athlete accelerates powerfully from a standing staggered start, continuing for 15 to 20 yards (or meters).

Coaching Points

- Attain the acceleration posture described in chapter 4.
- Emphasize a powerful driving action, with full triple extension of the ankle, knee, and hip.
- A powerful arm action complements the driving action of the legs.

▶ RUGBY

Ian Jeffreys and P.J. Wilson

Rugby union is a team-based collision sport, widely believed to have originated at Rugby School in England in 1823 when William Webb Ellis, during a game of association football, picked up the ball and ran with it toward the opponent's goal line. Today the game is played in over 100 countries by over 6 million people. At the senior level the game is played by two teams of 15 athletes for a total duration of 80 minutes (two halves of 40 minutes). Junior games are played by fewer athletes and for briefer durations as dictated by the athlete pathways in different countries. While the 15-a-side game is the dominant format, rugby union also has a 7-a-side format, played on the same size pitch over far briefer durations (10-14 min), and typically in a 1- or 2-day knockout format. This version is now a part of the Olympic games. This section will look at the 15-a-side game, but many of the exercises listed also transfer well to the 7-a-side format.

SPEED IN RUGBY

Rugby involves intermittent high-intensity activities interspersed with varying rest periods (1). Given the locomotor nature of rugby union, the ability to move effectively over the duration of the game is important, and high-speed running is an integral part of the game (1). As a result, speed has always been a highly prized commodity, especially in certain positions. The collision nature of the game also brings another potential advantage of speed: momentum. In rugby, gaining an edge in collision situations is a key aspect of the game, and the momentum an athlete has in these situations is a contributory factor. Given that momentum is a product of mass and velocity, having greater speed capacity can proffer advantages in these situations over and above the more obvious offensive and defensive patterns seen in the game.

Analysis of the speed patterns of the game demonstrate that backs carry out more high-speed running actions than forwards and are generally faster (1, 8, 9). There is also a difference between how the athletes commence their sprints, with forwards more likely to initiate their sprint from a standing start, whereas backs start their sprinting actions from more varied starts including standing, walking, jogging, and striding (3). Both forwards and backs have been shown to achieve speeds of over 90% of their maximum velocity on a number of occasions during a game, but backs achieve this almost twice as often as forwards (3). Sprint distances vary between positions and also in relation to the location on the field. On the ball and off the ball, sprints tend to be shorter for forwards than backs (3).

Interestingly, while speed is often considered an important performance variable, a number of studies have indicated that speed actions and the peak velocities achieved are actually lower at higher performance levels when compared to the level or age group below (1, 7). However, care must be taken not to interpret this as an indicator that speed is less important at the highest level. High speeds require distance to achieve, and because at the highest level the space available is often less due to the organization of defenses, these figures may be an indication of the tactical nature of the game rather than an indicator that speed is less important. It is also important to note that averages may not demonstrate the full extent of sprint actions used in a game (2), so it is often informative to also consider the worst-case scenarios in order to fully understand the nature of speed actions in the game.

It is important to keep in mind that the application of movements will occur within the game, and as a result, it is also paramount that rugby union athletes have a good understanding of the sport itself. This includes the ability to scan and understand rugby scenarios, recognize patterns in athlete and ball movement, and make decisions based on this information. This is often referred to via vague terms such as *gamesense* or *rugby intelligence*. In relation to gamespeed, this requires the athlete to span the continuum between the skills of speed and the skills of the game; in other words, athletes must be able to make effective game decisions while having the movement capacities to execute these decisions successfully. This is a critical component to consider when designing a holistic speed program for rugby union, because it depends on the integration of rugby-specific capacities at perceptual, cognitive, technical, and tactical levels with the physical capacities to execute, which is itself built on a range of fitness components. In collaboration with coaches, designing integrated drills focused on gamespeed can provide athletes with the opportunity to develop these skills deliberately. This will ensure athletes have ample opportunity to develop their pattern recognition and experience-based intuition to make rapid-response decisions in complex, dynamic environments, as has been demonstrated in other fast-moving environments (6). This underscores the importance of gamespeed and pattern recognition skills in rugby union, which requires an understanding of the underpinning objectives of these movements.

IMPLICATIONS OF SPEED IN RUGBY

While identifying the speed actions in rugby can help inform training, in itself it is insufficient. What is also needed is an understanding of the underpinning goals of the actions: the "why" behind the movement (5). Only when this is understood and acknowledged can a fully coherent speed development program be established.

To get to the why, it is useful to reverse engineer the goals of speed application in rugby. Here it is useful to differentiate between *structured phase* play and *broken* play. This classification is not binary, and in some situations play will take on the characteristics of both, but it does provide a useful framework around which to build an effective rugby speed analysis (see table 9.2).

Essentially, structured phase play occurs between set pieces (scrums and lineouts) and breakdowns (rucks and mauls), with the team in possession trying to gain ground while also maintaining possession of the ball. Structured phase play refers to situations where both the offense and defense are in position and thus well structured. As a result, both are well organized and able to use a range of planned and unplanned strategies, much of which involves the goal of dominating the gain line. The *gain line* is an imaginary line drawn across the pitch at the point of a set piece or scrum and halfway between the opposing teams. Crossing the gain line represents an advance in territory and becomes a crucial consideration where, given the objectives of play and the tackle rules, the ability to advance over the gain line allows the team to move forward into any breakdowns. Offensive athletes therefore will try to advance over the gain line with the ball, while the defense will try to move forward to tackle the offensive athletes and drive them back behind the gain line. In both of these instances speed can be an advantage, allowing the offensive athlete to advance toward the gain line as quickly as possible, whereas for the defensive team, what is termed *line speed*, or the ability to move the defensive line forward, is crucial. High levels of line speed help ensure that athlete engagement occurs in as advanced a position as possible. In both instances, momentum is crucial, and as stated previously, speed plays an important role.

The need to dominate the tackle area also brings key considerations for both the offense and defense. For the defense, line speed is clearly crucial, allowing the tackle area to be advanced as far as possible, but another important factor must be considered. This rapid advancement must be followed by a deceleration into a position to make the tackle, as if the tackle is missed, then all the advantage immediately goes to the offensive team. Indeed, the number of missed tackles is considered a key metric that influences game success. For the offensive athlete, advancing rapidly and building momentum is key. An important skill allied to speed is the ability to adjust the point of contact. Offensive athletes should always aim to run at space and, at a minimum, the opponent's arms and not their shoulders, thereby increasing the likelihood of winning the contact situation by facilitating getting over the gain line. Here, athletes who can rapidly build momentum have a potential advantage, but there is a further consideration. Athletes who can use movement adjustments (shape-shifting) to wrong-foot the defense while maintaining momentum have the greatest advantage (4). How this momentum is built is very much dependent on the proximity to the set piece or break-down. In tight situations runs are likely to be initiated from standing starts, requiring speed to be built over very short distances. In wider situations, speed is more likely to be initiated from rolling starts and combined with more marked offensive shape and speed shifts in an attempt to wrong-foot the opposition. The precise strategies used will vary depending on the specific scenario facing the athlete, and while some may be preplanned to a degree, even these will vary as the play evolves, so most speed skills in rugby lie toward the open side of the open- to closed-skill continuum.

Broken play refers to situations where the ball has been lost or kicked away or where the gain line has been broken. In these situations, defenses are less organized and the potential for greater space is present. Offensively, these situations provide an opportunity to achieve greater speeds as both a ballcarrier and a support runner. Importantly, many of these situations require adjustments of the run to manipulate the opponent's position and to exploit space. As a result, the ability to adjust speed and direction is crucial. This results in many runs being curved rather than linear and the use of sharp direction changes when facing an opponent.

Table 9.2 Key Speed Capacities for Rugby

		STRUCTURED PHASE PLAY		BROKEN PLAY	
		Offense	Defense	Offense	Defense
KEY GOAL		To cross the gain line and break the defense	To move the defensive line rapidly forward toward and potentially across the gain line	To exploit space to create running lines and try scoring opportunities	To close down space rapidly, make tackles, and channel offensive athletes into low-risk areas
KEY CAPACITIES	**Tight situations**	The ability to rapidly accelerate toward the gain line	The ability to rapidly accelerate toward the gain line	---	---
		The ability to use shape-shifting moves to run at arms	The ability to decelerate to an effective tackle position	---	---
		The ability to run supporting runs to clear out at the breakdown or support a line break	The ability to ensure line integrity and targeting the correct attacker	---	---
	Wide situations	The ability to create and accelerate into space	The ability to rapidly accelerate according to the defensive system being used	To create and rapidly accelerate toward space	To accelerate to rapidly close down space and channel offensive athletes into low-risk areas
		To use shape-shifting and change-of-speed and direction capacities to beat an opponent	The ability to decelerate to an effective tackle position	To rapidly achieve a supporting position	To decelerate to an effective defensive position to make tackles
		To run supporting lines to receive a pass, clear out at a breakdown, or support a line break	To ensure line integrity, horizontally and vertically shifting lines where needed, and targeting the correct attacker	To accelerate to an optimal speed to run attacking and supporting lines to create scoring opportunities	To rapidly establish effective defensive horizontally and vertically shifting lines where needed and to target the correct attacker

Defensively, the goals are the opposite of those of the offense. In these situations, the need to close down space, reduce offensive options, and channel the offense are important. Here again, while acceleration and top speed are important, these need to be developed with appropriate levels of movement control, and the ability to adjust speed, directions, and body orientation are important.

Based on this analysis, the following key areas need to be addressed in a comprehensive rugby speed development program:

▶ Accelerative ability from both static and rolling starts, with the emphasis depending on the playing position (i.e., the ability to maintain momentum while performing shapeshifting actions that facilitate success at the gain line)

▶ Direction-change ability, both sharp (cutting) and more gentle (curved running) with an emphasis on their use to achieve rugby-specific tasks

▶ Maximum-speed ability in a linear and curved directions, predominantly for outside backs

▶ Decelerative ability linked to the ability to assume positions from which to undertake key sport-skills and tasks

RUGBY-SPECIFIC DRILLS

Although the following drills improve rugby speed, they should be seen as part of a bigger recipe for success. Speed can never be isolated from agility, and hence it is important that rugby speed development is never considered in isolation but is built around enabling athletes to effectively navigate the tasks they face in a game (4). Speed is also dependent on a range of physical abilities, including maximum-force capacity, the rate of force development, and the effectiveness of the stretch-shortening cycle. Therefore, coaches and athletes should supplement this work with a strength and power program to maximize its effectiveness.

Rugby drills	Page number
Build-up runs	193
Decelerate to a staggered defensive stance	188
Get past (defender moving forward)	192
Get up and go	185
Harness drive (single exchange down and up)	184
Linear acceleration: standing start	186
Linear rolling start	187
Rugby-specific curved running	191
Run and cut	189
Run to daylight	190

Harness Drive (Single Exchange Down and Up)

Aim

To develop the ability to drive the knee of the lead leg forward and up while simultaneously driving the opposite leg down into the ground, holding an acceleration posture.

Action

The athlete stands facing forward with a belt around the waist. The belt is linked to a rope that is held firmly by a partner. This allows the athlete to assume a 45-degree angle. From this posture, the athlete lifts one knee forward and up into a knee-drive position, briefly holding this position (photo *a*). The athlete drives the same leg down into the ground, simultaneously driving the other leg forward and up, again briefly holding this position (photo *b*). The athlete performs this three to five times with each leg. The actions result in forward movement by the athlete.

Knee-drive position.

Driving the leg down and bringing the other leg up.

Coaching Points

- The athlete maintains a straight-line posture with no break at the hip.
- The drive knee moves forward and up with the foot dorsiflexed.
- The exchange of legs should be forceful and rapid without a change in posture.

Variation

This can be developed to double (two actions, ending up in the same start position) and triple (three actions) exchanges.

Get Up and Go

Aim

To develop the ability to accelerate from a low body position, which is especially important when accelerating into a potential contact situation.

Action

The athlete lies prone on the ground (photo *a*). On a self-start or a signal from the coach, the athlete lifts out of the start position and sprints forward for a given distance, such as 10 yards (photo *b*).

Starting position.

Sprinting.

Coaching Points

- The athlete maintains a straight-line posture, with no break at the hip.
- The athlete maintains a low position throughout the initial acceleration.
- The athlete drives forward and up and should never rise straight up.
- The drive knee moves forward and up, and the foot is dorsiflexed.

Variation

This drill can be performed in competition against other athletes. Athletes line up on a start line, and on a signal from the coach they sprint for a given distance, such as 10 yards, and try to get to the finish line first.

Linear Acceleration: Standing Start

Aim
To develop linear accelerative ability from a standing start.

Action
Two cones are placed 10 to 30 yards apart. The distance reflects the requirements of the athlete's playing position. The athlete assumes a defensive position, normally a staggered standing start. On a self-start or signal, the athlete accelerates as quickly as possible for the given distance. The athlete assumes an acceleration posture, with the center of mass ahead of the base of support. The athlete focuses on taking powerful, fast strides. The leading knee drives forward and up, and the foot is dorsiflexed through this process.

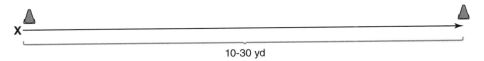

10-30 yd

Coaching Points
- A powerful arm drive through the full range of motion (hip to shoulder) contributes to the ground forces. The arm angle can open slightly on the backward movement to allow more time for force application.
- Foot contact is on the balls of the feet.
- The eyes focus forward, not down, enabling the athlete to see the sport action on the field.

Variations
Distances can be varied, and athletes can start to the front, to the side, and to the rear. Once athletes have developed the technique, the coach can encourage the development of shape-shifting actions that can facilitate success at the gain line.

Linear Rolling Start

Aim

To develop the ability to accelerate from a rolling start.

Action

Three cones are placed in a line; the distance between the first two cones is an initial movement zone, and the distance between the second and third cones is an acceleration zone. The athlete moves between the first two cones and on reaching the second cone, accelerates for the given distance. The lengths of the zones reflect typical movement patterns. For example, distances for tight forwards might be 5 yards for initial movement and 5 yards for a sprint. Distances for wingers might be a 15-yard build-up and 15 to 30 yards for the sprint. As competence increases, coaches can encourage the development of shape-shifting actions that can facilitate success at the gain line.

Coaching Points

- The athlete maintains control during the initial movement.
- The athlete drives the legs and arms powerfully when accelerating.

Variation

The athlete can vary the distance for the initial movement and subsequent movement. The change in pace can be self-directed or triggered by an external signal.

Decelerate to a Staggered Defensive Stance

Aim
To develop the ability to decelerate into a staggered defensive stance.

Action
The athlete assumes an athletic position at cone 1, facing a second cone placed 5 yards away. The athlete runs forward toward cone 2 and decelerates on approaching the cone by lowering the center of mass and shortening the stride (photo *a*). At the cone, the athlete assumes a staggered athletic position with either foot leading (photo *b*). This replicates a defensive position, where a defender tries to channel the offensive athlete in a given direction.

Athlete decelerates.   **Staggered athlete position.**

Coaching Points
- The feet are wider apart in an athletic position (hip width or slightly wider) and body weight is over the balls of the feet.
- In a staggered athletic stance, one foot is slightly in front of the other, resulting in the body facing toward the left or right.

Run and Cut

Aim

To develop the ability to change direction through a cut step and then to accelerate.

Action

Two cones are set up 5 yards apart. The athlete assumes an athletic position at cone 1 and then runs toward cone 2, decelerating to make a cut step at the cone. After making the cut step, the athlete immediately accelerates away at approximately 45 degrees. The athlete plants the cutting foot wider than the knee, which is in turn wider than the hips. The drill maximizes the lateral distance the athlete can move and resembles trying to avoid a tackle. Repetitions alternate between cuts to the right and cuts to the left.

Coaching Points

- The foot is planted straight ahead and lands nearly flat but with weight toward the ball of the foot.
- The body weight stays within the base of support, allowing the athlete to maintain an effective line of force.
- Acceleration should take place immediately after the cut.
- As an athlete becomes more adept at the run and cut, the run in can start to incorporate a number of shape-shifts, adjustments of the running posture aimed to wrong-foot the defense. These moves can be used in a game to effectively set up the cut.

Run to Daylight

Aim

To develop the ability to make a cut step in response to a stimulus and to accelerate from this direction change.

Action

The athlete assumes an athletic position on cone 1, facing cone 2, which is 8 yards away. The coach stands 2 yards behind cone 2. The athlete runs toward cone 2 and decelerates on approaching the cone. As the athlete nears cone 2, the coach makes a lateral move to one side of the cone. The athlete makes a cut step and accelerates in the direction opposite the coach's movement.

Coaching Points

- The cutting foot is planted wider than the knee, which is in turn wider than the hip. The foot is planted straight ahead and almost flat but with weight toward the ball of the foot.
- The body weight stays within the base of support, allowing the athlete to maintain an effective line of force.
- The athlete accelerates immediately after the cut.

Rugby-Specific Curved Running

Aim

To develop the ability to run in curved patterns and to perfect gentle changes in direction with high levels of control as required during a rugby game.

Action

A series of poles are set up to simulate the curved running patterns found in a rugby game (e.g., running at, pinning, and then running around a defender). The athlete sprints through the course, maintaining speed through all of the sections. The athlete leans into the curve. The foot lands under the center of mass, on the ball of the foot, and toward the outside of the foot. The recovery leg rapidly cycles, creating a rapid cadence.

Coaching Points

- The athlete's posture is upright or leaning slightly forward in a straight line.
- The body lean into the curve should be through the whole body.
- The arms swing through the full range of motion, with the hands moving from the hip to shoulder level.
- The knee of the lead leg drives forward and up, and the foot is dorsiflexed during this action.
- Focus initially on control and increase speed over time while ensuring control in maintained.

Variation

The coach or athlete can set up a variety of patterns that replicate given tasks in rugby. For example, the coach can set up a pattern that mimics the wide arc movement that a hooker would take on a lineout to receive a pass off the scrum half.

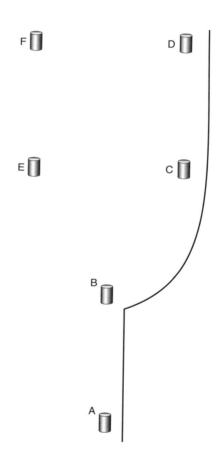

Get Past (Defender Moving Forward)

Aim
To develop the ability to beat a defender and accelerate and to develop the ability to track an opponent's movements forward while maintaining a defensive position.

Action
Two athletes perform the drill, one assuming an offensive role and the other a defensive role. A zone approximately 10 to 20 yards long and 15 to 20 yards wide is marked. The offensive athlete stands at one end of the marked area at cone 1, which is placed in the middle of that side of the area. The defensive athlete assumes an athletic position at cone 2, at the other end of the zone from the offensive athlete. The offensive athlete moves forward and tries to get to the opposite end of the zone without being tagged by the other athlete. This should require a change of direction followed by a rapid acceleration. The defensive athlete moves forward and makes movement adjustments to try to tag the offensive athlete. Athletes should reverse roles on subsequent repetitions.

Coaching Points
- The defender decelerates to a jockeying position and adjusts this in response to the attacker's movements.
- When changing direction, athletes use the cutting action described in the run and cut drill.
- Athletes accelerate immediately after the cut.
- As an athlete becomes more adapt, the run in should incorporate a number of shape-shifts, adjustments of the running posture aimed to wrong-foot the defense. These moves can be used in a game to effectively set up the cut.

Build-Up Runs

Aim
To develop the running action and to learn to change gears at pace.

Action
A series of four cones are set up 20 yards apart. The athlete runs the 60-yard course, increasing running speed in each 20-yard section and attaining maximum speed in the last section. Emphasis is on attaining maximum speed in the last 20 yards and to changing gears in the earlier sections.

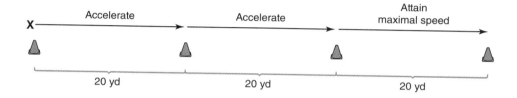

Coaching Points
- The athlete's posture is upright or slightly forward, with the body in a straight line.
- The arms swing through a full range of motion, with the hands moving from the hip to shoulder level.
- The knee drives forward and up, and the foot is dorsiflexed during this action. The recovery leg cycles rapidly to create a rapid cadence.
- The foot lands under the center of mass and on the ball of the foot.

Variation
The distances can be varied to reflect the specific requirements of different positions. The outside backs run the greatest distances.

▶ *SOCCER*

Irineu Loturco and Ian Jeffreys

The game of soccer (or, outside the United States, football) is played in over 200 countries and generally regarded as the world's most popular sport. Played between two teams of 11 athletes and over a 90-minute duration (two halves of 45 minutes) at the senior level, the aim is to score more goals than the opposition. Soccer presents a great challenge to any strength and conditioning coach given that success depends on a range of physical and physiological attributes together with a series of technical and tactical capabilities. However, speed is generally considered a crucial component in soccer, playing a key role in determining success in a number of soccer-specific tasks, especially in decisive moments of the game such as fast counterattacks and goal-scoring situations (5, 15). Whether it is a goalkeeper sprinting off the line to smother the ball at the feet of the oncoming striker or a striker surging to the near post to head home a corner, it is clear that greater speed can significantly enhance the physical, technical, and tactical performance of any athlete.

SPEED IN SOCCER

Speed has long been considered a highly desirable physical attribute in soccer, with athletes possessing superior speed often deemed to have an advantage in both offensive and defensive actions (12). This is further emphasized by the fact that straight-line sprinting speed (both acceleration and maximal sprinting speed) has been shown to be an indicator of playing ability in both the male (8) and female game (6). Data indicate that sprint distance and number of sprints per game have been progressively increasing over the years in the most important leagues in the world, further emphasizing the importance of speed for modern soccer athletes (1, 13, 14).

Time–motion analysis of speed application within games suggests that the majority of sprinting actions are short (8), with the majority (approximately 60%) initiated in a forward direction (3) and others initiated in lateral, diagonal, or posterior directions (3). Maximal and submaximal sprints tend to be frequent and performed over short distances (up to 10 yards) (1). Additionally, most sprints are initiated when the athlete is already in motion (i.e., a rolling start), with athletes predominantly accelerating from low to moderate velocities (<9.5 mph [<15 km/h]) (3, 16) and from a linear initiation position, with a range of prior movements and changes in sprint trajectories being observed (3, 16). A significant feature is that the vast majority of sprints in soccer occur with a degree of curvature (about 85%) and are rarely purely linear in nature (3). Importantly, approximately 50% of these short and multidirectional sprints end with some form of interaction with the ball or opponent (3). This often requires the ability to effectively decelerate to a position where the performance of such a skill is optimized (9, 10).

The importance of sprinting speed in soccer is further emphasized by the fact that it is closely linked to scoring opportunities in both the men's (5, 8) and women's game (6, 7). Indeed, sprinting is the most common action before a goal for both the goal scorer and the athlete making the assist (5, 8). While acceleration and speed performance are important for all athletes, differences can be observed in the patterns of acceleration and sprint activities between distinct playing positions and their on-pitch roles. Specifically, wide midfielders tend to make the most frequent sprints, followed by attackers, then wide defenders, then central midfielders, and finally central defenders (4). Also, attackers and central defenders tend to perform more maximal accelerations before sprint efforts than midfielders and wide defenders (17). Therefore, the maximal speed achieved by athletes will be affected not only by the relative distances covered while sprinting, but also by their positional acceleration profiles (10). In a more simplistic view, athletes covering greater distances or starting from higher speeds (with higher acceleration rates) are likely to achieve higher speeds while sprinting (10). Despite these particularities, accelerations and sprinting actions are somewhat homogeneous across all playing positions, these being characterized by high degrees of variability and unpredictability (2, 17). This, in turn, requires the use of a wide variety of speed training strategies, which should be balanced and prescribed according to individual needs, irrespective of playing position (11).

IMPLICATIONS OF SPEED IN SOCCER

Speed is clearly a highly desirable capacity in soccer, but it would be a mistake to presume that simply by increasing linear speed capacity that this will always fully transfer to enhanced soccer-specific performance (9, 10). Instead, it is crucial to not only consider how athletes sprint in soccer but also why they sprint (11). When viewed from a soccer perspective, speed is a multifaceted and complex skill, requiring the combination of physical, perceptive, cognitive, technical, and tactical capabilities (10, 12), all of which affect how speed is deployed and, by design, how it should be trained and developed. Ultimately, the great advantage of speed to soccer performance is how it enhances the athlete's capacity to successfully negotiate soccer-related tasks; therefore, we must be able to identify the underpinning goals of soccer-specific speed—understanding the context is key.

Appropriate contextualization of speed requires a system via which the specific application of speed can be determined (11). Here the gamespeed reverse engineering process is extremely valuable. Using this process, a soccer game can be broken down into two main phases, *transition* and *organization* (10, 12), with both of these phases having offensive and defensive categories. In transition situations, possession has been lost by one team and gained by another (12). Given that these involve a turnover in possession and the team losing possession is out of its defensive shape, these situations represent defensive risks while similarly presenting offensive opportunities for the team winning possession. The principles and subprinciples of play at this time revolve around exploiting these opportunities in the case of the offensive team or mitigating against the risk in relation to the defensive team (12). The nature of how the team will attempt to achieve the principles will, to an extent, depend on its tactical approach, but generally the offensive team will attempt to move the ball away from the place where it was won as rapidly as possible. This requires moving the ball into different channels to fill unoccupied channels, which is dependent on the athletes' ability to move rapidly into and between these channels. These situations often afford greater space, which in turn requires well-developed acceleration capacities along with the potential to achieve higher speeds. The defensive team at this time will generally use one of two approaches: They will either press rapidly, attempting to win the ball back as quickly as possible, or will retreat into a defensive organization. As such, the ability to accelerate rapidly in different directions is critical. Additionally, the ability to use high speeds to channel the offense into lower-risk areas is advantageous. In all of these instances, the ability to sprint over a curved paths and to orient the body to be able to perceive and manipulate the environment is crucial. The offensive athletes will similarly require this curved sprinting ability to move between channels while similarly perceiving and manipulating the environment.

Organization settings are quite different and present distinctive movement challenges. Once again, these will differ to some extent based on the tactical approach taken. A low block, for example, provides far less space behind a defense when compared to a high block. In general, the defensive teams' principles will revolve around defending as a block, maintaining distances between defenders, and channeling the play into low-risk areas with the aim of preventing goals. Here a far greater emphasis will be on the ability to maintain effective position during what are termed *transition movements* and the capacity to initiate acceleration from a range of these patterns and in all three primary directions (linear, lateral, and posterior) (10). In the gamespeed system, *transition movement* refers to movements where the athlete is in motion but the goal is to maintain a position from where they are able to read the game and make appropriate responses, rather than trying to necessarily move at high speeds (10). Given the defensive organization, the opportunities for the attacking team are reduced, and offensive strategies typically revolve around manipulating the environment by moving defenders out of position through movement of the ball and athletes. Here again, acceleration is important with this needing to be achieved from a range of initial speeds and prior movements in multiple directions, and often combined with *shape-shifting actions* (i.e., actions where the athlete makes deliberate adjustments in body position designed to either disguise movement or to deliberately try to fool an opponent with the goal of gaining a first step on the defense).

The reverse engineering process allows for a greater contextual awareness not of just what movements are used but crucially why they are used. This can ensure that the full gamut of movements relevant to soccer performance can be developed while also making sure that they are developed in a manner that reflects how they are used to carry out soccer-related tasks. Based on the previously discussed reverse engineering process, the following key areas need to be addressed:

▶ Accelerative ability from both static and rolling starts, using rolling starts in a variety of directions and using varied movement patterns

▶ Change-of-direction ability, both sharp (cutting) and gentle (curved sprinting)

▶ Maximum-speed ability for athletes covering greater distances, such as wingbacks, wingers, and central midfielders

▶ Decelerative ability and the ability to control running speed to optimize skill execution

SOCCER-SPECIFIC DRILLS

Many of the basic speed requirements from the analysis can be developed through the drills in chapter 3. These should form the backbone of a program.

Soccer drills	Page number
Build-up run	205
Decelerate to a skill	208
Decelerate to a staggered defensive stance	207
Get past (defender moving backward)	204
Ins and outs	206
Linear ball drop	199
Multidirectional rolling starts	200
Run to space	202
Side shuffle and cut	201
Soccer-specific curved sprinting	203
Wall drive (single exchange)	198

While the drills outlined in this section improve soccer speed, they are part of a bigger recipe for success. It is crucial to remember that speed can never be separated from agility, and, consequently, many of the drills here have elements of both qualities involved (i.e., they work on soccer gamespeed [10]). Speed is also dependent on a range of physical abilities, including maximum strength capacity, muscle power, rate of force development, and stretch-shortening cycle function, as highlighted in earlier chapters. Therefore, this work needs to be supplemented by a strength-power based program to maximize its effectiveness.

ACCELERATION DRILLS

Wall Drive (Single Exchange)

Aim

To develop the ability to drive the knee of the lead leg forward and up while holding an acceleration posture.

Action

The athlete stands approximately a yard away from a wall and assumes a 45-degree body lean, with the hands against the wall, supporting the body. From this posture, the athlete lifts the right knee forward and up toward the wall and into a knee-drive position, briefly holding this position. The athlete drives the right leg down into the ground, simultaneously driving the left leg forward and up, again briefly holding this position.

Coaching Points

- The athlete maintains a straight-line posture with no break at the hip.
- The drive knee moves forward and up with the foot dorsiflexed.
- The exchange of legs should be forceful and rapid but should not result in a change in posture.

Variation

This can be developed to double (two actions, where the athlete returns to the start position) and triple exchanges (three actions).

Linear Ball Drop

Aim

To develop the ability to accelerate in reaction to a stimulus and to control speed to enable a skill to be performed.

Action

The athlete assumes a staggered stance, and a coach or partner faces the athlete from a position 5 yards in front of the athlete. The coach or partner holds a soccer ball out to the side at shoulder height, and the athlete faces forward (photo *a*). The coach or partner drops the ball and, on that signal, the athlete accelerates forcefully to reach and control the ball before it bounces a second time by driving the outside leg forward and up (photo *b*) and accelerating forward.

Starting position.   **Hip turn.**

Coaching Point

- The athlete accelerates forcefully using an effective acceleration action.

Variations

The distance between the athlete and partner is increased after each successful attempt. The athlete can perform a variety of skills, such as shooting, passing, and initiating a dribble. This drill also can be performed in a lateral and posterior manner to replicate the initiation movements required in soccer. Additionally, where equipment and numbers permit, reactive choices can be set up where the athlete assumes a jockeying action rather than a static start position.

Multidirectional Rolling Starts

Aim
To develop the ability to accelerate from a range of rolling starts.

Action
Two cones are placed to mark an initial movement zone, with a further cone placed to represent an acceleration zone. The setup depends on the choice of initial movement and subsequent movement. The athlete moves between the first two cones and on reaching the second cone, accelerates in a given direction for a given distance toward the third cone. Soccer movement is characterized by multiple movement combinations. Therefore, rolling starts can be initiated from a range of directions and into a range of subsequent directions, and the subsequent direction of acceleration (to the side or straight ahead) can vary depending on the aim of the drill.

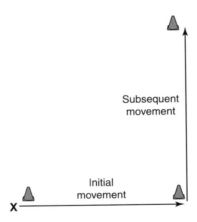

Coaching Points
- The athlete maintains a position of control during the initial movement.
- The athlete drives the legs and arms powerfully when accelerating.

Variations
A variety of patterns can be developed by adjusting the initial movement and subsequent movement. Similarly, a range of paces can be used to replicate the acceleration patterns of the game. The change in pace itself can be self-directed or initiated by an external signal.

CHANGE-OF-DIRECTION DRILLS

Side Shuffle and Cut

Aim

To develop an effective cutting step to change direction.

Action

The drill uses two cones set up 5 yards apart. The athlete assumes an athletic position facing one cone, with the other cone to the athlete's side. The athlete side shuffles to the other cone (photo a) and at the second cone, performs a cutting action and side shuffles back to the first cone (photo b). When cutting, the cutting foot plants wider than the knee, which is in turn wider than the hip. The athlete plants the foot pointed straight ahead and nearly flat, with weight toward the ball of the foot to allow a greater force to be applied. The athlete pushes aggressively with this foot to side shuffle back in the opposite direction.

Side shuffle.
Cutting and shuffling back.

Coaching Points

- During the side shuffle, the body weight stays within the base of support, allowing the athlete to maintain an effective line of force.
- The foot does not flair out when planted. It stays pointing straight ahead.

Variations

The athlete can perform the drill as a single repetition or as a series of repetitions, ensuring that an equal number of cuts are performed on each leg during the practice. Once the athlete masters the original drill, change of direction can be initiated on an external signal.

Run to Space

Aim
To develop the ability to accelerate to a given point in a soccer-specific context.

Action
A 10-yard-square is marked with cones at each corner. Two athletes stand facing each other within the square. One assumes an offensive role and the other a defensive role. The offensive athlete's aim is to create space and accelerate to a cone, while the defensive athlete aims to maintain the initial distance between them and, if possible, prevents the offensive athlete from getting to the cone or getting to the cone first. The offensive athlete moves first, trying to manipulate the defender in order to create space (photo a) and subsequently accelerate to one of the four cones (photo b). The drill ends after 3 seconds or whenever the athlete reaches the cone. Athletes reverse roles on subsequent repetitions.

Cut to create space.   **Accelerate into space.**

Coaching Points
- Both athletes maintain jockeying positions before the movement.
- The athlete accelerates as described in chapter 3.

Variation
This drill can be varied by changing the area covered or the position the athlete tries to get to (this may be random or predetermined by the coach) or by adding a skill requirement such as receiving a pass on reaching the cone.

Soccer-Specific Curved Sprinting

Aim

To develop the ability to sprint over curved paths and to perfect gentle changes in direction.

Action

A series of poles are placed in a pattern simulating the curved sprinting typical of soccer. For example, the drill can replicate the pattern center forwards may run in creating space as they move toward the near post to receive a cross. The athlete sprints through the course, maintaining speed through all the sections. Throughout the pattern, the athlete's posture is tall but leaning into the curve with the lean being a whole body lean and the focus is on controlled speed.

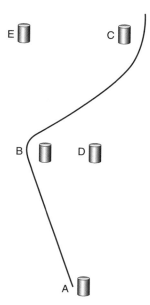

Coaching Points

- The arm swings through a full range of motion, with the hands moving from the hip to shoulder level.
- Any lean should be initiated through the whole body and with the athlete still running tall.
- The knee drives forward and up, and the foot on that leg is dorsiflexed during this action. The recovery leg cycles through rapidly to create a quick cadence.
- The foot lands under the center of mass and on the ball of the foot a little toward the outside as the athlete leans into the curve.

Variation

A variety of patterns can be set up to replicate different tasks in soccer, such as a wing back running an arc outside a full back or a central midfielder running a curve away from a defender. Varying speeds can be used to encourage the ability to switch between speeds and to run with a high level of control.

Get Past (Defender Moving Backward)

Aim
To develop the offensive ability to beat a defender and accelerate and to develop the defensive ability to track an opponent's movements while moving backward and then to accelerate.

Action
Two athletes perform the drill, one assuming an offensive role and the other a defensive role. A zone approximately 15 yards wide and 20 yards long is marked, although the size can vary depending on the specific aim of the exercise. For example, smaller areas stress the need to create space in a tight area. The offensive athlete stands at one end of the marked area at cone 1, which is placed in the middle of that side of the area. The defensive athlete assumes an athletic position at cone 2, which is placed 2 yards in front of the offensive athlete. The drill starts on the first movement of the offensive athlete, who moves forward trying to get to the end of the zone by making a rapid acceleration at some point in the drill. The defensive athlete initially backpedals and then adjusts between movements, tracking the offensive athlete's movements, attempting to stay close to the offensive athlete through the drill. The athlete accelerates in response to the attacker's movement. Athletes reverse roles on subsequent repetitions.

Coaching Points
- Effective postures are maintained during the initial movements. For the defensive athlete this requires an athletic position while backtracking. For the offensive athlete this requires an adjustment between a running pattern and a deceleration pattern to enable an effective cut to take place.
- Direction changes are performed with a cutting action, and athletes accelerate using proper form.

Variations
Variations can be introduced, including changes in distances, changes in directions, different instructions to the athletes, and the addition of skills such as reacting to the ball.

MAXIMUM-SPEED DRILLS

Build-Up Run

Aim

To develop a maximum-speed running action and the ability to change gears at pace.

Action

A series of cones 20 yards apart creates a 60-yard course. The athlete runs the course, increasing speed in each 20-yard section so that maximum speed is attained in the last section. The goal is to attain maximum speed in the last 20 yards by changing gears effectively in the earlier sections. During the pattern, the athlete's posture is upright or leaning slightly forward in a straight line.

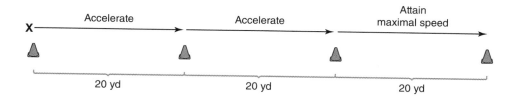

Coaching Points

- The arm swings through a full range of motion, with the hands moving from the hip to shoulder level.
- The knee of the lead leg drives forward and up, and the foot is dorsiflexed during this action. The recovery leg cycles through rapidly to create a quick cadence.
- The foot lands under the center of mass and on the ball of the foot.

Variation

The distances can be varied.

Ins and Outs

Aim

To develop the ability to relax at speed and to develop the ability to control running speeds.

Action

Five cones are placed 15 yards apart. Athletes run the 60-yard course increasing running speed in each 15-yard section so that they attains their highest speed in the second to last (penultimate) 15-yard section. In the final section, the athlete maintains speed while remaining relaxed, pulling back the effort to 90% to 95%.

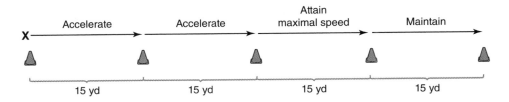

Coaching Points

- The athlete's posture is upright or leaning slightly forward in a straight line.
- The arm swings through a full range of motion, with the hands moving from the hip to shoulder level.
- Remind the athlete to relax.
- The knee of the lead leg drives forward and up, and the foot is dorsiflexed during this action.
- The foot lands under the center of mass and on the ball of the foot.
- The recovery leg cycles through rapidly, creating a quick cadence.

Variation

The in and out phases of the drill can be varied, with the athlete encouraged to run in a controlled manner for parts of the drill and at higher speeds in others. This helps develop the ability to run at varying paces while maintaining control of the movement.

DECELERATION DRILLS

Decelerate to a Staggered Defensive Stance

Aim

To develop the ability to decelerate into a staggered defensive stance.

Action

The athlete assumes an athletic position at cone 1, facing a second cone placed 5 yards away. The athlete runs forward toward cone 2 and decelerates on approaching the cone by lowering the center of mass and shortening the stride (photo a). At the cone, the athlete assumes a staggered athletic position with either foot leading (photo b). This replicates a defensive position, where a defender tries to channel the offensive athlete in a given direction.

Athlete decelerates.   **Staggered athlete position.**

Coaching Points

- The feet are wider apart in an athletic position (hip width or slightly wider), and the body weight is over the balls of the feet.
- In a staggered athletic stance, one foot is slightly in front of the other, resulting in the body facing toward the left or right.

Decelerate to a Skill

Aim
To develop the ability to decelerate and carry out a soccer skill.

Action
The athlete assumes an athletic position at cone 1. Cone 2 is 5 to 10 yards ahead. A coach or partner stands with a soccer ball near cone 2. The athlete runs toward cone 2 (photo *a*) and then decelerates to be able to carry out a soccer skill (e.g., making a shot, controlling a pass ball, making a save). As the athlete decelerates, the coach or partner feeds the ball in a manner appropriate to the desired skill, and the athlete performs the skill (photo *b*). This skill can be predetermined or the athlete can be given options and asked to respond according to what evolves as the ball is delivered.

Athlete accelerates to the ball.

Athlete decelerates to shoot the ball.

Coaching Points
- The athlete lowers the center of mass while decelerating and rapidly adjusts the stance in preparation for the skill.
- The athlete shortens the stride on the approach to the cone.
- The feet are placed wider apart (hip width or slightly wider) to assume an athletic position, and the body weight is over the balls of the feet.

Variations
Variations can be made in the distances used, the initial speeds of movement, and the skill performed.

▶ *TENNIS*

W. Britt Chandler

Tennis is a multidirectional sport consisting of short sprints, rapid changes of direction, and intermittent short recovery periods, all interspersed with tennis-specific skills. The specific movements vary from point to point and are dictated by the requirements of the game. The sprints are determined by anticipating the opponent's next action as well as the subsequent flight and speed of the ball. Because this creates a context-specific speed requirement, this section focuses on developing sport-specific speed for the tennis athlete.

SPEED IN TENNIS

Given the specificity of tennis speed, it is vital to evaluate the movement demands of competitive tennis matches. It is important to note that point lengths and movement requirements will vary depending on court surface and the athlete's sex, style of play, and level of play (1, 2, 4, 6).

Typical Movement Distances

The average point length is typically between 5 and 8 seconds, with most points lasting less than 10 seconds (1, 2, 4). Athletes are allowed 20 to 25 seconds between points and 90-second rest periods on changeovers, which occur every 2 games. During a point, the tennis athlete travels an average distance of 7 to 9 yards and averages two to four changes of direction (1, 2, 6). Each change of direction averages between 2 and 4 yards, with maximum distances covered per stroke typically between 9 and 13 yards (9, 11). Due to the size of the court and the number of direction changes required, high acceleration and deceleration movements occur more frequently than high-velocity movements (3).

Typical Movement Directions

In evaluating the movements common to tennis, we see sprints forward to the net (less than 20%), sprints back to the baseline (less than 8%), sprints laterally to cover the width of the court (more than 70%), and a combination of those that run in a diagonal direction to cover the shortest distance to the ball (11).

Typical Starting Patterns

All movements in tennis begin with the *split step*, which is a small hop that occurs around the time the opponent contacts the ball and allows the athlete to get into a balanced position and move explosively toward the ball. This strategy to break inertia and produce a powerful first step has gone through an evolution in higher levels of play (10). Instead of landing simultaneously and parallel, elite

---

The author would like to acknowledge the significant contribution of Diane Vives to this section.

athletes use the modern split step in which the athlete reacts in the air during the split and lands with the foot farthest from the ball a split second before the opposite foot (10). Following the split step, the athlete will move toward the direction of the ball with either a pivot step or gravity step, which are used for lateral acceleration (5). In a *gravity step*, the lead foot is brought in toward the body as the hips turn. This moves the body's center of mass outside the base of support, which allows gravity to assist the movement. As the athlete begins to hit the ball, deceleration must occur. The ability to decelerate properly determines how effective the athlete can load and prepare for a movement, how powerfully the movement is expressed, and how safely the movement is decelerated. Following the execution of the stroke, a recovery movement occurs when the athlete turns towards the net and performs a *lateral cross-over* or *shuffle* back toward the center of the court, before performing a split-step to prepare for the next stroke.

Based on the tennis movement analysis, the following key areas need to be addressed:

▶ Acceleration over short distances from a lateral start position
▶ Change-of-direction speed
▶ Lateral speed training in the form of shuffling and crossover steps
▶ Deceleration ability
▶ Reactive open-skill movements

IMPLICATIONS OF SPEED IN TENNIS

Tennis is a combination of stops, starts, changes of direction, and short sprints. Both linear speed and change-of-direction speed have been found to correlate with performance, but change-of-direction speed has a stronger correlation with level of play than linear speed (7, 8, 12). The athlete who moves faster and more efficiently will be able to get to more shots, which makes it more difficult for the opponent to hit a winner. In addition, an athlete who moves faster can get to the ball earlier and, as a result, is in a better position to execute successful strokes than an athlete who gets to the ball later and is rushed when hitting the ball. Finally, speed can be used to take time away from the opponent. By moving forward, faster athletes can hit the ball earlier, thus giving their opponent less time to prepare for their shot.

TENNIS-SPECIFIC DRILLS

This section focuses on drills that enhance speed as it relates to tennis. Although the basic skills and mechanics of linear acceleration are not dominant movements in tennis, training these skills is beneficial when developing an athlete. Training in forward sprinting can benefit the foundational mechanics for multidirectional speed. Therefore, many of the drills highlighted in chapter 4 can be used in a tennis speed program. Four types of drills are presented in this section: deceleration, acceleration, change of direction, and reactive open skills. These movement patterns reflect the way speed is applied in a tennis context. These are just examples, so coaches and athletes can add or alter drills that address these basic abilities. In addition, all the movement drills can be performed on clay courts so the athletes can practice sliding, which is an essential skill for clay court tennis.

Tennis drills	Page number
Competitive fire feet to sprint	219
Drop jump with sprint	215
Drop squat	212
Hurdle jump	216
Lateral wall drill	214
Medicine ball toss and sprint	220
Spider drill	218
Skater for stability	213
Skater to sprint	217

To maximize the benefit of these drills, it is important to first use *closed-skill drills*, where the athlete performs a set movement pattern in an unchanging environment. This allows the athlete to develop and stabilize key movement patterns before focusing on more complex, reactive drills. For tennis, reactive training covers movements specific to tennis play on the court and the skills needed to improve performance. This allows the athlete to put skills and movement patterns together in a predictable setting to optimize development of coordination and specific training components. Once the athlete has mastered the closed-skill drills these can be progressed to *open-skill drills* in which unpredictable stimuli, such as a tennis ball toss, a coach's verbal cue, or a gesture with the racket, are added. This allows the coach to provide a game-like atmosphere in training while knowing that time is being invested in skills that will translate to the tennis court.

Progression of drills is an important element of speed development. The drills presented in this section have been constructed to follow a general progression that both reduces the chance of injury and maximizes the development of tennis-specific speed. The progressions are as follows:

▶ Slow and stable to fast and explosive
▶ Simple to complex
▶ Single direction to multidirectional
▶ Closed skill to open skill
▶ Body weight to external resistance

DECELERATION DRILLS

Drop Squat

Aim
To train the ability to drop the center of mass quickly and under control in a two-point stance while maintaining proper position and dynamic balance.

Action
The athlete starts with the feet hip-width apart in an upright position. The athlete drops the hips back quickly into a squat position, finishing with the thighs just above parallel to the ground and with the feet in a shoulder-width stance. The athlete comes to a complete stop, showing balance and control, before returning to an upright position for the next repetition.

Coaching Points
- The movement emphasizes the hips dropping back.
- The eyes are forward, the chest is up, and the feet are facing forward (not rotated outward).
- The drop is as fast as the athlete can control, and the finish is in a balanced and stable position.

Variations
Use a partner's hands for resistance on the shoulders to produce a slight overload to the movement. Progress to band resistance at the hips with a 45-degree angle to an anchor on the ground. Light resistance is sufficient to create a significant load. Another variation of this exercise involves the athlete finishing in a split-stance position with the front leg's thigh just above parallel to the ground and the torso upright. For advanced athletes, the drop squat can be done on a single leg while maintaining strict ankle, knee, and hip alignment.

Skater for Stability

Aim
To train the strength and stability needed for powerful change of direction.

Action
The athlete starts in a single-leg stance (photo *a*) and bounds onto the opposite leg in a directly lateral position, landing in a single-leg power position (photo *b*) and not too upright. The athlete pauses in the final position with no movement to demonstrate stability and control. The athlete can start with narrow bounds and progress to wider bounds. A countermovement may be used to initiate the lateral bound if it is quick and crisp with no delay before takeoff.

a Single-leg starting stance.

b Single-leg power position.

Coaching Points
- The body's center of gravity and shoulders are over the base of support at landing.
- The feet face forward and do not rotate outward.
- The drill focuses on the stability of the landing position rather than reducing ground contact time and explosiveness.

Variations
The athlete can progress to a diagonal skater by bounding forward and laterally in a zigzag pattern. For more advanced athletes this drill can focus more on acceleration focused by reducing ground contact time and increasing explosiveness of the movement.

ACCELERATION DRILLS

Lateral Wall Drill

Aim
To develop lateral acceleration and powerful lateral takeoffs.

Action
The athlete leans sideways into a wall, with the inside arm extended and palm against the wall. The athlete lifts the leg closest to the wall with the knee up to hip height and maintains the leaning position (photo a). Keeping the upper body still, the athlete drives the flexed, or drive, leg down so that the hip and knee are extended. Simultaneously, the athlete drives the trail leg up and across toward the wall so that the hip and knee on that leg flex to 90 degrees and the ankle remains dorsiflexed (photo b). This is the single-response version. Then the athlete repeats the drill facing the opposite direction with the other arm against the wall.

Starting stance.   **Lateral leg drive.**

Coaching Points
- The hips do not shift laterally during the drill.
- The dynamic crossover action of the leg away from the wall simulates the crossover movement commonly seen in tennis.

Variations
To simplify the movement, the athlete can start by holding each position: inside knee up, then outside knee up, then repeating facing the opposite direction on each leg, holding each position for 15 seconds. To increase the difficulty, the athlete can use a double response (where two actions are performed consecutively ending up in the same start position), a triple response (three actions performed consecutively), and finally a rapid fire for a set time (usually just 5 sec).

Drop Jump With Sprint

Aim

To develop the ability to accelerate into a sprint from a split step.

Action

The athlete begins standing on a box 2 to 24 inches (5-61 cm) high depending on the athlete's training history, experience, and progression (photo *a*). The athlete drops from the box and lands in a split-step position (photo *b*). Upon landing the athlete sprints forward for 5-10 yards (photo *c*).

Starting stance.   **Split-step landing.**   **Forward sprint.**

Coaching Points

- Athletes may use either the standard version of the split step or the modern split step, depending on their experience and level of play.
- While sprinting, the athlete drives the arm forward and up to shoulder level and pulls the arm back so the hand is at the hip.

Variations

To simulate more tennis-specific movement patterns on landing, the athlete performs a crossover step and turns then sprints for 5-10 yards. This lateral start sprint more closely resembles the lateral movement required to get in position to perform a stroke.

Hurdle Jump

Aim
To improve the athlete's strength and power for acceleration.

Action
Five hurdles are placed approximately 2 feet (61 cm) apart. The hurdles are 2 to 18 inches (5-46 cm) high depending on the athlete's training history, experience, and progression. The coach approaches the initial height and progression conservatively for beginners. From a shoulder-width stance, the athlete jumps over the hurdles, maintaining a continuous jumping pattern over the series of hurdles. Athletes focus on jumping over the hurdles in a consistent rhythm. As athletes becomes more experienced, they focus on spending as little time on the ground as possible, as if landing on hot coals.

Coaching Points
- Use no more than five hurdles to ensure the athlete reaches full amplitude on each jump. Limiting the number of hurdles negates the effects of fatigue.
- The progression to higher hurdles should occur in small increments to gradually increase the amplitude and intensity of the jumps.

Variations
To regress the exercise the athlete can pause between jumps and focus on proper landing technique. This shifts the focus of the exercise to deceleration.

After mastering forward jumps, the athlete can also incorporate lateral jumps.

After athletes master forward and lateral jumps (this could take several weeks), they can perform single-leg hops over the hurdles. The progression starts with single-leg forward hops over lower hurdles and progresses to single-leg lateral hops (lead with both the inside edge of the foot and the outside edge of the foot). Again, the progression to higher hurdles is incremental.

CHANGE-OF-DIRECTION DRILLS

Skater to Sprint

Aim
To train lateral changes of direction and improve dynamic balance.

Action
The athlete performs a skater squat or lateral bound (photo *a*) as described previously. On landing the athlete immediately performs a crossover step (photo *b*) to turn to sprint in the opposite direction of the jump. The athlete sprints for a distance of 5 yards. Jumps should be performed from right to left leg and left to right leg.

Lateral bound landing.

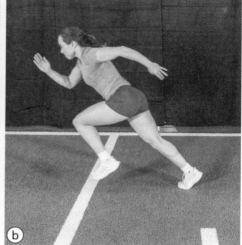

Start of crossover step to begin sprint in the opposite direction.

Coaching Point
The athlete lands from the skater jump in a single-leg power position and attempts to transition rapidly into the crossover step.

Variation
The athlete lands from the skater jump and performs a crossover step, but instead of turning and performing a sprint she transitions to a lateral shuffle. This movement simulates the movement back to the center of the court that occurs after an athlete performs a stroke.

Spider Drill

Aim
To train lateral changes of direction, improve the mechanics of changing direction, and improve the strength and power needed for faster reaction and lateral starts.

Action
Set up five cones on a tennis court: one at the intersection of the baseline and singles line on each side, one at the intersection of the service line and singles line on each side, and one at the intersection of the service line and center line. Athletes begin on the center of the baseline facing the net. To begin, they turn and sprint toward cone 1 and then immediately turn and sprint back to the starting position. This is repeated for cones 2 through 5. The drill concludes when the athlete returns to the start position after cone 5.

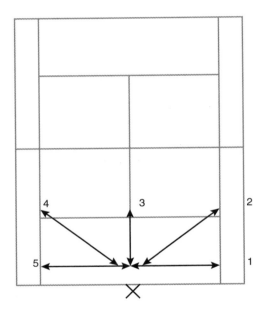

Coaching Point
Coach the athlete to lower the center of mass and decelerate quickly to load the body for the change of direction.

Variation
To emphasize tennis-specific movement patterns the athlete must face the net when returning to the start position after reaching each of the cones. This will require shuffle, crossover, and backpedal movements when returning to the middle of the court after hitting a shot.

REACTIVE OPEN-SKILL DRILLS

Competitive Fire Feet to Sprint

Aim
To improve reaction time and improve the strength and power needed for changes of direction.

Action
Four cones are set up to create a box. A fifth cone sits in the center of the square. Each side of the square is 10 yards long. Two athletes start on either side of the cone in the center of the square (photo a). On the coach's command both athletes begin quick "fire feet" movements in place. When the coach gives the command of "up," "middle," or "back," both athletes sprint either laterally or diagonally to the designated cone on their side of the square (photo b). The athletes touch the cone, change direction, race the opponent back to the starting position, and immediately resume the "fire feet" movements. This is repeated four to six times to complete the drill. Athletes stay on their side of the square and do not cross the middle cone.

Starting positions.

Racing to touch cone.

Coaching Points
- Use clear verbal or visual cues.
- Encourage the use of good form on changes of direction and a full-speed sprint to and from the cones.

Variation
More complex cues can be used for target cones. The athlete can begin the sprint with a split step.

Medicine Ball Toss and Sprint

Aim
To incorporate a more sport-specific skill while training reaction and speed.

Action
The athlete starts at the center of the baseline within a designated area that mimics the size of the court. Using a light medicine ball (generally 4-8 lbs [2-4 kg]), the coach tosses the ball 4 to 8 yards in any direction within the area. The athlete sprints to the ball, letting the ball bounce only once, and then catches and side tosses the ball back to the coach. The toss action should be similar to a forehand or backhand action. At that point the athlete performs a shuffle or crossover back to the starting location and split steps in preparation for the next toss. This is repeated for four to eight tosses. The coach should change the distances and direction of the toss to remain as unpredictable as possible.

Coaching Points
- The athlete should use proper body position and correctly set up for the side toss.
- When moving back to the center of the court following the side throw the athlete should keep the head and eyes forward on the ball to be prepared to react for the next throw.

Variations
The coach can use commands to designate different tosses, such as overhead toss or chest pass. As the athletes progress different stances and movement patterns also can be required. Finally, this drill can be used as a competitive game in which two athletes play against each other. They must throw the ball over the net and use the dimensions of the tennis court.

▶ *FIELD HOCKEY*

Christina Rasnake

Field hockey is a physically demanding intermittent team sport that combines aerobic and anaerobic fitness (8). In the United States, the majority of participants are female, but the sport is played at the international level by both sexes (11). The playing area in field hockey is a rectangular field that measures 100 yards long by 60 yards wide (91 m by 55 m). The field is marked with boundaries and has 11 athletes, including a goalie, on the field for each team. The athletes use sticks and a ball to maneuver and score goals at the opposing team's goal cage. The game involves strategic movements, passes, and shots as the athletes work together to outscore their opponents and secure victory. At the international and collegiate level, the game is played in four 15-minute quarters with rolling substitution, which has enhanced the importance of speed in the sport.

SPEED IN FIELD HOCKEY

Speed development is categorized as an essential factor for success in the sport due to the repeated high-intensity running bouts and rapid acceleration and deceleration (5). During a match, athletes cover an average of 4.1 miles (6.6 km) of distance, with a range of 2.1 to 5.9 miles (3.4-9.5 km) (2). High-velocity and high-acceleration activities commonly occur up to 20 yards among forwards, midfielders, and defenders. Midfielders cover the most distance and high-intensity efforts during a match compared to other positions, with high-intensity running occurring at speeds greater than 5.5 meters per second (18.0 ft/sec) (2). In female athletes, sprints normally last 2.5 seconds at a high intensity level greater than 4.4 meters per second (14.4 ft/sec) (9). Maximum acceleration training and the ability to sprint in a semi-slouched position is vital for success in high-speed dribbling with the ball. Development of speed in different postural positions with rapid change of direction increases an athlete's ability to perform at an optimal level (7). Additionally, the ability to adapt to the change from offense to defense rapidly and to respond to the evolving game requires that each position group has effective first-step quickness capacities.

The structure of game play provides 2 minutes' rest between the quarters and a 10-minute halftime period for both teams (4). Unlike soccer, the use of substitutions is unlimited. The ability to substitute on the fly provides an advantage for more recovery time. The varying rest in games provides the opportunity for aerobic recovery and the ability to maintain maximal effort sprints when using pacing strategies. Use of a rotation strategy for substitution will assist in recovery and is vital for tactical play with 15% to 20% of match play occurring at high-intensity speeds at or above 5.5 meters per second (18.0 ft/sec) or based on individual athlete thresholds (6).

It is vital to place an athlete under a load level that is game specific during training, and proper work-to-rest ratios are key in acclimatization during preseason (1). Repeat sprint ability in field sports should be ramped up after periods of inactivity based on best practices established. Training volume in repeat sprint ability should demonstrate a 20% and 10% reduction in week one and week two, respectively (1). The phosphagen system will be the primary system stressed during short high-intensity activities such as sprinting (3). Repeated sprint training will encompass brief maximal effort sprints lasting 3 to 7 seconds separated by short rest periods of less than 60 seconds (10). Maintaining exercise time between 5 and 10 seconds with a work-to-rest period ratio of 1:12 to 1:20 is important in developing the phosphagen system with interval training to adapt to expected competition workload (3). Varying the rest during training creates a more game-paced training environment that will provide transfer of training to competition.

IMPLICATIONS OF SPEED IN FIELD HOCKEY

The activities in a field hockey match demonstrate short bursts of high-intensity speed paired with longer periods of lower- to moderate-intensity activities (6). Speed is a high-priority attribute for each position in the game. Although goalkeepers may not be researched as highly when it comes to speed, their ability to react quickly and perform quick, powerful first step movements will also help dictate success in the position. Although speed and acceleration are highly trained in most developmental programs, deceleration training is also important, especially for midfielders since they perform a higher number of deceleration movements compared to forwards and defensive athletes (6). Training proper deceleration mechanics assists in proper movement, which may assist in decreasing non-contact injuries. Midfielders see more action on both an offensive and defensive side of the ball and are on the field longer than other positions (6). Forwards' main role is to create opportunities to score, and to assist in this they must have the ability to beat defenders and sprint into space (6). Defensive athletes should be trained based on the tactical play of the game, and outside backs need to produce higher intensity levels of activity compared to central backs since they play higher into the offensive zone along the sideline (6). Training lateral, linear, and backward speed movements will provide a greater ability to dominate on the offensive side by beating out opponents and on defensive by managing transitional moments in the game.

FIELD HOCKEY-SPECIFIC DRILLS

The following drills focus on sport-specific speed development that will provide the best opportunity for speed to transfer to the game. Each drill can be progressed by implementing a stick and ball for more specific postural speed as the athlete becomes technically sound in movement patterns. The drills provided should be part of a periodized strength and power program that focuses on the musculature that enhances speed and rate of force development. The pace of each drill can be increased or decreased depending on the skill level of the individual athlete, and these can also be effective drills for implementation in a return to sport progression.

Field hockey drills	Page number
Forward-backward cone drill	224
Hour glass	225
Progressive sprints	226
Snake drill	223

Snake Drill

Aim

To develop the ability to accelerate into curved sprinting and to decelerate.

Action

Eight cones will be used in the drill, with cone 1 and cone 2 approximately 5 yards apart. Cones 2 through 7 are approximately 3 yards apart, and cone 8 is approximately 5 yards from cone 7. At cone 1, the athlete begins a flying start toward cone 2 and begins to accelerate to cone 3. The athlete continues to sprint in a curved manner around each cone. At cone 7 the athlete begins decelerating toward cone 8.

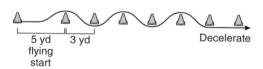

Coaching Points

- The athlete should remain close to the cones and not swing too far away from the cones as speed is built up.
- Deceleration should embody an athletic position at the end of the drill.

Variations

Distance of the flying start and deceleration zone can vary. Different starting stances can be used, and use of a ball and stick can be included once technique is sound.

Forward-Backward Cone Drill

Aim

To develop the ability to create force into the ground and accelerate in a small space moving forward and backward.

Action

Eight cones will be used in the drill, with the first two cones lined up parallel to each other approximately 5 yards apart. The next set of two cones are spaced 3 yards to the right, and the setup is repeated for the remainder of cones. The athlete starts the drill outside the first set of cones in the middle. On a command the athlete sprints to the last set of cones and turns toward the right cone, circles it, and then sprints forward to the top cone. The athlete begins to decelerate at the top cone while shifting toward the left to the next set of cones and begins to backpedal toward the bottom cone before shifting toward the left to sprint forward again. The athlete then begins to decelerate and drops the hips when turning around the final top cone before sprinting past the final bottom cone to end the drill. Perform the same pattern sequence starting from the other side to focus on both left- and right-side movement patterns.

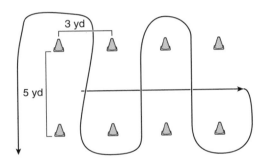

Coaching Points

- The athlete should keep the hips low during the drill and stay close to the cones while rounding them.
- Eye focus should be forward, looking up the field rather than down at the cones.
- Accelerate after each cone.

Variations

Different starting stances can be used, and the use of a ball and stick can be included once technique is sound.

Hour Glass

Aim

To develop the ability to accelerate, decelerate, and change direction while maintaining a sport-like posture.

Action

Five cones will be used in the drill, with two cones at the base, approximately 10 yards apart. Two more cones are spaced approximately 10 yards above the base cones in a box grid. The fifth cone is placed in the middle of the grid approximately 5 yards from the base and top of the grid. The athlete starts on the right side of cone 1 and sprints to cone 5, planting the outside foot to perform a change of direction toward cone 3. The athlete sprints toward cone 3 and plants the outside foot to perform a sprint toward cone 4 before planting the outside foot and sprinting toward cone 5. The athlete plants the outside foot and sprints toward cone 2, finishing the drill by planting the outside foot and sprinting through cone 1. Perform the same pattern sequence starting from the other side to focus on both left- and right-side change-of-direction patterns.

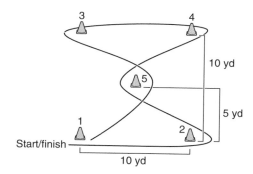

Coaching Points

- Drop and load the hips with each deceleration.
- The planted foot should be wider than the knee.
- Acceleration should occur after each cone.

Variations

Different starting stances can be used, and the use of a ball and stick can be included once technique is sound.

Progressive Sprints

Aim
To develop the ability to accelerate and decelerate at a game-like pace.

Action
Five cones will be used in the drill, with each cone spaced approximately 10 yards apart. The athlete starts at cone 1, jogs to cone 4, and immediately accelerates to cone 5. The athlete then turns and cuts toward cone 3 at a jog pace. As the athlete approaches cone 3, the athlete begins to accelerate to cone 1. Upon approaching cone 1, the athlete cuts and turns to cone 2 at a jog pace. When reaching cone 2, the athlete accelerates and sprints to cone 5 and finally performs one more cut, then turns and sprints through cone 1.

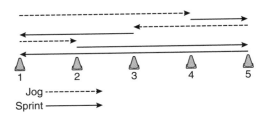

Coaching Points
- Drop and load the hips with each cut and turn.
- Maintain control and posture during the jog pace.

Variations
Distance between cones can be decreased to make the acceleration and deceleration more intense in smaller spaces. Use of a ball and stick can be included once technique is sound.

▶ *LACROSSE*

Jeffrey Kipp

Lacrosse, in its modern form, has its origins in games played by North America's Indigenous communities and is considered one of the oldest team sports in North America (1, 6). A quick internet search reveals that W. Wilson Wingate, a Baltimore sportswriter, is credited with labeling lacrosse as "the fastest game on two feet," a moniker that is still in use today (7). Whether this nickname is objectively justified can be debated. However, the aggressive intensity of play, the speed of the athletes and ball moving up and down the field, and the velocity of the shots in lacrosse performed at a high rate give the sport its fast-paced tempo (1, 2, 6).

SPEED IN LACROSSE

Comparable to other field-based, invasion-style team sports, including soccer, rugby, and hockey, lacrosse is comprised primarily of repeated bouts of high-intensity bursts of speed, combined with moderate running, jogging, and walking, with the purpose of one team possessing and moving the ball into the opposing team's area to score a goal (1, 5, 6). Athletes rely more on anaerobic power and bursts of high-intensity sprints during a lacrosse game compared to soccer and rugby (7). While maximal linear speed is an important component of lacrosse, there is much more to the game than moving in a straight line. An athlete's ability to have an explosive first step, accelerate rapidly, decelerate and stop suddenly, change speeds and directions fluently, and react to situations quickly, all while handling the ball and managing the opponent, may be a greater predictor of success in lacrosse (1, 8). A speed development program for lacrosse athletes must address many characteristics that encompass an athlete's performance on the field.

According to the NCAA Men's Lacrosse Rule Book, the official size of the collegiate lacrosse field measures 110 yards (101 m) in length by 60 yards (55 m) in width with a 5-yard (5 m) side and end run-off area. Women's lacrosse field measurements vary and are generally slightly larger (1). Movements and requirements of speed for an athlete vary by position and situation. In a lacrosse game, each team has 10 athletes divided into four main positions on the field: three midfielders, three defenders, three attackers, and one goalie. Goalies typically cover the least amount of distance but are very explosive in their movements. Attackers typically remain in the offensive end of the field or attack area, where an athlete's use of speed can help create space and time, giving teammates the opportunity to score. Defenders, on the other hand, typically remain in their team's defensive area where their use of speed is instrumental in defending their goal, reducing their opponent's capability to score by taking away their space, and not giving them time to make effective passes or shots. Midfielders cover the most ground on the lacrosse field, because they can travel anywhere on the field. They are required to support the defenders when the opposing team has the ball, as well as operate in the offensive end with the attackers to create scoring opportunities (1, 3, 4, 6).

With the needs of lacrosse in mind, the following areas should be addressed in a comprehensive speed development program:

- ▶ Explosive starts and acceleration in various directions or along a curve and initiated from a standing position, a moving start, or a rolling start
- ▶ Deceleration from different speeds and angles, which is an important factor in preparing for change-of-direction drills in training and the stress of full-speed reactions in game situations
- ▶ Change of direction, both at an angle (hard cut) and on a curve (speed cut)
- ▶ Change of speed (acceleration and deceleration) while already moving

IMPLICATIONS OF SPEED IN LACROSSE

Lacrosse is a game of time and space, both of which can be gained or taken away, with respect to an athlete's speed to create or reduce opportunities to score. Whether in the attack area or defensive area, increasing a lacrosse athlete's speed and anaerobic power can be instrumental to success and create important advantages on the field (8). An athlete's ability to gain possession on a loose or ground ball, move the ball up the field, avoid opponents, and run to open field to receive a pass or create a lane for shooting are all affected by speed. Additionally, speed can give the defensive athlete an upper hand by cutting off an attacking athlete's advancement, pressuring an opponent's pass, moving to intercept a pass, or getting to a ground ball first.

LACROSSE-SPECIFIC DRILLS

In combination with a comprehensive and appropriate strength and conditioning program, these drills can effect specific adaptations in key lacrosse-specific speed development areas. Visual cues and reactions incorporated into drills are important stimuli for a lacrosse athlete's improvement. With some of these drills, it is useful for the athlete to include his stick after proficiency of the drill's movement technique has been met. Additionally, as the athlete becomes more efficient, adding a ball and cradling throughout the drill will add difficulty and variety.

Wall Drive

Aim

To develop proper mechanics for acceleration, including knee drive, body posture and position, upper and lower leg positioning, and speed through appropriate ranges of motion.

Action

The athlete stands in front of an appropriate wall or vertical support and leans forward as near a 45-degree angled body position as can be maintained, with the arms extended and the palms of the hands flat against the wall. The athlete raises one knee so that the hip and knee are flexed to about 90 degrees. With a stationary upper torso, the athlete drives the flexed or raised leg down into the ground so that the hip and knee become extended. Concurrently, the athlete will drive the down leg or trail leg up so that the hip and knee on that leg are flexed to 90 degrees. After leaving the ground, the ankle of the raised leg immediately returns to dorsiflexion. The result of this movement is that the legs switch positions in a quick and powerful action.

Coaching Points

- The athlete should keep the body in a straight-line position from the ankle up to the head.
- The athlete should keep the heel of the trail leg close to the ground, with pressure on the ball of the foot.
- The straight-line posture should be maintained throughout the drill.

Variations

To modify the movement for novice athletes, the athlete can begin by using a simple marching pattern: Begin with both legs straight, then right knee up, then both legs straight, then left knee up, holding each position for 5 to 10 seconds. The athlete can progress to a tempo march and then move on to a single-leg tap, in which the lead leg drives down to tap the ground next to the trail leg and immediately returns to the knee-drive position.

To amplify the difficulty, a progression of double response (two actions performed consecutively, returning to the same start position), triple response (three actions performed consecutively), and rapid fire (3-5 sec) may be used. Ultimately, the athlete may remove one arm from the wall to perform an arm drive while executing the drill.

Falling Start

Aim
To develop first-step explosion leading into acceleration while maintaining a straight-line posture.

Action
The athlete begins in a tall, standing position with the feet even and directly under the hips, chest up, head neutral, and eyes focused straight ahead. The athlete falls forward, maintaining a straight-line posture, not flexing at the waist or hips or rounding the back, before forcefully flexing the hip and knee of the lead leg to 90 degrees and driving the arms. The lead leg continues into a first step by propelling the hips forward explosively while maintaining the straight-line posture. This step is immediately followed by an explosive second step while maintaining the posture. The athlete should master the technique and posture first, then increase the speed and explosive nature of the drill. The athlete performs the drill using the natural drive leg and then using the other leg as the drive leg. The athlete needs to be able to take an explosive first step from either leg.

Coaching Points
- The athlete should begin with the body straight and tall.
- The athlete falls as far as possible before initiating the drive leg.
- The athlete keeps a straight-line posture with the hips in line through the entire movement.
- The athlete should drive the lead leg explosively into the ground, pushing the hips as far forward as possible.

Variations
After the athlete masters the technique of the first two or three steps, progress can be made to use a more explosive start, increase the distance of the drill, perform the drill on a slight uphill (2-3 degrees) or slight downhill angle, or use other forms of lightly resisted or assisted falling starts.

Attack, Dodge, Attack

Aim
Develop the ability to change speeds and accelerate after a dodge or a reaction to visual cues.

Action
Five cones or barriers are set up 10 yards apart on a line. The athlete begins the drill from a two-point start position. On the coach's signal, the athlete makes a move around the first cone or barrier and accelerates toward, or attacks, the second cone. Upon reaching the second cone, the athlete performs a dodge to avoid the cone or barrier. This process is repeated with each subsequent cone without stopping. Emphasis should be placed on the acceleration toward the next cone.

Change of speed with dodge

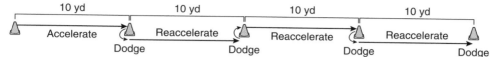

Coaching Points

- Attack each cone or barrier as aggressively and quickly as possible.
- Explode out of each dodge or cut and drive toward the next cone or barrier.
- Use a variety of cuts, dodges, and fakes.

Variations

The drill may be varied by changing the distances for any of the segments of the drill, creating more emphasis on acceleration, lengthening or shortening the full-speed segment, or allowing less stride time. As the athlete gets more proficient with the drill, add a stick and ball. In place of the barriers, other athletes may be positioned at intervals to add visual cues and additional interference.

Modified T-Drill with Arch Pattern

Aim

To develop the athlete's ability to combine explosive starts with lacrosse-specific reactions, changes of direction, and nonlinear acceleration.

Action

Set up three cones in a line 10 yards apart from each other for a total of 20 yards (cones D, B, C). Place a fourth cone (A) 5 yards perpendicular from the middle cone. The athlete begins at the bottom of the T at cone A. On the coach's signal, the athlete attacks the middle cone (B), quickly stops, and bounces back to the starting cone (A). The athlete then sprints to the right in an arch toward cone C, stops, changes direction, and accelerates on an arch past A to cone D (diagram a).

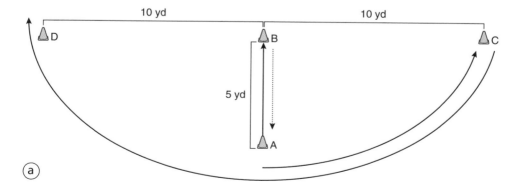

Coaching Points

- Attack cone B as explosively as possible.
- Return to cone A using a quick backpedal step or turning and running.
- Maintain good mechanics (arm, leg, and body angle positions) while accelerating through arches.

Variations

Once the athlete acclimates to the patterns, the coach can vary the drill by moving the attack and bounce portion to one side of the arch (diagram a) or inverting the drill so the athlete is on the inside of the arch facing the opposite direction (diagram b). As with other lacrosse drills, adding a stick and ball after the athlete is proficient with the drill can add variety and difficulty and make the drill resemble game situations.

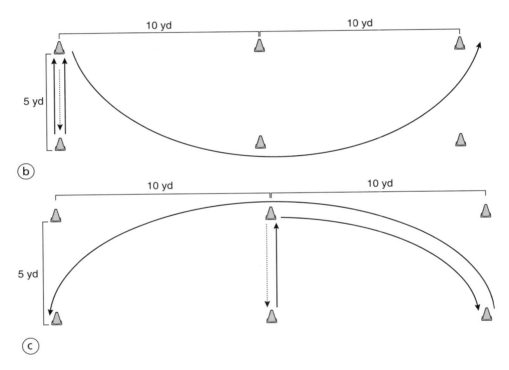

Circle Drill

Aim

To develop the athlete's ability to maintain body control and position while increasing speed when performing nonlinear acceleration and deceleration patterns.

Action

Set up two circles (cones, mobile creases, or similar-sized circles) with a 2-yard gap between them. Place cones 2 yards to the side of each circle and cones 5 yards from each of the circles as shown. The athlete begins the drill 5 yards from one side of the first circle. The athlete attacks a point 2 yards outside of the circle and should immediately bounce back to the starting position. The athlete then attacks the same position again, this time transitioning to an arch around the first circle (diagram a).

Coaching Points

- The attack and bounce segment should be as aggressive and explosive as possible.
- The athlete should maintain good running mechanics for acceleration and body control through the arch.

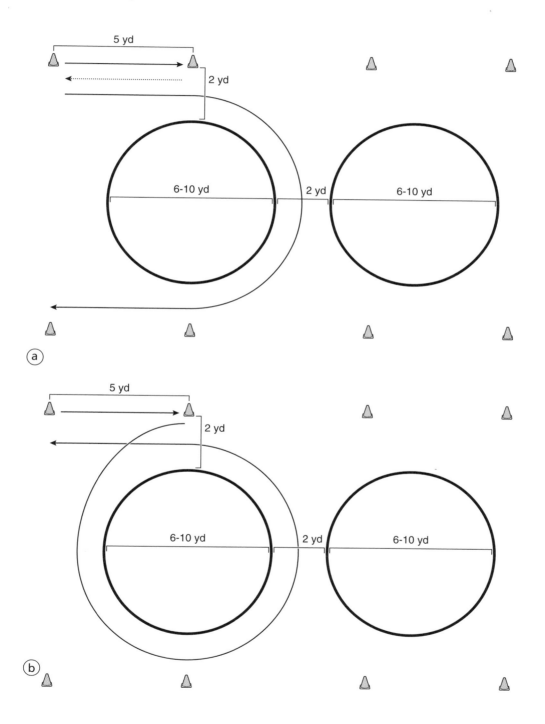

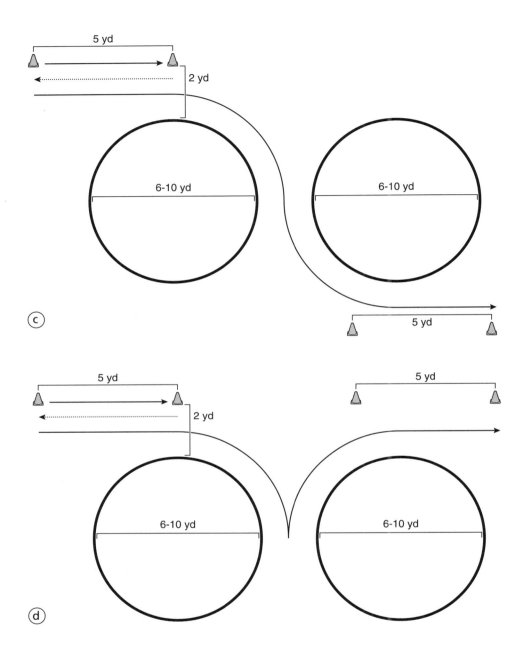

Variations

This drill can be manipulated to progress to more difficult patterns reactions or accelerations after the circles. With the same setup, the athlete can reverse direction after the attack (diagram *b*). The drill can progress to use both circles, transitioning between two different arches (diagram *c*). Additionally, the drill can include a change of direction between the two circles (diagram *d*). Sticks, balls, and additional athletes can be added for difficulty and game situation replication.

Ins and Outs

Aim

To develop the athlete's ability to develop, change, and maintain linear speed while retaining correct form over a large area.

Action

The entire drill should be performed on a 100-yard field with 20-yard increments indicated. The athlete begins in a two-point start stance at the 0-yard mark. On the coach's signal, the athlete will perform a build-up through the 20-yard mark, reaching about 75% of full speed. At the 20-yard mark the athlete will transition to a full-speed sprint. At the 40-yard mark, the athlete should transition to strides, maintaining correct posture and running form. From the 60-yard mark to the 80-yard mark, the athlete will again sprint at full speed. From the 80-yard mark to the 100-yard mark, the athlete will stride while slowing down.

Linear change of speed

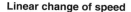
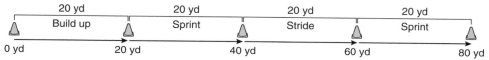

Coaching Points

- Athlete should maintain good sprinting mechanics with positive shin angles, dorsiflexed ankles, and straight-line body position.
- Athlete should swing the arm from the shoulder with a loose 90-degree elbow.
- Remind the athlete not to overstride or reach for the forward step.

Variations

The drill may be varied by changing the distances for any of the segments of the drill, creating more emphasis on acceleration, lengthening, or shortening the full-speed segment or allowing less stride time. Care should be taken in allocating sets, repetitions, and recovery time to ensure that quality work is maintained, thus ensuring a focus on speed development.

▶ *SPRINT (TRACK) CYCLING*

Brentan Parsons

Sprint (track) cycling primarily consists of three events at the Olympic level: the team sprint, the individual sprint, and the Keirin. All three events are characterized by high-intensity, repeatable maximal strength and power efforts that require a well-trained neuromuscular system. Because a premium is placed on repeated maximal efforts, strength and power training and its application form a significant part of a rider's training.

SPEED IN SPRINT (TRACK) CYCLING

To determine the speed requirements for track cycling, it is important to determine the nature of each of the three events. First, the team sprint (TS) is a three-lap all-out sprint raced between two teams of three riders. After each lap, the leading rider from each team leaves the race by going up the embankment until the last remaining rider is left to cross the finish line. Races at the elite level last for around 42 to 43 seconds for the men and around 45 to 47 seconds for the women. The first lap, which lasts around 17 to 18 seconds for male athletes and around 18 to 19 seconds for female athletes, is the slowest because the athletes are starting from stationary. The second and third laps are similar in time at approximately 12 to 13 seconds for men and 13 to 14 seconds for woman, with the third lap being slightly slower due to fatigue. The physical requirements for the race differ between the three individual athletes, and this can affect the type of track and resistance training undertaken. The starter needs to have an excellent rate of force development and speed strength to push a large gear from a stationary start, and the second and third riders need more speed strength to keep a fast cadence on a big gear as well as great neuromuscular coordination with speed frequency to maintain the high output over an extended period. This event requires great skill, coordination of movements, and teamwork while maintaining an aerodynamic posture (8, 10).

Next up is the individual sprint (IS). This is different from the other two events in that it has a separate qualification event or round to seed the riders for racing. The IS qualification process includes a flying 200-m sprint in which the athlete undertakes a two-lap rolling speed build-up that reaches maximal velocity at the start mark with the goal of holding this pace to the finish line. The time is recorded for the flying 200-meter and is used to rank competitors. The all-out maximal effort usually lasts between 11 seconds and low-10-second mark for elite female cyclists and between low 10 seconds through the low 9-second mark for elite male athletes; these are similar to times of a 100-meter track and field sprint. Once the athlete is seeded, he or she races over the same distance against an inversely seeded racer over three races if needed. Depending on the field, competition, and classification, the athlete may have to repeat the racing numerous times, which may include back-to-back races up to several races during the day or over a few days. This makes high-intensity repeatability essential to the IS athlete, especially one with a full program. Smaller competitions or carnivals can be crammed into 1 or 2 days, or in the case of World Cups and Olympic Games the competition duration is lengthened to accommodate several days of racing, so the rest and recovery is dependent on the number of events, number of competitors, and how full a program an individual rider chooses to ride. Riders work with their coach to use knowledge of their personal and opponents' abilities along with perceived riding skill to determine sprint length, sprint timing, and race tactics (10).

Finally, in the Keirin six to eight riders are paced behind a Derny (motorcycle) for a few laps until the speed has risen from 12 miles per hour to 31 miles per hour (20-50 km/h); this usually occurs around 600-700 meters (approximately 650 to 750 yards) from the finish. As soon as the Derny leaves the track, it is a race until the finish. This popular Japanese form of sprint (track) cycling is characterized by daring racing and numerous crashes. The sprints can sometimes last a little longer than the IS and may be dictated more by tactics (due to more riders) rather than an all-out sprint; however, sprints can last up to around 40 seconds (10).

IMPLICATIONS OF SPEED IN SPRINT (TRACK) CYCLING

Sprint (track) cycling efforts are short, high-intensity affairs, and because winning sprints can last a few seconds up to 40 seconds, a strong development of both the phosphagen system (PC) and glycolytic energy system is required. An emphasis on maximal efforts on the bike and in the weight room is necessary, so full recovery of the PC system is necessary to ensure intensity of effort (5).

Now that the events of sprint (track) cycling have been explained, it is important to understand the rationale and direction of strength exercises to enhance speed. In the next section we will discuss the anatomy, physiology, and methodologies underpinning starting strength, strength speed, and cadence speed and how they affect speed in track cycling.

Muscles Used in Cycling

As seen in the physiques of elite sprint (track) cyclists, the quadriceps (especially vastus medialis) as well as the gluteals and hamstrings are highly developed. Because the sole propelling forces for cycling are generated by the legs, the previously mentioned muscles and the others shown in figure 9.1 all become primary and secondary movers for cycling.

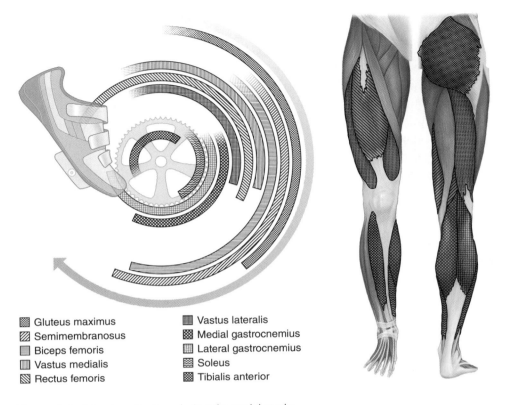

Gluteus maximus
Semimembranosus
Biceps femoris
Vastus medialis
Rectus femoris

Vastus lateralis
Medial gastrocnemius
Lateral gastrocnemius
Soleus
Tibialis anterior

Figure 9.1 Muscle activation during the pedal stroke.
Reprinted by permission from S. Sovndal, *Cycling Anatomy*, 2nd ed. (Champaign, IL: Human Kinetics, 2020), 188.

Exercise and Intensity Programming for Cycling

The intensity of the training is of high importance, because increased intensity and intent leads to higher recruitment of motor units and the intensity and frequency of neural firing (2, 4, 16). A strong upper body and a rigid midsection is also of importance to attenuate and control the powerful leg forces; however, that is beyond the purview of this section. The neurological pathways and muscle-usage sequence of strength and power exercises can mimic the specific neuromuscular coordination of track cycling or enable general preparation for athlete development. The integration of the neuromuscular system is of high importance because the skillful nature of sprint cycling requires sequential and seamless maximal contraction, from the start through acceleration to maintaining top speed. An example of this high neural demand is cadence power, which is built on the foundation of high neural capacity that supports the gym-to-bike adaptations (3, 11, 12, 13, 15, 18).

The following section of this chapter are classified into specific components of sprint (track) cycling racing. These classifications include starting strength, acceleration and speed strength, and neuromuscular coordination for cadence speed, and specific strength training and methodology are outlined in detail.

Starting Strength

Starting strength is needed during the first 20 meters (22 yards) of the TS start and is characterized by a rapid, high-concentric strength component focusing primarily on front kinetic chain muscle groups during the first few downward pedal strokes (see figure 9.1). They are assisted by the gluteal muscles and posterior kinetic chain (on recovery) (7, 8). This can be trained using the following exercises with the precise choice and loading dependent on the specific athlete development and injury status and history (figure 9.2):

- Maximal barbell squat at a velocity of 1.0 to 1.6 feet per second (0.3-0.5 m/sec)
- Maximal trap bar deadlift at a velocity of 0.5 to 1.3 feet per second (0.15-0.4 m/sec)
- Single-leg 45-degree leg press at 100% of the 1RM
- Trap bar clean pull at 80% to 90% of the 1RM at a velocity between 3.3 to 3.9 feet per second (1.0-1.2 m/sec)

Training volume and intensity for starting strength will differ depending on many variables such as athlete training status, training block, competition schedule, and coaching style. Keeping this in mind, repetition ranges are from 1 to 5, with sets ranging from 2 to 8. The high intensity and near-maximal

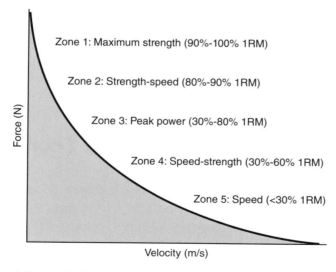

Figure 9.2 A force-velocity curve with specific training zones. (**Note**: the velocity varies based on the exercise; the velocities seen in the figure are for the trap bar clean pull.)

Adapted by permission from S. Marohn and Z. Gjestvang, "Sport-Specific Program Design Guidelines," in *Strength Training for Baseball*, edited for the National Strength and Conditioning Association by A.E. Coleman and D.J. Szymanski (Champaign, IL: Human Kinetics, 2022), 71.

load of the exercises reflect the event's requirement to overcome inertia quickly, using a high neural drive and muscle mechanical output, and thus exercises that prioritize these qualities are preferred (1, 10, 16, 19).

A primary exercise to improve starting strength or power is the barbell back squat. Use a range of 1 to 5 repetitions and a set range of 1 to 8. The load should be 85% to 100% of the 1RM depending on individual training and competition focus. Strength testing or velocity-based training (see figure 9.2) can determine the ideal loading (19).

Acceleration and Speed Strength

Acceleration within the TS occurs primarily from the 20 meters (22 yards) through to the 120 meter to 150 meter (approximately 130 to 165 yards) mark and is determined by the athlete or opponent during the Keirin and IS (10). The main purpose within this phase is to accelerate as fast as possible, so speed is a priority often to the detriment of form, cycle position, and aerodynamics. This speed-strength phase is similar to the back end of the starting phase in the TS when the athlete transitions from a stationary start to one at a building speed. Within this phase the athlete transfers the body position from acceleration (nonstreamlined and out of the saddle) into an aerodynamic position. Once again here, the following exercises are recommended:

▶ Trap bar clean pull at 75% to 90% of the 1RM at a velocity between 3.3 to 3.9 feet per second (1.0-1.2 m/sec) (19)

▶ Single-leg 45-degree leg press at 50% to 75% of the 1RM focusing on concentric intent (2, 16)

A primary exercise to improve acceleration and speed strength is the single leg 45-degree leg press. Use a range of 2 to 6 repetitions and a set range of 1 to 8 at 50% to 75% of the 1RM, focusing on concentric intent. This type of training is commonly used before competition and in between competitions to maintain a high neural output, while also reducing muscle damage with a reduction in the eccentric component (19).

Cadence Speed for Neuromuscular Coordination

For the third speed training component it is essential that the body position is aerodynamic and rigid through the upper body; however, through the lower body the intent is to maintain a high strength or power neural output. The athlete should maintain not only cadence (pedal speed) but also the watts (power) produced with every rotation of the pedals. For this power output the athlete focuses on the speed of movement rather than the resistance force. For example, in this training block the athlete concentrates on a trap bar block pull or jump squat with a lighter resistance 30% to 50% of the 1RM and aims for a mean power of 4.6 feet per second (1.4 m/sec) or greater, depending on the phase of training (i.e., use a higher load for building and a lower load for actualization phases) (1, 2, 3, 4, 14, 17, 19).

A primary exercise to improve neuromuscular coordination is the trap bar clean-pull. Use a range of 2 to 6 repetitions and 2 to 4 sets depending on training focus.

Other Sprint (Track) Cycling Speed Training Modalities

The art of coaching allows for emphasizing certain training elements within the year or training block on and off the bike. For example, the following bike-specific exercises are used for speed and strength speed development on the bike:

- ▶ *Isometric pedal push.* Maximal isometric pedal push from 5 to 15 seconds
- ▶ *Isokinetic pedal push.* Pushing a set wattage at a predetermined cadence
- ▶ *Eccentric pedal push.* Resisted-load pedal push
- ▶ *Hill sprints.* In and out of the saddle over various distances
- ▶ *Riding a larger gear.* Various on-track sprint distances
- ▶ *Riding a smaller gear.* Muscle firing coordination and neural development

The variations for speed development in the weight room are also numerous and commonly include but are not limited to the following:

- ▶ *Isometric-specific exercises.* Tendon and ligament strength (6)
- ▶ *Concentric-specific exercises.* Supramaximal and reduced-range neural drive (17)
- ▶ *Eccentric-specific exercises.* Supramaximal and building phases
- ▶ *Jumps and plyometric training.* Tendon stiffness and neural drive (17)
- ▶ *Leg press variations at 45-degree angle.* Single leg, throws, isometric, pure concentric, eccentric (10)
- ▶ *Olympic lifts and their derivatives*

Flexibility and joint range of motion vary in importance depending on the sport, and sprint (track) cycling is no different. Due to the specific nature of being on a bike to generate speed, the body position and technique is more important to most sprinting sports to generate speed. Bike setup is key, as is the reduced-drag air-flow qualities of athletes in their streamlined position. To attain this body position, cycling athletes need a good range of motion through dominant movement joints such as ankle, knee, hip, lower back and mid-back, and shoulder. Not only do they need range but they need to express strength and power in this aerodynamic posture. They also need the strength to hold posture while transferring great forces from the upper body to the lower and vice versa, especially on longer sprints. Therefore, sprint (track) cycling is one sport in which flexibility and its application in concert with strength and bike-specific training can have a direct impact on speed (7, 9).

SPRINT (TRACK) CYCLING-SPECIFIC EXERCISES

Sprint (track) cycling drills	Page number
Barbell back squat	243
Single-leg 45-degree leg press	244
Trap bar clean pull	245

Barbell Back Squat

Aim

Leg and mid-section muscular and nervous system development.

Action

Step into the power rack and center the bar across the upper trapezius muscle. Set the hands on the bar slightly wider than shoulder width. Feet should be shoulder-width apart or slightly wider depending on anthropometry and joint range, and the eyes should look forward in normal a posture. Step away from the rack to leave clearance to move comfortably (photo a). Start the movement by breaking at the hips first, flex the knees, and squat down to where the top of the thighs are parallel to the ground (deeper or shallower depending on the individual athlete), evenly distributing the weight through both feet (photo b). Keep the chest out and the head neutral, and make sure that spine position is neutral throughout the movement. On ascension, push evenly through the feet, maintaining posture and extending through the knees and hips until returning to the starting position.

Coaching Points

- Use a power rack and a spotter to ensure the exercise is as safe as possible, especially while lifting maximal efforts.
- Control the descent to ensure a strong platform for ascent.
- Push through the whole of the foot, with a focus on the imaginary triangle that forms from the heel and the balls of your feet.
- Keep the knees and ankles aligned.
- Concentrate on intent of movement and drive the feet through the floor.

Variation

Squat technique will depend on many factors, the main points being the athlete's anthropometry, joint range, and training history. The athlete should be technically proficient at lighter loads for several months before squatting lower repetitions at near to maximal loads.

Single-Leg 45-Degree Leg Press

Aim
Cycling-specific single-leg muscular strength and neuromuscular development.

Action
While sitting in the machine, place two feet in the center position of the machine's sled platform in a similar fashion to squats. From this position, depending on knee joint angles, either push off with two legs and then take one leg off the machine and rest on the floor or undertake the exercise straight from the resting position (normally 80-90 degrees at the knee). The athlete pushes with maximal effort through the whole foot, while maintaining a straight line of power from the foot through the knee and aligning with the hip joint (watch for misalignment, especially at the knee). The athlete is assisted with the eccentric component by coaches and assistants taking most of the load back to the start position.

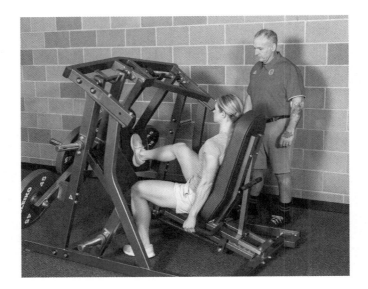

Coaching Points
- Because this exercise focuses on the concentric component, the machine's specific mechanisms needs to help catch the weight after the concentric or up phase.
- Initially, set up the angle of the seat to ensure comfort as well as similar hip joint angles to on-bike position.
- Have a coach or assistant on either side of the machine to assist with returning the weight sled to the starting position, thus minimizing the athlete's eccentric exertion with this exercise.
- Concentrate on intent of movement of every repetition.

Variations
Many variations of purely concentric, eccentric, and isometric muscle actions can be used depending on training goals. Coaches can manipulate the load to also train along the force and velocity curve to emphasize various strength and power modalities as the competition schedule dictates.

Trap Bar Clean Pull

Aim

High-speed neuromuscular development promoting the recruitment of higher threshold motor units when done with maximal voluntary effort and the intent to move the weight rapidly.

Action

Squat down and grab the handles while keeping a higher hip position, shoulders set back and down (engage latissimus dorsi), and head looking forward (photo *a*). Breathe in while bracing the core and keeping tension in the arms, drive the feet through the floor, and start the bar moving while maintaining a strong neutral spine position (photo *b*). Once the bar moves past the knees rapidly triple extend the ankle, knee, and hips while shrugging and keeping the arms straight at the apex of the movement (photo *c*).

Coaching Points

- Setup is similar to that of a trap bar deadlift; step inside the trap bar and set up the feet similar to a squat.
- Make sure technique and movement are accurate before adding speed.
- Concentrate on intent of movement; nervous system development is key.
- Powerful athletes should generate enough force with this movement for the feet to leave the floor momentarily. This is fine and even encouraged to fully express the maximal power output, but make sure the athlete is competent to land in a safe manner.

Variations

This exercise can be done off weightlifting blocks for taller athletes or to reduce total distance moved. The load lifted can be changed to reflect the force and velocity profile a coach may wish to emphasize: heavier for building phases and lighter and faster for actualization and competition phases.

▶ *SPEED SKATING*

Andrew Stuart

Speed skating is a time trial–based sport performed on an indoor or outdoor ice-covered track that requires skill, strength, power, speed, and capacity. The distances that are covered can be classified into three different events: sprint (500 m and 1,000 m [547 and 1,093 yards]), middle distance (1,500 m [almost 1 mile]), and long distance (3,000 m, 5,000 m, and 10,000 m [1.9, 3.1, and 6.2 miles]). Although speed skating does not share the exact same ground contact times, technical cues, or movement patterns as off-ice speed training, research has investigated the benefits of off-ice speed training modalities such as Olympic weightlifting derivatives (11), plyometric training (12), and sprint training (8) to the development of speed and on-ice skating performance of the speed skating athlete.

SPEED IN SPEED SKATING

As previously mentioned, it is important to implement speed and power training in the strength and conditioning program to enhance on-ice performance. In speed skating the main goal is to maintain a high power output over the entire duration of the competitive distance.

The start of a speed skating race will largely depend on the competitive distance that is being raced (long distance vs. sprint); however, for most races the start mimics a static two-point position similar to many off-ice sprinting drills (4, 9, 10). Following an external stimulus from the official's gun, the skater must use more force and higher anaerobic work initially to accelerate off the line during the start.

The initial start in speed skating has a relatively short ground contact time, which is the opposite of traditional off-ice sprinting. After the initial start, the strokes will begin to shift toward more of a gliding motion with faster knee extension. The skater's torso angle will become more horizontal, enabling the skater to prepare for acceleration around the first corner. After the initial start and leaving the first corner of the track, the skater's movement begins to emulate a wave-like motion as the skater's stroke shifts into the three different phases: glide, push-off, and reposition (1, 2, 3, 9, 13). Similar to ice hockey, speed skating uses the push-off phase to create acceleration and increase skating speed.

IMPLICATIONS OF SPEED IN SPEED SKATING

For the sport of speed skating, the tactics—namely, the pacing strategy used during a race—will dictate the need for skating speed. The sprinting event distances of the 500- and 1,000-meter races typically last 33.6 to 71.6 seconds; speed is needed to produce the high power outputs needed to complete the event. The middle-distance event of the 1,500-meter race typically lasts 1:40 to 1:49 (minutes:seconds) (13). The strategies that have been used successfully in international competition seem to be focused on using the skater's maximum sprint speed and sustainable pace (13). Theoretically, this has been accomplished by rapidly applying a significant amount of force in the shortest period of time to minimize friction on the ice and achieve a maximal horizontal velocity, which in turn creates higher top-end speed (4). This increase in top-end speed will create a greater point from which speed will drop at the onset of fatigue. For the long-distance events of the 3,000-meter to 10,000-meter races that typically last 6:01 to 12:30 (minutes:seconds), the need for speed is not as advantageous to competitive success as it is in the sprint distances (13). For these distances, the oxidative system development is more of a physiological driver for sport success (6, 7).

SPEED SKATING-SPECIFIC DRILLS

The key qualities of speed development drills for speed skaters focus on acceleration, top-end speed, starting strength, and power. These drills supplement a strength and conditioning program that is designed to produce the required physical qualities to increase skating speed. The following drills are categorized into on-ice drills, off-ice skill, and off-ice physical development.

Speed skating drills	Page number
Assisted sprinting (overspeed)	248
Incline sprinting	253
Push-up starts (prone start)	252
Rolling starts	248
Sled pull	251
Slide board	249
Zig-zag bounding skater bounds	250

ON-ICE DRILLS

Assisted Sprinting (Overspeed)

Aim

To isolate acceleration mechanics through designated zones such as acceleration midpoint (50 m [55 yards]), preparation for corner entry (70 m [77 yards]), corner entry (100 m [109 yards]), or corner exit (200 m [219 yards]). Success in these designated zones will be attributed to the skater who maintains proper posture and effective push-off and reposition mechanics (13). Less efficient skaters may rush through the reposition phase of the stroke in attempts to increase maximum velocity by attacking the ice. This will allow the athlete more exposure to acceleration and maximum velocity training while reinforcing technique.

Action

The athlete assumes a skate position stance and attaches him- or herself to the assisted apparatus such as a winch system or a cable or band via a handle or waist belt. After confirming that the athlete is ready, a coach initiates the sprint by the apparatus. If using a cable or band, the coach maintains a distance of 10-20 yards from the athlete to maintain tension on the cable or band. Once ready the coach accelerates over 10 yards to ensure that tension remains on the cable or band. Once pulled up to speed, the athlete detaches from the apparatus and accelerates over the designated zone.

Coaching Points

- Using an assisted winch machine or a cable or band apparatus, the athlete will accelerate to a maximum speed.
- Once the athlete has been pulled to the designated zone, the coach provides cueing to encourage the athlete to maintain proper technique.
- Athletes should focus on maintaining patience and focus on maintaining a stacked position with knees directly under shoulders during the glide and reposition phase of skating.

Rolling Starts

Aim

To isolate maximum velocity mechanics through designated zones such as acceleration midpoint (50 m [55 yards]), preparation for corner entry (70 m [77 yards]), and corner entry (100 m [109 yards]).

Action

The athlete performs a build-up to approximately 75% speed through the initial movement of the drill at approximately 15-30 yards. Once athletes reach the designated zone they will accelerate and maintain maximum velocity for the given distance.

Coaching Points

- The athlete should demonstrate good skating position and mechanics.
- The athlete should focus on maintaining a stable torso angle while focusing on strong, aggressive pushes from the knee and hip complex.

OFF-ICE DRILLS

Slide Board

Aim

To rehearse technical proficiency and lateral lower body power while using a similar movement pattern to on-ice skating.

Action

The athlete starts in a low skate position on the slide board and laterally pushes off explosively by initiating the movement with the outside leg from a flexed position and a powerful extension. The athlete then decelerates the body while transferring from one limb to the other, similar to the push-off, glide, and reposition phase of on-ice skating. The athlete should move rhythmically while holding shoulders, knees, and arms similar to on-ice skate position.

Coaching Points

- The athlete should emphasize driving off the outside of the leg to propel across the slide board.
- The athlete should maintain a horizontal hip perpendicular to the floor.
- The athlete should emphasize staying stacked, with knees directly in line with shoulders.

Variation

If maintaining shoulder, knee, and arm position is difficult, a regression is to have the athlete perform alternating single-leg lift-offs in the posterior-lateral plane from a static skate position, often called *weight transfer*.

Zig-Zag Bounding Skater Bounds

Aim
This exercise develops lower body horizontal power while using a similar movement pattern to ice skating.

Action
The athlete stands on one foot and repeatedly bounds both forward and laterally from that foot (photo *a*) to the opposite foot (photo *b*) as quickly and explosively as possible. The typical distance for this exercise is 20-40 yards but can be increased or decreased to develop power or endurance.

Coaching Points
- Athletes should be focused on optimizing flight time during this exercise.
- Proper landing mechanics at the knee and hip should be visually inspected to ensure the decreased risk of injury.

Variations
A regression for this drill is to include a static hold on landing. This would increase the static stability of the athlete. A progression for this drill is to include an angled board with a low-grade incline and a static hold on landing.

OFF-ICE PHYSICAL DEVELOPMENT

Sled Pull

Aim

To develop lower body rate of force development, horizontal power, and effective start mechanics.

Action

The athlete wears a shoulder or waist harness attached to a sled. The athlete accelerates with maximal effort from a standing staggered start position for the desired distance of 10-20 yards. A variety of loads can be used for this drill and will depend on the goal of the training sessions. However, load selection should be conservative to maintain similar kinematics and elastic mechanisms similar to what is demonstrated during unresisted sprinting and on-ice starts. A moderate load of roughly 55% body weight could be a starting point to effectively increase ground contact time while decreasing total force (5).

Coaching Points

- Attain an acceleration posture: forward torso lean, minimal knee-gap at touchdown, neutral pelvic position, shins pushing back, and stiff ankles.
- Emphasize a powerful punch and drive action, with full extension of the ankle, knee, and hips.
- Use a powerful arm action that complements the leg action.

Push-Up Starts (Prone Start)

Aim

To develop proper acceleration mechanics and propulsive ability as a beginning teaching tool for more traditional starts.

Action

The athlete assumes the position as at the bottom of a push-up (photo *a*). Initially, the athlete may use a self-start to build confidence and technical mastery of the drill. Once athletes have demonstrated appropriate technical ability, they can respond to an external cue (clap, whistle, or audible command) and immediately push the center of mass up and out of the starting position (photo *b*). The emphasis should be to maintain a long torso. The athlete should focus on aggressive, rapid footstrikes with long arm actions.

Starting position.

Sprinting.

Coaching Points

- Explode off the ground and drive the knee toward the chest.
- Maintain a long and braced torso.
- Aggressively and rapidly strike the ground.
- Keep arms long and strong.

Incline Sprinting

Aim

To address the execution of proper acceleration mechanics and propulsive abilities.

Action

Using a slope of 5 degrees allows for imitation of the first five steps from the start (5).

Coaching Points

- Attain an acceleration posture.
- Emphasize a powerful punch and drive, with full triple extension (hip, knee, and ankle).
- The athlete should focus on leading into the natural lean of the slope through the hips.
- The athlete should maintain a forward lean of the torso.
- The athlete should be cued to "punch the ground hard and fast."

References

Chapter 1

1. Deacon, J. Acceleration: Theory and practice. *Prof Strength Cond J* 21:16-21, 2011.

2. Goodwin, J. Maximum velocity is when we can no longer accelerate. *Strength Cond J* 21:3-9, 2011.

3. Jeffreys, I. *Total Soccer Fitness*. Monterey, CA: Coaches Choice.

4. Jeffreys, I. Utilising motor learning methods in the development of physical skills. *Strength Cond J* 21:33-35, 2011.

5. Jeffreys, I. The structure and function of the neuromuscular system. In *Strength and Conditioning for Sports Performance*. 2nd ed. Jeffreys, I, and Moody, J, eds. London: Routledge, 43-61, 2021.

6. Jeffreys, I, and Goodwin, J. Developing speed and agility for sports performance. In *Strength and Conditioning for Sports Performance*. 2nd ed. Jeffreys, I, and Moody, J, eds. London: Routledge, 342-367, 2021.

7. Jeffreys, I. *Gamespeed: Movement Training for Superior Sports performance*. 3rd ed. Monterey, CA: Coaches Choice, 2021.

8. Jeffreys, I. Use context and gamespeed to transform speed and agility training. *Strength Cond J* 67:29-35, 2022.

9. McGinnis, PM. *Biomechanics of Sport and Exercise*. 4th ed. Champaign, IL: Human Kinetics 2020.

10. Schmidt, RA, and Lee, TD. *Motor Control and Learning: A Behavioral Emphasis*. 5th ed. Champaign, IL: Human Kinetics 2011.

11. Stoyanov, H. Competition model characteristics of elite male sprinters. *New Stud Athl* 29:57-58, 2014.

12. Weyand, PG, Sternlight, DB, Bellizzi, MJ, and Wright, S. Faster top running speeds are achieved with greater ground forces not more rapid leg movements. *J Appl Physiol* 89(5):1991-1999, 2000.

13. Weyand, PG, and Davis, JA. Running performance has a structural basis. *J Exp Biol* 208:2625-2631, 2005.

14. Weyand, PG, Sandell, RF, Prime, DN, and Bundle, MW. The biological limits to running speed are imposed from the ground up. *J Appl Physiol* 108(4):950-961, 2010.

Chapter 2

1. Best, CH, and Partridge, RC. The equation of motion of a runner, exerting a maximal effort. *Proc R Soc London Ser B* 103:218-225, 1928.

2. Cavagna, GA, Komarek, L, and Mazzoleni, S. The mechanics of sprint running. *J Physiol* 217:709-721, 1972.

3. Clark, KP, and Weyand, PG. Are running speeds maximized with simple-spring stance mechanics? *J Appl Physiol* 117:604-615, 2014.

4. Clark, KP, Meng, CR, and Stearne, DJ. "Whip from the hip": Thigh angular motion, ground contact mechanics, and running speed. *Biol Open* 9:1-51, 2020.

5. Colyer, SL, Nagahara, R, Takai, Y, and Salo, AIT. How sprinters accelerate beyond the velocity plateau of soccer players: Waveform analysis of ground reaction forces. *Scand J Med Sci Sport* 28:2527-2535, 2018.

6. Dorn, TW, Schache, AG, and Pandy, MG. Muscular strategy shift in human running: Dependence of running speed on hip and ankle muscle performance. *J Exp Biol* 215:1944-1956, 2012.

7. Furusawa, K, Hill, AV, and Parkinson, JL. The dynamics of "sprint" running. *Proc R Soc London Ser B* 102:29-42, 1927.

8. Hicks, D, Schuster, JG, Samozino, P, and Morin, JB. Improving mechanical effectiveness during sprint acceleration: Practical recommendations and guidelines. *Strength Cond J* 42:45-62, 2020.

9. Jiménez-Reyes, P, Cross, M, Ross, A, Samozino, P, Brughelli, M, Gill, N, and Morin, JB. Changes in mechanical properties of sprinting during repeated sprint in elite rugby sevens athletes. *Eur J Sport Sci* 19:585-594, 2019.

10. Mendiguchia, J, Castaño-Zambudio, A, Jiménez-Reyes, P, Morin, JB., Edouard, P, Conceição, F, Tawiah-Dodoo, J, and Colyer, SL. Can we modify maximal speed running posture? Implications for performance and hamstring injury management. *Int J Sports Physiol Perform* 17:374-383, 2022.

11. Morin, JB, Edouard, P, and Samozino, P. Technical ability of force application as a determinant factor of sprint performance. *Med Sci Sports Exerc* 43:1680-1688, 2011.

12. Morin, JB, Samozino, P, Edouard, P, and Tomazin, K. Effect of fatigue on force production and force application technique during repeated sprints. *J Biomech* 44:2719-2723, 2011.

13. Morin, JB, Bourdin, M, Edouard, P, Peyrot, N, Samozino, P, and Lacour, JR. Mechanical determinants of 100-m sprint running performance. *Eur J Appl Physiol* 112:3921-3930, 2012.

14. Morin, JB, Gimenez, P, Edouard, P, Arnal, P, Jiménez-Reyes, P, Samozino, P, Brughelli, M, and Mendiguchia, J. Sprint acceleration mechanics: The major role of hamstrings in horizontal force production. *Front Physiol* 6:404, 2015.

15. Morin, JB, Samozino, P, Murata, M, Cross, MR, and Nagahara, R. A simple method for computing sprint acceleration kinetics from running velocity data: Replication study with improved design. *J Biomech* 94:82-87, 2019.

16. Rabita, G, Dorel, S, Slawinski, J, Sàez-de-Villarreal, E, Couturier, A, Samozino, P, and Morin, JB. Sprint mechanics in world-class athletes: A new insight into the limits of human locomotion. *Scand J Med Sci Sport* 25:583-594, 2015.

17. Saeterbakken, AH, Stien, N, Andersen, V, Scott, S, Cumming, KT, Behm, DG, Granacher, U, Prieske, O. The effects of trunk muscle training on physical fitness and sport-specific performance in young and adult athletes: A systematic review and meta-analysis. *Sport Med* 52:1599-1622, 2022.

18. Schache, AG, Dorn, TW, Williams, GP, Brown, NAT, and Pandy, MG. Lower-limb muscular strategies for increasing running speed. *J Orthop Sports Phys Ther* 44:813-824, 2014.

19. Schache, AG, Lai, AKM, Brown, NAT, Crossley, KM, and Pandy, MG. Lower-limb joint mechanics during maximum acceleration sprinting. *J Exp Biol* 222:Pt2, 2019.

20. Slawinski, J, Termoz, N, Rabita, G, Guilhem, G, Dorel, S, Morin, J-B, and Samozino, P. How 100-m event analyses improve our understanding of world-class men's and women's sprint performance. *Scand J Med Sci Sport* 27:45-54, 2017.

Chapter 3

1. Baker, D, and Newton, RU. Comparison of lower body strength, power, acceleration, speed, agility, and sprint momentum to describe and compare playing rank among professional rugby league players. *J Strength Cond Res* 22:153-158, 2008.

2. Barr, MJ, Sheppard, JM, and Newton, RU. Sprinting kinematics of elite rugby players. *J Aust Strength Cond* 21:14-20, 2013.

3. Barr, MJ, Sheppard, JM, and Newton, RU. The effect of ball carrying on the sprinting speed of international rugby union players. *Int J Sports Sci Coach* 10:1-9, 2015.

4. Clark, K, and Weyand, P. Are running speeds maximized with simple-spring stance mechanics? *J Appl Physiol* 117(6):604-615, 2014.

5. Colyer, SL, Nagahara, R, and Salo, AIT. Kinetic demands of sprinting shift across the acceleration phase: Novel analysis of entire force waveforms. *Scand J Med Sci Sports* 28:1784-1792, 2018.

6. Dardouri, W, Selmi, MA, Sassi, RH, Gharbi, Z, Rebhi, A, Yahmed, MH, and Moalla, W. Relationship between repeated sprint performance and both aerobic and anaerobic fitness. *J Hum Kinet* 40:139-148, 2014.

7. Gambetta, V. *Athletic Development*. Champaign, IL: Human Kinetics, 2007.

8. Matsuo, A, Mizutani, M, Nagahara, R, Fukunaga, T, and Kanehisa, H. External mechanical work done during the acceleration stage of maximal sprint running and its association with running performance. *J Exp Biol* 222(5), 2019.

9. Mendiguchia, J, Castano-Zambudio, A, Jimenes-Reyes, R, Morin, J, Edouard, P, Conceicao, F, Tawiah-Dodoo, J, and Colyer, S L. Can we modify maximal speed running posture? Implications for performance and hamstring injury management. *Int J Sports Physiol Perform* 17:374-383, 2022.

10. Miller, R, Balshaw, TG, Massey, GJ, Maeo, S, Lanza, MB, Johnston, M, Allen, SJ, and Folland, JP. The muscle morphology of elite sprint running. *Med Sci Sports Exerc* 53:804-815, 2021.

11. Miyashiro, K, Nagahara, R, Yamamoto, K, and Nishijima, T. Kinematics of maximal speed sprinting with different running speed, leg length, and step characteristics. *Front Sports Act Living* 1, 2019.

12. Murata, M, Takai, Y, Kanehisa, H, Fukunaga, T, and Nagahara, R. Spatiotemporal and kinetic determinants of sprint acceleration performance in soccer players. *Sports* 6:169, 2018.

13. Nagahara, R. Ground reaction force across the transition during sprint acceleration. *Scand J Med Sci Sports* 30:450-461, 2020.

14. Nagahara, R, Amini, E, Marcon, KCC, Chen, P-W, Chua, J, Eiberger, J, Futalan, NJC, Lye, J, Pantovic, MM, Starczewski, M, Sudsa-Ard, K, Sumartiningsih, S, Wang, CY, William, TB, Kasujja, T, and Gujar, TA. Influence of the intention to lean the body forward on kinematics and kinetics of sprinting for active adults. *Sports* 7:133, 2019.

15. Nagahara, R, Kanehisa, H, Matsuo, A, and Fukunaga, T. Are peak ground reaction forces related to better sprint acceleration performance? *Sports Biomech* 20:360-369, 2021.

16. Nagahara, R, Matsubayashi, T, Matsuo, A, and Zushi, K. Kinematics of transition during human accelerated sprinting. *Biol Open* 3:689-699, 2014.

17. Nagahara, R, Matsubayashi, T, Matsuo, A, and Zushi, K. Kinematics of the thorax and pelvis during accelerated sprinting. *J Sports Med Phys Fitness* 58:1253-1263, 2018.

18. Nagahara, R, Mizutani, M, Matsuo, A, and Kanehisa, H. Step-to-step spatiotemporal variables and ground reaction forces of intra-individual fastest sprinting in a single session. *J Sports Sci* 36:1392-1401, 2018.

19. Nagahara, R, Mizutani, M, Matsuo, A, Kanehisa, H, and Fukunaga, T. Association of step width with accelerated sprinting performance and ground reaction force. *Int J Sports Med* 38:534-540, 2017.

20. Nagahara, R, Naito, H, Morin, JB, and Zushi, K. Association of acceleration with spatiotemporal variables in maximal sprinting. *Int J Sports Med* 35:755-761, 2014.

21. Nagahara, R, Takai, Y, Kanehisa, H, and Fukunaga, T. Vertical impulse as a determinant of combination of step length and frequency during sprinting. *Int J Sports Med* 39:282-290, 2018.

22. Nagahara, R, and Zushi, K. Development of maximal speed sprinting performance with changes in vertical, leg and joint stiffness. *J Sports Med Phys Fitness* 57:1572-1578, 2017.

23. Newell, K. Constraints on the development of coordination. In *Motor development in children: Aspects of coordination and control*. Wade, M, and Whiting, H, eds. Leiden: Martinus Nijhoff Publishers, 341-360, 1986.

24. Schache, AG, Lai, AKM, Brown, NAT, Crossley, KM, and Pandy, MG. Lower-limb joint mechanics during maximum acceleration sprinting. *J Exp Biol* 222(Pt 22):jeb209460, 2019.

25. Seitz, LB, Barr, MJ, and Haff, GG. Effects of sprint training with or without ball carrying in elite rugby players. *Int J Sports Physiol Perform* 10(6):761-766, 2015.

26. Stoyanov, H. Competition model characteristics of elite male sprinters. *New Stud Athl* 29:57-58, 2014.

27. Uth, N. Anthropometric comparison of world-class sprinters and normal population. *J Sports Sci Med* 4:608-616, 2005.

28. Weyand, P, Sandell, R, Prime, D, and Bundle, M. The biological limits to running speed are imposed from the ground up. *J Appl Physiol* 108:950-961, 2010.

29. Wild, JJ, Bezodis, IN, North, JS, Bezodis, NE, Wild, JJ, and Bezodis, IN. Differences in step characteristics and linear kinematics between rugby players and sprinters during initial sprint acceleration players and sprinters during initial sprint acceleration. *Eur J Sport Sci* 18(10):1-11, 2018.

Chapter 4

1. Dietz, V. Neuronal control of functional movement. In *Strength and Power in Sport*. 2nd ed. Komi, PV, ed. Oxford: Blackwell Scientific Publications, 11-26, 2003.

2. Duchateau, J, and Hainaut, K. Mechanisms of muscle and motor unit adaptation to explosive power training. In *Strength and Power in Sport*. 2nd ed. Komi, PV, ed. Oxford: Blackwell Scientific Publications, 315-330, 2003.

3. Hinricks, RN. Whole body movement: Coordination of arms and legs in walking and running. In *Multiple Muscle Systems*. Winters, JM, and Woo, S, eds. New York: Springer Verlag, 694-705, 1990.

4. Magill, RA. *Motor Learning: Concepts and Applications*. Columbus, OH: McGraw Hill, 284-296, 2001.

5. Winckler, G. An examination of speed endurance. *New Studies in Athletics* 6(1):27-33, 1991.

Chapter 5

1. Barnes, C, Archer, DT, Hogg, B, Bush, M, and Bradley, PS. The evolution of physical and technical performance parameters in the English Premier League. *Int J Sports Med.* 35: 1095-1100, 2014.

2. Castagna, C, Lorenzo, F, Krustrup, P, Fernandes-da-Silva, J, Póvoas, SC, Bernardini, A, and D'Ottavio, S. Reliability characteristics and applicability of a repeated sprint ability test in young male soccer players. *J Strength Cond Res* 32(6):1538-1544, 2018.

3. Castro-Piñero, J, González-Montesinos, JL, Keating, XD, Mora, J, Sjöström, M, and Ruiz, JR. Percentile values for running sprint field tests in children ages 6-17 years: Influence of weight status. *Res Q Exerc Sport* 81:143-151, 2010.

4. Faude, O, Koch, T, and Meyer, T. Straight sprinting is the most frequent action in goal situations in professional football. *J Sports Sci* 30:625-631, 2012.

5. Fernandes-Da-Silva, J, Castagna, C, Teixeira, AS, Carminatti, LJ, Francini, L, Póvoas, SC, and Guglielmo, LGA. Ecological and construct validity of a repeated sprint test in male youth soccer players. *J Strength Cond Res* 35(7):2000-2009, 2021.

6. Fílter, A, Olivares, J, Santalla, A, Nakamura, FY, Loturco, I, and Requena, B. New curve sprint test for soccer players: Reliability and relationship with linear sprint. *J Sports Sci* 38(11-12):1320-1325, 2020.

7. Fukuda, D. *Assessment for Sport and Athletic Performance*. Champaign, IL: Human Kinetics, 122, 125-127, 2019.

8. Graham, J. Guidelines for providing valid testing of athletes' fitness levels. *Strength Cond J* 16(6):7-14, 1994.

9. Hoffman, J. *Norms for Fitness, Performance, and Health*. Champaign, IL: Human Kinetics, 110, 2006.

10. Little, T, and Williams, AG. Specificity of acceleration, maximum speed, and agility in professional soccer players. *J Strength Cond Res* 19:76-78, 2005.

11. Loturco, I, Pereira, L, Freitas, TE, Alcaraz, P. Zanetti, V, Bishop, C, and Jeffreys, I. Maximum acceleration performance of professional soccer players in linear sprints: Is there a direct connection with change-of-direction ability? *PLOS ONE* 14(5):e0216806, 2019.

12. Loturco, I, Pereira, L, Fílter, A, Olivares-Jabalera, J, Reis, VP, Fernandes, V, Freitas, TT, and Requena, B. Curve sprinting in soccer: Relationship with linear sprints and vertical jump performance. *Biol Sport* 37(3):277-283, 2020.

13. McBurnie, AJ, Parr, J, Kelly, DM, and Dos'Santos, T. Multidirectional speed in youth soccer players: Programming considerations and practical applications. *Strength Cond J* 44(2):10-32, 2022.

14. McGuigan, M. Principles of test selection and administration. In *Essentials of Strength Training and Conditioning*. 4th ed. Haff, GG, and Triplett, NT., eds. Champaign, IL: Human Kinetics, 249-258, 2016.

15. Rovan, K, Kugovnik, O, Holmberg, LJ, and Supej, M. The steps needed to perform acceleration and turning at different approach speeds. *Kinesiol Slov* 20(1):38-50, 2014.

16. Wong del, P, Chan, GS, and Smith, AW. Repeated-sprint and change-of-direction abilities in physically active individuals and soccer players: Training and testing implications. *J Strength Cond Res* 26:2324-2330, 2012.

17. Wong del, P, Hjelde, GH, Cheng, CF, and Ngo, JK. Use of the RSA/RCOD index to identify training priority in soccer players. *J Strength Cond Res* 29:2787-2793, 2015.

18. Young, W, Benton, D, Duthie, G, and Pryor, J. Resistance training for short sprints and maximum speed sprints. *Strength Cond J* 23(2):7-13, 2001.

Chapter 6

1. Bezodis, NE, Willwacher, S, and Salo, AIT. The biomechanics of the track and field sprint start: A narrative review. *Sports Med* 49(9):1345-1364, 2019.

2. Bissas, A, Walker, J, Paradisis, GP, Hanley, B, Tucker, CB, Jongerius, N, Thomas, A, Merlino, S, Vazel, PJ, and Girard, O. Asymmetry in sprinting: An insight into sub-10 and sub-11 s men and women sprinters. *Scand J Med Sci Sports* 32(1):69-82, 2022.

3. Bret, C, Rahmani, A, Dufour, AB, Messonnier, L, and Lacour, JR. Leg strength and stiffness as ability factors in 100 m sprint running. *J Sports Med Phys Fitness* 42(3):274, 2002.

4. Clark, KP, and Weyand, PG. Are running speeds maximized with simple-spring stance mechanics? *J Appl Physiol* 117:604-615, 2014.

5. Clark, KP, and Weyand, PG. Sprint running research speeds up: A first look at the mechanics of elite acceleration. *Scand J Med Sci Sports* 25(5):581-582, 2015.

6. Clark, KP, Ryan, LJ, and Weyand, PG. A general relationship links gait mechanics and running ground reaction forces. *J Exp Biol* 220(2):247-258, 2017.

7. Clark, KP, Meng, CR, and Stearne, DJ. 'Whip from the hip': Thigh angular motion, ground contact mechanics, and running speed. *Biol Open* 9(10):053546, 2020.

8. Clark, KP, Ryan, LJ, Meng, CR, and Stearne, DJ. Evaluation of maximum thigh angular acceleration during the swing phase of steady-speed running. *Sports Biomech* 1-14, 2021.

9. Clark, KP, Ryan, LJ, Meng, CR, and Stearne, DJ. Horizontal foot speed during submaximal and maximal running. *J Hum Kinet* 87:1-9, 2023.

10. Colyer, SL, Nagahara, R, and Salo, AI. Kinetic demands of sprinting shift across the acceleration phase: Novel analysis of entire force waveforms. *Scand J Med Sci Sports* 28(7):1784-1792, 2018.

11. Colyer, SL, Nagahara, R, Takai, Y, and Salo, AI. How sprinters accelerate beyond the velocity plateau of soccer players: Waveform analysis of ground reaction forces. *Scand J Med Sci Sports* 28(12):2527-2535, 2018.

12. Delecluse, CH, Coppenolle, HV, Willems, E, Diels, R, Goris, M, Leemputte, MV, and Vuylsteke, M. Analysis of 100 meter sprint performance as a multi-dimensional skill. *J Hum Mov Stud* 28(2):87, 1995.

13. Douglas, J, Pearson, S, Ross, A, and McGuigan, M. Kinetic determinants of reactive strength in highly trained sprint athletes. *J Strength Cond Res* 32(6): 1562-1570, 2018.

14. Faude, O, Koch, T, and Meyer, T. Straight sprinting is the most frequent action in goal situations in professional football. *J Sports Sci* 30(7):625-631, 2012.

15. Gleadhill, S, and Nagahara, R. Kinetic and kinematic determinants of female sprint performance. *J Sports Sci* 39(6):609-617, 2021.

16. Healy, R, Kenny, IC, and Harrison, AJ. Profiling elite male 100-m sprint performance: The role of maximum velocity and relative acceleration. *J Sport Health Sci* 11(1):75-84, 2022.

17. Haugen, T, Danielsen, J, Alnes, LO, McGhie, D, Sandbakk, Ø, and Ettema, G. On the importance of "front-side mechanics" in athletics sprinting. *Int J Sports Physiol Perform* 13(4):420-427, 2018.

18. Jeffreys, I, Huggins, S, and Davies N. Delivering a gamespeed focused speed and agility development programme in an English Premier League Soccer Academy. *Strength Cond J* 40(3):23-32, 2018.

19. Jeffreys, I. *Effective Coaching in Strength and Conditioning: Pathways to Superior Performance*. London: Routledge, 2019.

20. Jeffreys, I. *Gamespeed: Movement Training for Superior Sports Performance*. 3rd ed. Monterey, CA: Coaches Choice, 2021.

21. Jeffreys, I. Use context and gamespeed to transform speed and agility training. *Strength Cond J* 67:29-35, 2023.

22. Kakehata, G, Goto, Y, Iso, S, and Kanosue, K. The timing of thigh muscle activity is a factor limiting performance in the deceleration phase of the 100-m dash. *Med Sci Sports Exerc* 54(6):1002-1012, 2022.

23. King, D, Burnie, L, Nagahara, R, and Bezodis, NE. Relationships between kinematic characteristics and ratio of forces during initial sprint acceleration. *J Sports Sci* 1-9, 2023.

24. Kugler, F, and Janshen, L. Body position determines propulsive forces in accelerated running. *J Biomech* 43(2):343-348, 2010.

25. Mann RV, and Murphy, A. *The Mechanics of Sprinting and Hurdling*. Self-published: CreateSpace Independent Publishing Platform, 2022.

26. Mendiguchia, J, Castaño-Zambudio, A, Jiménez-Reyes, P, Morin, JB, Edouard, P, Conceição, F, Tawiah-Dodoo, J, and Colyer, SL. Can we modify maximal speed running posture? Implications for performance and hamstring injury management. *Int J Sports Physiol Perform* 17(3):374-383, 2021.

27. Miyashiro, K, Nagahara, R, Yamamoto, K, and Nishijima, T. Kinematics of maximal speed sprinting with different running speed, leg length, and step characteristics. *Front Sports Act Living* 1:1-10, 2019.

28. Morin JB, Edouard, P, and Samozino, P. Technical ability of force application as a determinant factor of sprint performance. *Med Sci Sports Exerc* 43(9):1680-1688, 2011.

29. Morin, JB, Bourdin, M, Edouard, P, Peyrot, N, Samozino, P, and Lacour, JR. Mechanical determinants of 100-m sprint running performance. *Eur J Appl Physiol* 112:3921-3930, 2012.

30. Morin, JB, Slawinski, J, Dorel, S, Couturier, A, Samozino, P, Brughelli, M, and Rabita, G. Acceleration capability in elite sprinters and ground impulse: Push more, brake less? *J Biomech* 48(12):3149-3154, 2015.

31. Murphy, A, Clark, KP, Murray, N, Melton, B, Mann, R, and Rieger, R. Relationship between anthropometric and kinematic measures to practice velocity in elite American 100 m sprinters. *J Clin Transl Res* 7(5):682, 2021.

32. Nagahara, R, Matsubayashi, T, Matsuo, A, and Zushi, K. Kinematics of transition during human accelerated sprinting. *Biol Open* 3(8):689-699, 2014.

33. Nagahara, R, and Zushi, K. Development of maximal speed sprinting performance with changes in vertical, leg and joint stiffness. *J Sports Med Phys Fitness* 57(12):1572-1578, 2016.

34. Nagahara, R, Kanehisa, H, and Fukunaga, T. Ground reaction force across the transition during sprint acceleration. *Scand J Med Sci Sports* 30(3):450-461, 2020.

35. Nagahara, R, and Girard, O. Alterations of spatiotemporal and ground reaction force variables during decelerated sprinting. *Scand J Med Sci Sports* 31(3):586-596, 2021.

36. Rabita, G, Dorel, S, Slawinski, J, Sàez-de-Villarreal, E, Couturier, A, Samozino, P, and Morin, JB. Sprint mechanics in world-class athletes: A new insight into the limits of human locomotion. *Scand J Med Sci Sports* 25(5):583-594, 2015.

37. Slawinski, J, Termoz, N, Rabita, G, Guilhem, G, Dorel, S, Morin, JB, and Samozino, P. How 100-m

event analyses improve our understanding of world-class men's and women's sprint performance. *Scand J Med Sci Sports* 27(1):45-54, 2017.

38. von Lieres Und Wilkau, HC, Irwin, G, Bezodis, NE, Simpson, S, and Bezodis, IN. Phase analysis in maximal sprinting: An investigation of step-to-step technical changes between the initial acceleration, transition and maximal velocity phases. *Sports Biomech* 19(2):141-156, 2020.

39. von Lieres Und Wilkau, HC, Bezodis, NE, Morin, JB, Irwin, G, Simpson, S, and Bezodis, IN. The importance of duration and magnitude of force application to sprint performance during the initial acceleration, transition and maximal velocity phases. *J Sports Sci* 38(20):2359-2366, 2020.

40. Walker, J, Bissas, A, Paradisis, GP, Hanley, B, Tucker, CB, Jongerius, N, Thomas, A, von Lieres Und Wilkau, H', Brazil, A, Wood, M, Merlino, S, Vazel, PJ, Bezodis, IN. Kinematic factors associated with start performance in world-class male sprinters. *J Biomech* 124:110554, 2021.

41. Weyand, PG, Sternlight, DB, Bellizzi, MJ, and Wright, S. Faster top running speeds are achieved with greater ground forces not more rapid leg movements. *J Appl Physiol* 89(5):1991-1999, 2000.

42. Weyand, PG, Sandell, R.F, Prime, DN, and Bundle, MW. The biological limits to running speed are imposed from the ground up. *J Appl Physiol* 108(4):950-961, 2010.

Chapter 7

1. Aagaard, P, Simonsen, EB, Andersen, JL, Magnusson, P, and Dyhre-Poulsen, P. Increased rate of force development and neural drive of human skeletal muscle following resistance training. *J Appl Physiol* 93(4):1318-1326, 2002.

2. DeWeese, BH, and Nimphius, S. Program design and technique for speed and agility training. In *Essentials of Strength Training and Conditioning*. 4th ed. Haff, GG, and Triplett, NT, eds. Champaign, IL: Human Kinetics, 521-558, 2016.

3. Francis, C, and Patterson, P. *The Charlie Francis Training System*. TBLI Publications, 1992.

4. Girard, O, Mendez-Villanueva, A, and Bishop, D. Repeated-sprint ability—part I. *Sports Med* 41(8):673-694, 2011.

5. Hansen, DM. Successfully translating strength into speed. In *High-Performance Training for Sports*. Joyce, D, and Lewindon, D, eds. Champaign, IL: Human Kinetics, 145-166, 2014.

6. Haugen, T, Seiler, S, Sandbakk, Ø, and Tønnessen, E. The training and development of elite sprint performance: An integration of scientific and best practice literature. *Sports Medicine - Open* 5(1), 2019.

7. Jeffreys, I. Warm-up and flexibility training. In *Essentials of Strength Training and Conditioning*. 4th ed. Haff, GG, and Triplett, NT, eds. Champaign, IL: Human Kinetics, 317-350, 2016.

8. Lockie, RG, Murphy, AJ, Knight, TJ, and De Jonge, XAJ. Factors that differentiate acceleration ability in field sport athletes. *J Strength Cond Res* 25(10):2704-2714, 2011.

9. McBride, JM. Bioenergetics of exercise and training. In *Essentials of Strength Training and Conditioning*. 4th ed. Haff, GG, and Triplett, NT., eds. Champaign, IL: Human Kinetics, 43-64, 2016.

10. Morin, JB, Petrakos, G, Jiménez-Reyes, P, Brown, SR, Samozino, P, and Cross, MR. Very-heavy sled training for improving horizontal-force output in soccer players. *Int J Sports Physiol Perform* 12(6):840-844, 2017.

11. Taylor, JB, Wright, AA, Dischiavi, SL, Townsend, MA, and Marmon, AR. Activity demands during multi-directional team sports: A systematic review. *Sports Med* 47(12):2533-2551, 2017.

Chapter 8

1. Jeffreys, I. Optimising speed and agility development using target classifications and motor control principles Part One. *Prof Strength Cond* (3):11-14, 2006.

2. Jeffreys, I. A motor development approach to enhancing agility Part One. *Strength Cond J* 28(5):72-76, 2006.

3. Jeffreys, I. *Gamespeed: Movement Training for Superior Sports Performance.* 3rd ed. Monterey, CA: Coaches Choice, 2021.

4. Jeffreys, I. Use context and gamespeed to transform speed and agility training. *Prof Strength Cond* 67:29-35, 2023.

Chapter 9

Baseball and Softball

1. Bristow, C. Baserunning & times. March 2018. https://cdn4.sportngin.com/attachments/document/0149/2160/008off_BaserunningTimes_1_.pdf. Accessed February 20, 2023.

2. Coleman, AE. *52-week Baseball Training.* Champaign, IL: Human Kinetics, 2000.

3. Coleman, AE. *In-Season Base Running Speed Drills.* Unpublished manuscript, 2009.

4. Coleman, AE, and Dupler, TL. Changes in running speed in game situations during a season of Major League Baseball. *J Exerc Physiol Online* 7(3):89-93, 2004.

5. Coleman, AE, and Dupler, TL. Differences in running speed among major league players in game situations. *J Exerc Physiol Online* 8(2):10-15, 2005.

6. Coleman, AE, and Lasky, L. Assessing running speed and body composition in professional baseball players. *Health* 6:207-213, 1992.

7. Crotin, R. (2009). Game speed training in baseball. *Strength Cond J* 31:13-25, 2009.

8. Gambetta, V. *Athletic Development: The Art and Science of Functional Sports Conditioning.* Champaign, IL: Human Kinetics.

9. Hoffman, JR, Vazquesz, J, Pichardo, N, and Tenenbaum, G. Anthropometric and performance comparisons in professional baseball players. *J Strength Cond Res* 23:2173-2178, 2009.

10. Magrini, M, Dawes, JJ, Spaniol, FJ, and Roberts, A. Speed and agility training for baseball/softball. *Strength Cond J* 40(1):68-74, 2018.

11. Sheppard, JM and Young, WB. Agility literature review: Classifications, training and testing. *J Sports Sci* 24:919-932, 2006.

12. Spaniol, FJ. Body composition and baseball performance. *NSCA Performance Training Journal* 4(1):10-11, 2005.

13. Spaniol, FJ, Melrose, D, Bohling, M, and Bonnette, R. Physiological characteristics of NCAA Division I baseball players [abstract]. *J Strength Cond Res* 19(4):e34, 2005.

14. Spaniol, FJ. Physiological characteristics of NAIA intercollegiate baseball players [abstract]. *J Strength Cond Res* 21(4):e25, 2007.

15. Spaniol, FJ. Baseball athletic test: A baseball-specific test battery. *Strength Cond J* 31:26-29, 2009.

Basketball

1. Boyle, M. *New Functional Training for Sports.* Champaign, IL: Human Kinetics, 2016.

2. Stojanović, E, Stojiljković, N, Scanlan, AT, Dalbo, VJ, Berkelmans, DM, and Milanović, Z. The activity demands and physiological responses encountered during basketball match-play: A systematic review. *Sports Med* 48:111-135, 2018.

Gridiron Football

1. Berry, J, Hepner, J, Burghardt, B, Myslinski, T, and Zimmer, A. Player movement profiles across three levels of American football: Academy high school, NCAA division 1 college, and National Football League. World Congress of Science and Football conference presentation, Melbourne, Australia, June, 2019.

2. Fitzgerald, CF, and Jensen, RL. A comparison of the National Football League's annual National Football League combine 1999-2000 to 2015-2016. *J Strength Cond Res* 34(3):771-781, 2020.

3. Hedlund, DP. Performance of future elite players at the National Football League scouting combine. *J Strength Cond Res* 32(11):3112-3118, 2018.

4. Hoffman, JR. The applied physiology of American football. *Int J Sports Physiol Perform* 3(3):387-392, 2008.

5. Hoffman, JR. Physiological demands of American football. *Sports Science Exchange* 28(143):1-6, 2015.

6. Landow, L, and Jarmon, C. *All-Pro Performance Training: An Insider's Guide to Preparing for the Football Combine.* Champaign, IL: Human Kinetics, 2020.

7. Robbins, DW, Goodale, TL, Kuzmits, FE, and Adams, AJ. Changes in the athletic profile of elite college American football players. *J Strength Cond Res* 27(4):861-874, 2013.

8. Tomlin, DL, and Wenger, HA. The relationship between aerobic fitness and recovery from high intensity intermittent exercise. *Sports Med* 31:1-11, 2001.

9. Vermeil, AHE, and Gattone, M. *Vermeil's Sports and Fitness Training System for Enhancing Athletic Performance.* Deerfield, IL: Vermeil's Sports and Fitness, 1999.

Ice Hockey

1. Budarick, AR, Shell, JR, Robbins, SM, Wu, T, Renaud, PJ, and Pearsall, D.J. Ice hockey skating sprints: Run to glide mechanics of high calibre male and female athletes. *Sports Biomech* 19(5):601-617, 2020.

2. Jackson, J, Snydmiller, G, Game, A, Gervais, P, and Bell, G. Movement characteristics and heart rate profiles displayed by female university ice hockey players. *Int J Kinesiol Sports Sci* 4(1):43-54, 2016.

3. Lentz, D, and Hardyk, A. Speed training. In *Training for Speed, Agility, and Quickness.* 2nd ed. Brown, LE, and Ferrigno, VA, eds. Champaign, IL: Human Kinetics, 2005.

4. Manners, TW. Sport–specific training for ice hockey. *Strength Cond J* 26(2):16-22, 2004.

5. Peterson, BJ. *Repeated sprint ability: The influence of aerobic capacity on energy pathway response and fatigue of hockey players* (PhD diss., University of Minnesota), 2014.

6. Thompson, KM, Safadie, A, Ford, J, and Burr, JF. Off-ice resisted sprints best predict all-out skating performance in varsity hockey players. *J Strength Cond Res* 36(9):2597-2601, 2022.

7. Upjohn, T, Turcotte, R, Pearsall, DJ, and Loh, J. Three-dimensional kinematics of the lower limbs during forward ice hockey skating. *Sports Biomech* 7(2):206-221, 2008.

8. Warren, YB, McDowell, MH, and Scarlett, BJ. Specificity of sprint and agility training methods. *J Strength Cond Res* 15(3):315-319, 2001.

Rugby

1. Cunningham, DJ, Shearer, DA, Drawer, S, Pollard, B, Eager, R, Taylor, N, Cook, CJ, and Kilduff, LP. Movement demands of elite under-20s and senior international rugby union players. *PLoS One* 11(11):e0164990, 2016.

2. Cunningham, DJ, Shearer, DA, Carter, N, Drawer, S, Pollard, B, Bennett, M, Eager, R, Cook, CJ, Farrell, J, Russell, M, and Kilduff, LP. Assessing worst case scenarios in movement demands derived from global positioning systems during international rugby union matches: Rolling averages versus fixed length epochs. *PLoS One* 13(4):e0195197, 2018.

3. Duthie, GM, Pyne, DB, Marsh, DJ, and Hooper. SL. Sprint patterns in rugby union players during competition. *J Strength Cond Res* 20(1):208-214, 2006.

4. Jeffreys, I. *Gamespeed: Movement Training for Superior Sports Performance.* 3rd ed. Monterey CA: Coaches Choice, 2021.

5. Jeffreys, I. Use context and gamespeed to transform speed and agility training. *Professional Strength and Conditioning* 67: 29-35, 2023.

6. Klein, G. Naturalistic decision making. *Hum Factors* 50(3):456-460, 2008.

7. Peeters, A, Piscione, J, Lacome, M, Carling, C, and Babault, N. A comparison of running and contact loads in U18 and U20 international rugby union competition. *Biol Sport* 40(1):149-160, 2022.

8. Sheppy, E, Hills, SP, Russell, M, Chambers, R, Cunningham, DJ, Shearer, D, Heffernan, S, Waldron, M, McNarry, M, and Kilduff, LP. Assessing the whole-match and worst-case scenario locomotor demands of international women's rugby union match-play. *J Sci Med Sport* 23(6):609-614, 2020.

9. Suarez-Arrones L, Portillo J, Pareja-Blanco F, Sáez de Villareal E, Sánchez-Medina L, and Munguía-Izquierdo D. Match-play activity profile in elite women's rugby union players. *J Strength Cond Res* 28(2):452-458, 2014.

Soccer

1. Barnes, C, Archer, DT, Hogg, B, Bush, M, and Bradley, P. The evolution of physical and technical performance parameters in the English Premier League. *Int J Sports Med* 35(13):1095-1100, 2014.

2. Bloomfield, J, Polman, R, and O'Donoghue, P. Physical demands of different positions in FA Premier League soccer. *J Sports Sci Med* 6(1):63, 2007.

3. Caldbeck, P, and Dos'Santos, T. A classification of specific movement skills and patterns during sprinting in English Premier League soccer. *PLoS One* 17(11):e0277326, 2022.

4. Di Salvo, V, Baron, R, González-Haro, C, Gormasz, C, Pigozzi, F, and Bachl, N. Sprinting analysis of elite soccer players during European Champions League and UEFA Cup matches. *J Sports Sci* 28(14):1489-1494, 2010.

5. Faude, O, Koch, T, and Meyer, T. Straight sprinting is the most frequent action in goal situations in professional football. *J Sports Sci* 30(7):625-631, 2012.

6. Griffin, J, Larsen, B, Horan, S, Keogh, J, Dodd, K, Andreatta, M, and Minahan, C. Women's football: An examination of factors that influence movement patterns. *J Strength Cond Res* 34(8):2384-2393, 2020.

7. Griffin, J, Newans, T, Horan, S, Keogh, J, Andreatta, M, and Minahan, C. Acceleration and high-speed running profiles of women's international and domestic football matches. *Front Sports Act Living* 25(3):2021604605, 2021.

8. Haugen, T, Tønnessen, E, Hisdal, J, and Seiler, S. The role and development of sprinting speed in soccer. *Int J Sports Physiol Perform* 9(3):432-441, 2014.

9. Jeffreys, I. Soccer. In *Developing Agility and Quickness.* 2nd ed. Dawes, J, ed. Champaign, IL: Human Kinetics, 2019.

10. Jeffreys, I. *Gamespeed: Movement Training for Superior Sports Performance.* 3rd ed. Monterey, CA: Coaches Choice, 2021.

11. Jeffreys, I. Use context and gamespeed to transform speed and agility training. *Professional Strength and Conditioning* 47:29-35, 2022.

12. Jeffreys, I, Huggins, S, and Davies, N. Delivering a gamespeed focused speed and agility development programme in an English premier League Soccer Academy. *Strength Cond J* 40(3):23-32, 2018.

13. Lago-Peñas, C, Lorenzo-Martinez, M, López-Del Campo, R, Resta, R, and Rey, E. Evolution of physical and technical parameters in the Spanish LaLiga 2012-2019. *Sci Med Footb* 7(1):41-46, 2023.

14. Loturco, I, Nimphius, S, Kobal, R, Bottino, A, Zanetti, V, Pereira, LA, and Jeffreys, I. Change-of-direction deficit in elite young soccer players. *Ger J Exerc Sport Res* 48(2):228-234, 2018.

15. Loturco, I, Pereira, LA, Freitas, TT, Alcaraz, PE, Zanetti, V, Bishop, C, and Jeffreys, I. Maximum acceleration performance of professional soccer players in linear sprints: Is there a direct connection with change-of-direction ability? *PloS One* 14(5):e0216806, 2019.

16. Loturco, I, Pereira, LA, Fílter, A, Olivares-Jabalera, J, Reis, VP, Fernandes, V, and Requena, B. Curve sprinting in soccer: Relationship with linear sprints and vertical jump performance. *Biol Sport* 37(3):277-283, 2020.

17. Varley, MC., and Aughey, RJ. Acceleration profiles in elite Australian soccer. *Int J Sports Med* 34(01):34-39, 2013.

Tennis

1. Fernandez-Fernandez, J, Mendez-Villanueva, A, Fernandez-Garcia, B, and Terrados, N. Match activity and physiological responses during a junior female singles tennis tournament. *Br J Sports Med* 11:711-716, 2007.

2. Giles, B, Peeling, P, and Reid, M. Quantifying change of direction movement demands in professional tennis match play: An analysis from the Australian Open grand slam. *J Strength Cond Res*, 2021. [e-pub ahead of print].

3. Hoppe, M, Baumgart, C, Bornefeld, J, Sperlich, B, Freiwald, J, and Holmberg, H. Running activity profile of adolescent tennis players during match play. *Pediatr Exerc Sci* 26:281-290, 2014.

4. Kovacs, M. Applied physiology of tennis performance. *Br J Sports Med* 40:381-386, 2006.

5. Kovacs, M. Movement for tennis: The importance of lateral training. *Strength Cond J* 30:77-85, 2009.

6. Kovalchik, S, and Reid, M. Comparing matchplay characteristics and physical demands of junior and professional tennis athletes in the era of big data. *J Sports Sci Med* 16:489-497, 2017.

7. Lambrich, J, and Muehlbauer, T. Physical fitness and stroke performance in healthy tennis players with different competition levels: A systematic review and meta-analysis. *PLoS One* 17(6):e0269516, 2022.

8. Munivrana, G, Filipčić, A, and Filipčić, T. Relationship of speed, agility, neuromuscular power, and selected anthropometrical variables and performance results of male and female junior tennis players. *Coll Antropol* 39(Suppl 1):109-116, 2015.

9. Pieper, S, Exler, T, and Weber, K. Running speed loads on clay and hard courts in world class tennis. *Med Sci Tennis* 12:14-17, 2007.

10. Roetert, E, and Ellenbecker, T. Biomechanics of tennis movements. *International Tennis Federation CSSR* 24:15-17, 2001.

11. Weber, K, Pieper, S, and Exler, T. Characteristics and significance of running speed at the Australian Open 2006 for training and injury prevention. *Med Sci Tennis* 12:14-17, 2007.

12. Vuong, J, Fett, J, Ulbricht, A, and Ferrauti, A. Physical determinants, intercorrelations, and relevance of movement speed components in elite junior tennis players. *Eur Jour Sport Sci* 22:1805-1815, 2022.

Field Hockey

1. Caterisano, A, Decker, D, Snyder, B, Feigenbaum, M, Glass, R, House, P, Sharp, C, Waller, M, and Witherspoon, Z. CSCCa and NSCA joint consensus guidelines for transition periods: Safe return to training following inactivity. *Strength Cond J* 41(3):1-23, 2019.

2. Gabbett, TJ. GPS analysis of elite women's field hockey training and competition. *J Strength Cond Res* 24(5):1321-1324, 2010.

3. Herda, TJ, and Cramer, JT. Bioenergetics of exercise and training. In *Essentials of Strength Training and Conditioning.* 4th ed. Haff, GG, and Triplett, NT, eds. Champaign, IL: Human Kinetics, 43-62, 2016.

4. International Hockey Federation. Rules of hockey. January 2022. www.fih.ch/inside-fih/our-official-documents/rules-of-hockey/. Accessed January 15, 2023.

5. Ishan M, Yeo V, Tan, F, Joseph, R, Lee, M, and Aziz, AR. Running demands and activity profile of the new four-quarter match format in men's field hockey. *J Strength Cond Res* 35:512-518, 2021.

6. Kapteijns, JA, Caen, K, Lievens, M, Bourgois, JG, and Boone, J. Positional match running performance and performance profiles of elite female field hockey. *Int J Sports Physiol Perform* 16(9):1295-1302, 2021.

7. Keogh, JWL., Weber, CL., and Dalton, CT. Evaluation of anthropometric, physiological, and skill-related tests for talent identification in female field hockey. *Can J Appl Physiol* 28:397-409, 2003.

8. Lythe, J, and Kilding, A. Physical demands and physiological responses during elite field hockey. *Int J Sports Med* 32(7):523-528, 2011.

9. McGuinness, A, Malone, S, Hughes, B, and Collins, K. Physical activity and physiological profiles of elite international female field hockey players across the quarters of competitive match play. *J Strength Cond Res* 33:2513-2522, 2019.

10. Spencer, M, Bishop, D, Dawson, B, and Goodman, C. Physiological and metabolic responses of repeated-sprint activities. *Sports Med* 35(12):1025-1044, 2005.

11. Wassmer, D, and Mookerjee, S. A descriptive profile of elite U.S. women's collegiate field hockey players. *J Sports Med Phys Fit* 42(2):165-171, 2002.

Lacrosse

1. Chorney, E, and Simonson, SR. Comprehensive needs analysis for women's collegiate lacrosse. *Strength Cond J* 44(2):1-9, 2022.

2. Collins, SM, Silberlicht, M, Perzinski, C, Smith, SP, and Davidson, PW. The relationship between body composition and preseason performance tests of collegiate male lacrosse players. *J Strength Cond Res* 28(9):2673-2679, 2014.

3. Gutowski, AE, and Rosene, JM. Preseason performance testing battery for men's lacrosse. *Strength Cond J* 33(2):16-22, 2011.

4. Hoffman, JR, Ratamess, NA, Neese, KL, Ross, RE, Kang, J, Magrelli, JF, and Faigenbaum, AD. Physical performance characteristics in National Collegiate Athletic Association Division III champion female lacrosse athletes. *J Strength Cond Res* 23(5):1524-1529, 2009.

5. Jeffreys, I. Delivering a gamespeed-focused speed and agility development program in an English Premier League soccer academy. *Strength Cond J* 40(3):23-32, 2018.

6. Polley, CS, Cormack, SJ, Gabbett, TJ, and Polglaze, T. Activity profile of high-level Australian lacrosse players. *J Strength Cond Res* 29(1):126-136, 2015.

7. Richard, H, and Harald, T. Physiological profile differences of male Austrian lacrosse athletes: A comparison to US collegian lacrosse athletes. *Kinesiol Slov* 23(3):18-31, 2017.

8. Sell, KM, Prendergast, JM, Ghigiarelli, JJ, Gonzalez, AM, Biscardi, LM, Jajtner, AR, and Rothstein, AS. Comparison of physical fitness parameters for starters vs. nonstarters in an NCAA Division I men's lacrosse team. *J Strength Cond Res* 32(11):3160-3168, 2018.

Sprint (Track) Cycling

1. Beattie, K, Carson, BP, Lyons, M, and Kenny, IC. The effect of maximal- and explosive-strength training on performance indicators in cyclists. *Int J Sports Physiol Perform* 12(4):470-480, 2017.

2. Bosch, F. *Strength Training and Coordination: An Integrative Approach.* Rotterdam, Netherlands: 2010 Publishers, 123-179, 2018.

3. Burnie, L, Barratt, P, Davids, K, Worsfold, P, and Wheat, JS. Effects of strength training on the biomechanics and coordination of short-term maximal cycling. *J Sports Sci* 40(12):1315-1324, 2022.

4. Douglas, J, Ross, A, and Martin, J. Maximal muscular power: Lessons from sprint cycling. *J Sports Med* 7(1):48, 2021.

5. Elliott, MC, Wagner, PP, and Chiu, L. Power athletes and distance training: Physiological and biomechanical rationale for change. *Sports Med* 37(1):47-57, 2007.

6. Kordi, M, Folland, JP, Goodall, S, Menzies, C, Patel, TS, Evans, M, Thomas, K, and Howatson, G. Cycling-specific isometric resistance training improves peak power output in elite sprint cyclists. *Scand J Med Sci Sports* 30(9):1594-1604, 2020.

7. Myers, MW. *Anatomy Trains: Myofascial Meridians for Manual & Movement Therapists.* London: Churchill Livingstone, 2014.

8. Padulo, J, Laffaye, G, Bertucci, W, Chaouachi, A, and Viggiano, D. Optimization of starting conditions in track cycling. *J Sport Sci Health* 10(3):189-198, 2014.

9. Page, P, Frank, C, and Lardner, R. *Assessment and Treatment of Muscle Imbalance: The Janda Approach.* Champaign, IL: Human Kinetics, 2010.

10. Parsons, B. Resistance training for elite-level track cyclists. *Strength Cond J* 32(5):63-68, 2010.

11. Paton, C, and Hopkins, WG. Combining explosive and high-resistance training improves performance in competitive cyclists. *J Strength Cond Res* 19(4):826-830, 2005.

12. Rønnestad, B, and Mujika, M. Optimizing strength training for running and cycling endurance performance: A review. *Scand J Med Sci Sports* 24(4):603-612, 2014.

13. Rønnestad, BR, Hansen, J, Hollan, I, and Ellefsen, S. Strength training improves performance and pedaling characteristics in elite cyclists. *Scand J Med Sci Sports* 25(1):e89-98, 2015.

14. Rønnestad, BR, Hansen, J, Hollan, I, Spencer, M, Ellefsen, S, and Rønnestad, BR. In-season strength training cessation impairs performance variables in elite cyclists. *Int J Sports Physiol Perform* 11:727-735, 2015.

15. Rønnestad, BR, Hansen, J, and Nygaard, H. 10 weeks of heavy strength training improves performance-related measurements in elite cyclists. *J Sports Sci* 35(14):1435-1441, 2017.

16. Rønnestad, BR, Hansen, EA, and Raastad, T. Effect of heavy strength training on thigh muscle cross-sectional area, performance determinants, and performance in well-trained cyclists. *Eur J Appl Physiol* 108:965-975, 2010.

17. Sale, DG. Neural adaptation to resistance training. *Med Sci Sports Exerc* 20(5):S135-145, 1988.

18. Sunde, A, Støren, Ø, Bjerkaas, M, Larsen, MH, Hoff, J, and Helgerud, J. Maximal strength training improves cycling economy in competitive cyclists. *J Strength Cond Res* 24(8):2157-2165, 2010.

19. Weakley, J, Mann, B, Banyard, H, McLaren, S, Scott, T, and Garcia-Ramos, A. Velocity-based training: From theory to application. *Strength Cond J* 43(2):31-49, 2021.

Speed Skating

1. Allinger, TL, and Van den Bogert, AJ. Skating technique for the straights, based on the optimization of a simulation model. *Med Sci Sport Exer* 29(2):279-286, 1997.

2. de Boer, RW, Ettema, GJ, Faessen, BG, Krekels, H, Hollander, AP, de Groot, G, and van Ingen Schenau, GJ. Specific characteristics of speed skating: Implications for summer training. *Med Sci Sport Exer* 19(5):504-510, 1987.

3. de Koning, JJ, Thomas, R, Berger, M, de Groot, G, and van Ingen Schenau, GJ. The start in speed skating: From running to gliding. *Med Sci Sport Exer* 27(12):1703-1708, 1995.

4. de Koning, JJ, and van Ingen Schenau, GJ. Performance-determining factors in speed skating. In *Biomechanics in Sport: Performance Enhancement and Injury Prevention.* Zatsiorsky, VM, and Kraemer, WJ, eds. Hoboken, NJ: Wiley-Blackwell, 232-246, 2000.

5. DeWeese, BH, Sams, ML, Williams, JH, and Bellon, CR. Speed play: Guiding skill through a seamlessly sequenced sprint curriculum. *Techniques* 22(4):9-24, 2019.

6. Foster, C, de Koning, JJ, Hettinga, F, Lampen, J, La Clair, KL, Dodge, C, Maarten, B, and Porcari, JP. Pattern of energy expenditure during simulated competition. *Med Sci Sport Exer* 35(5):826-831, 2003.

7. Foster, C, Schrager, M, Snyder, AC, and Thompson, NN. Pacing strategy and athletic performance. *Sports Med* 17(2):77-85, 1994.

8. Haug, WB, Drinkwater, EJ, Cicero, NJ, Barthell, AJ, and Chapman, DW. The impact of dry-land sprint start training on the short track speed skating start. *J Strength Cond Res* 33(2):544-548, 2017.

9. Houdijk, H, Bobbert, MF, De Koning, JJ, and de Groot, G. The effects of klapskate hinge position on push-off performance: A simulation study. *Med Sci Sports Exerc* 35(12):2077-2084, 2003.

10. Konings, MJ, Elferink-Gemser, MT, Stoter, IK, van der Meer, D, Otten, E, and Hettinga, FJ. Performance characteristics of long-track speed skaters: A literature review. *Sports Med* 45(4):505-516, 2014.

11. Laakso, LA, and Schuster, JG. Dynamic correspondence of the hang power clean to skating starts in men's ice hockey. *J Strength Cond* 43(4):1-8, 2021.

12. Liebermann, DG, Maitland, ME, and Katz, L. Lower-limb extension power: How well does it predict short distance speed skating performance? *Isokinet Exer Sci* 10(2):87-95, 2002.

13. Stuart, AC, and Snyman, K. Strength training and development in competitive speed skating. *J Strength Cond* 44(3):1-10, 2022.

Index

Note: Page references followed by an italicized *f* or *t* indicate information contained in figures or tables, respectively.

About the NSCA

The **National Strength and Conditioning Association (NSCA)** is the world's leading organization in the field of sport conditioning. Drawing on the resources and expertise of the most recognized professionals in strength training and conditioning, sport science, performance research, education, and sports medicine, the NSCA is the world's trusted source of knowledge and training guidelines for coaches and athletes. The NSCA provides the crucial link between the lab and the field.

About the Editor

Ian Jeffreys, PhD, CSCS,*D, NSCA-CPT*D, RSCC*E, FNSCA, is an internationally renowned and award-winning coach, educator, and author. He is regarded as a world authority in the development of speed and agility for team sports, where his unique Gamespeed system and RAMP warm-up protocols have been adopted by a wide range of coaches and organizations. A former professional rugby player, he played at the highest level for 15 years. Jeffreys is now the director of All-Pro Performance, a consultancy and education company based in Brecon, Wales. He is a professor emeritus in strength and conditioning and a visiting professor at Reykjavik University. He provides consulting services to several professional sports organizations. Jeffreys has worked with athletes, clubs, and sports organizations in over 20 countries.

Jeffreys holds the Emeritus Registered Strength and Conditioning Coach (RSCC*E), Certified Strength and Conditioning Specialist (CSCS,*D), and Certified Personal Trainer (NSCA-CPT*D) credentials from the National Strength and Conditioning Association (NSCA). He was on the board of directors of the NSCA between 2016 and 2019, was the vice president between 2018 and 2019, and in July 2024 begins serving a three-year term as the president of the organization. He was the NSCA's High School Professional of the Year in 2006, the first time the award had ever been presented to a coach working outside the United States. This was awarded for his pioneering work in developing a performance academy for youth athletes that produced numerous international performers and championship teams. In July 2009 Jeffreys was awarded a fellowship by the NSCA.

Jeffreys is a founding member of the United Kingdom Strength and Conditioning Association (UKSCA) and was a member of the board of directors from the organization's inception in 2004 until 2013. He holds the UKSCA's Accredited Strength and Conditioning Coach (ASCC) credential and is an honorary fellow of the association as well as being an assessor and tutor. In 2019 Jeffreys was made a lifetime member of the Polish Strength and Conditioning Association, and in 2021 he was awarded a Career Achievement Award by the Strength and Conditioning Society, recognizing his contribution to the profession of strength and conditioning.

Jeffreys has authored or edited 11 books, over 25 book chapters, and over 100 strength and conditioning articles, which have featured in the leading international journals. He is the editor of the UKSCA journal *Professional Strength and Conditioning* and is on the editorial board for the NSCA's *Strength and Conditioning Journal* and for *Journal of Australian Strength and Conditioning*. Jeffreys is a sought-after conference presenter and has given keynote presentations and hosted performance workshops at a host of major conferences around the world.

About the Contributors

Dana Agar-Newman, MSc, CSCS, RSCC, serves as a senior strength and conditioning coach at the Canadian Sport Institute Pacific. He is the head strength and conditioning coordinator at the University of Victoria, where he is also a lecturer. With a wealth of experience, he has provided tailored strength and conditioning support to numerous athletes across various sports, including rugby sevens, rugby union, diving, rowing, and swimming, and he has guided athletes to medals at the World Championships and Olympics. Agar-Newman is currently pursuing a PhD, focusing on lower-body mechanical diagnostics in athletic populations.

Matthew Barr, PhD, CSCS, is a strength and conditioning coach currently working with the New Zealand Warriors of the National Rugby League. He has previously worked with various national teams for Rugby Canada as well as the Toronto Argonauts of the Canadian Football League, the Canadian Sport Institute Pacific, the University of Manitoba, and York University. In addition to his coaching work, he has published several research papers exploring the influence of strength and power training on speed development as well as assessing sprinting kinematics using video and GPS.

Britt Chandler, PhD, CSCS, NSCA-CPT, is the managing editor of *Strength and Conditioning Journal* and is an adjunct instructor at the University of the Cumberlands and the University of Kansas–Edwards. He also works as a tennis coach and strength and conditioning coach, working primarily with junior tennis players.

Chris Chase, MS, CSCS, is a strength and conditioning coach who has spent his entire career coaching in the team sport environment. He has trained athletes in Division I collegiate athletics in a wide variety of Olympic sports, including, baseball, track and field, volleyball, and tennis. He has now spent close to a decade serving as a strength and conditioning coach for professional basketball teams in the NBA.

Ken Clark, PhD, is an associate professor in the kinesiology department at West Chester University (WCU), where he teaches biomechanics and motor learning. His research interests focus on sprinting biomechanics and speed development. Clark has two decades of performance coaching experience, including in the private sector and at high school and college levels. Additionally, he is a biomechanical consultant for USA Track and Field. Clark received his PhD in biomechanics from Southern Methodist University and his master's degree in kinesiology from WCU. He completed his bachelor's degree in psychology at Swarthmore College, where he was an All-Conference running back for the football team.

John F. Graham, MS, ACSM EP-C, CSCS,*D, RSCC*E, FNSCA, is the senior network administrator of fitness and sports performance at St. Luke's University Health Network in Pennsylvania and New Jersey. He is a fellow of the National Strength and Conditioning Association (NSCA). He holds the Certified Strength and Conditioning Specialist and Registered Strength and Conditioning Coach credentials from the NSCA as well as the Certified Exercise Physiologist credential from the American College of Sports Medicine. Graham has authored or contributed to local, regional, and national peer-reviewed and lay publications on metabolic training, management of chronic conditions, health, fitness, and sports conditioning. He has given local, regional, national, and international presentations on metabolic training, management of chronic conditions, health, fitness, and sports conditioning.

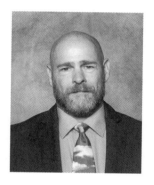

Jeff Kipp, MS, CSCS, RSCC*E, is the head performance coach, head hockey coach, and chair of the health and physical education department at Strake Jesuit College Preparatory in Houston, Texas. Kipp leads athletic development for 16 sports, over 450 athletes, and 360 freshmen PE students. Formerly coaching at the University of Kansas, the U.S. Air Force Academy, and the University of Denver, Kipp's expertise spans from collegiate to professional and Olympic levels, showcasing a diverse background in coaching and training.

Loren Landow, CSCS,*D is a movement, strength, and power development expert who currently serves as the director of football performance at Notre Dame. He has trained thousands of athletes of all ages and abilities, including over 700 professional athletes competing in the MLB, NHL, UFC, and WNBA, as well as Olympic medalists, 70 NFL All-Pros, and over 20 NFL Draft first-round selections. He served as the head strength and conditioning coach for the Denver Broncos from 2018 to 2023. Landow is the author of three books, including *All-Pro Performance Training: An Insider's Guide to Preparing for the Football Combine.* He is also the founder of Landow Performance in Centennial, Colorado.

Irineu Loturco, PhD, is a professor of methodology of sports training at the Federal University of São Paulo and director of sport science at the Nucleus of High Performance in Sport (NAR) in São Paulo, Brazil. NAR is a high-performance training center that serves hundreds of athletes from various sports and develops social projects to assist children from low-income families. Loturco has previously worked as a strength and conditioning coach in major Brazilian soccer clubs and with various Olympic and Paralympic sports, especially national teams. As a researcher, Loturco has published numerous studies focusing on strength and speed development, particularly among elite athletes.

Devan McConnell is the high-performance director for the Arizona Coyotes. In this role, he oversees all aspects of the performance department, including sport science, strength and conditioning, nutrition, and reconditioning. He handles much of the day-to-day sport science application while managing the performance development of all players in the organization. Before joining the Coyotes, McConnell was the director of performance science and reconditioning for the New Jersey Devils. In this role, he oversaw the integration and application of sport and performance science technologies, systems, and practices. In addition, he assisted with the day-to-day performance training of all National Hockey League (NHL) athletes within the organization, oversaw the return-to-play training of injured athletes, and assisted with the organizational vision and directive of the performance department, at both the NHL and AHL levels.

Jean-Benoit (J.B.) Morin, PhD, is a full professor at the University of Saint-Etienne (France), where he is also director of the sport science department and a member of the Interuniversity Laboratory of Human Movement Biology. He is also an associate researcher with Auckland University of Technology's Sports Performance Research Institute New Zealand and is a certified track and field coach. Morin's field of research is mainly human locomotion and performance, with a specific interest in running biomechanics and maximal power movements. He has published over 170 peer-reviewed scientific papers. He is also a consultant for professional sports groups.

Adam Noel, MA, CSCS, RSCC, is a seasoned strength and conditioning coach for the Texas Rangers; he has served in that role for over 8 years. Noel has a master's degree in kinesiology and exercise science from San José State University and a bachelor's degree in kinesiology and exercise science from California State University at Fullerton. Prior to his current role, Noel was the San José State University's head athletic performance coach for women's water polo, women's tennis, and women's golf, and he was the lead assistant for athletic performance for baseball, softball, and men's and women's basketball.

Brentan Parsons, MA, CSCS, is the head of strength and power for the Gold Coast Titans, a rugby league club in Australia. He has coached various international athletes across many sports—including basketball, volleyball, track and field, and sprint cycling—in both Australia and China. In China he coached Shanghai and National Cycling Team riders to national titles, World Cup success, world championships, and Olympic Gold medals. Previously Parsons worked with several clubs in AFL football and has coached numerous Olympic and Paralympic athletes at the Victorian Institute of Sport in Australia.

Christina Rasnake, MBA, MS, RSCC*D, CSCS, is the director of sport science and analytics at the University of Delaware. She oversees data collection, analysis, and performance technology utilization for the university's 22 sport teams. Rasnake has been a strength and conditioning coach for over 13 years, working specifically with field hockey athletes over the course of her career, and she played field hockey collegiately. She has completed her MBA in strategic leadership from the University of Delaware, her master's degree in exercise science from Bloomsburg University, and her BS in recreation management from Lock Haven University.

Adam M. Ross, EdD, CSCS, RSCC, currently serves as the chair and an associate professor of kinesiology at Dallas Baptist University. He began his career in athletic performance as a strength and conditioning coach for the Houston Astros organization in 2010. He then entered the world of collegiate strength and conditioning, serving at both Florida State University and Dallas Baptist University, aiding in the development of 78 players selected in the MLB Draft from 2011 to 2023. He has also served in a leadership capacity as the chair and vice chair of the Executive Council for the National Strength and Conditioning Association's Baseball Special Interest Group since 2018.

Irving "Boo" Schexnayder possesses 44 years of coaching and consulting experience, and he currently heads Schexnayder Athletic Consulting. He consults in a variety of sports with many professional teams, NCAA programs, and foreign sport organizations in areas such as speed, power, and strength development; biomechanics; restoration enhancement; and rehabilitation. He also frequently lectures and instructs classes in these topics. He is most noted for his career as a track and field coach; during this time he produced 26 NCAA champions, 18 Olympians, and 8 world champions and Olympic medalists. An educator by profession and mentor to hundreds of coaches, he also directs the Track and Field Academy, the educational branch of the U.S. Track & Field and Cross Country Coaches Association.

Andrew C. Stuart, MS, CSCS,*D, RSCC, is the assistant director of applied sport science at the University of Nebraska, contributing to athlete performance at the Nebraska Athletic Performance Lab. Previously, as the manager of applied sport science and performance at U.S. Speedskating, he collaborated on high-performance strategies for the 2022 Beijing Olympic Games. Awarded the 2019 Doc Counsilman Science Award by the U.S. Olympic & Paralympic Committee, Stuart has over 14 years of strength and conditioning expertise across various performance levels. Currently pursuing a doctoral degree in sport science at Charles University, his research centers on enhancing speed skating performance.

P.J. Wilson, MSc, is dedicated to the pursuit of excellence in the sports industry. Wilson's journey began with roles at renowned organizations such as Munster Rugby and Bath Rugby, where he played pivotal roles in leading the athletic performance departments. Through strategic leadership and innovative approaches to training and rehabilitation coordination, Wilson facilitated the development of athletes toward their true potential. Alongside Wilson's practical experience, he has pursued continuous learning, delving into the realms of psychology, particularly high-performance decision-making under uncertainty, which has culminated in the pursuit of a PhD in this field. With a commitment to continuous improvement and a passion for driving positive change in the sports industry, Wilson is dedicated to pushing boundaries and evolving with the ever-changing landscape of professional sports.

Contributors to the Previous Edition

Al Biancani, EdD, CSCS,*D
John Graham, MS, HFS, CSCS,*D, RSCC*D, FNSCA
Jeff Kipp, MS, CSCS
Jeremy Sheppard, PhD, CSCS
Frank Spaniol, EdD, CSCS,*D, FNSCA
Mark D. Stephenson, MS, ATC, CSCS,*D
Diane Vives

TAKE THE NEXT STEP

A continuing education exam
is available for this text.
Find out more.